Siblinghood and social relations in Georgian England

Manchester University Press

Siblinghood and social relations in Georgian England

Share and share alike

Amy Harris

Manchester University Press

Copyright © Amy Harris 2012

The right of Amy Harris to be identified as the author of this work has been asserted by her in accordance with the Copyright, Designs and Patents Act 1988.

Published by Manchester University Press
Altrincham Street, Manchester M1 7JA, UK
www.manchesteruniversitypress.co.uk

British Library Cataloguing-in-Publication Data is available

Library of Congress Cataloging-in-Publication Data is available

ISBN 978 1 7849 9364 1 *paperback*

First published by Manchester University Press in hardback 2012

This edition first published 2016

The publisher has no responsibility for the persistence or accuracy of URLs for any external or third-party internet websites referred to in this book, and does not guarantee that any content on such websites is, or will remain, accurate or appropriate.

Printed by Lightning Source

Dedicated to my late father, Alan L. Harris Sr. (1925–2011), who taught me how to dream big; and to my mother, Jenice Hardy Harris, who taught me why I should persevere in making big dreams a reality.

Contents

Abbreviations	viii
List of figures	ix
List of tables	x
Preface and acknowledgements	xi
Explanatory note on dates, ages, and names	xv
Introduction	1
Chapter 1: Learning to be a sibling	26
Chapter 2: Ties that bound	55
Chapter 3: Ties that cut	80
Chapter 4: Sibling economics	112
Chapter 5: Sibling politics	143
Conclusion	166
Appendix 1: Tables	175
Appendix 2: Family trees	177
Select bibliography	183
Index	203

Abbreviations

BAN   Bancroft Library (Berkeley, California)
BL   British Library (London)
BRO   Bristol Record Office
CALS   Cheshire Archives and Local Studies (Chester)
ECCO   Eighteenth Century Collections Online (Gale Group), accessed 2006–11
FHL   Family History Library (Salt Lake City, Utah)
GA   Gloucestershire Archives (Gloucester)
KCC   King's College Special Collections, Cambridge University
OBP   Old Bailey Proceedings Online (HRI Online Publications), accessed 2009–11
ORO   Oxfordshire Record Office (Oxford)
PWDRO   Plymouth and West Devon Record Office
SBTRO   Shakespeare Birthplace Trust Record Office (Stratford-upon-Avon)
STWY   Stanway House private collection (Stanway, Gloucestershire)
TNA   The National Archives/Public Record Office (Kew)
WFP   Witts Family Papers (private collection, catalogued in the GA)

List of figures

1. Thomas Gainsborough (1727–88), *Heneage Lloyd and his Sister [Lucy]*, c.1750 (oil on canvas). With permission from the Fitzwilliam Museum, University of Cambridge, UK. The Bridgeman Art Library International   *page* 32

2. Unknown British artist, eighteenth century (formerly attributed to William Hogarth, 1697–1764), *A Family Group Called 'The Stafford Family'*, c.1730. Yale Center for British Art, Paul Mellon Collection   39

3. Johan Joseph Zoffany, *The Sharp Family*, 1779–81. By courtesy of the National Portrait Gallery, London, and the Lloyd-Baker Trustees   60

4. Anne Travell's 1764 daybook, entry for Saturday 28 October describing moving to her new house in Cheltenham. Copyright Bowly Family and Gloucestershire Archives, D4582/4/17/1. Used with permission   115

List of tables

1. Gender composition of sibling probate disputes, Diocese of Gloucester, 1700–1842   *page* 175

2. Younger versus older siblings in probate disputes, Diocese of Gloucester, 1700–1842   175

3. Older versus younger siblings in probate disputes, Diocese of Gloucester, 1700–1842   176

4. Marital status of female litigants in probate disputes, Diocese of Gloucester, 1700–1842   176

Preface and acknowledgements

As best as I can remember this project began some time in 1977 or 1978. On a summer evening's walk, one of my older sisters decided to help me expand my vocabulary. Though I am sure that she eventually included additional words on the list, the original three were 'edifice', 'apparatus', and 'sibling' – pretty heady stuff for a pre-schooler. It would take a few years to learn the subtle different uses of edifice and building and to realize that 'apparatus' was not synonymous with 'monkey-bars'. But 'sibling' – that was something I immediately understood on many levels. As the youngest of nine children, I found that siblings formed the building blocks of my family experience and daily life, and at that time my family lived within two miles of no fewer than three of my father's siblings. Additionally, as a member of a religion that as a matter of practice and doctrine is based on a sibling model, I connected with and felt embedded in sibling-based kinship ties. The loss of a brother before my birth and the near loss of a sister in my teenage years imbued me with a keen sense of the importance and necessity of maintaining that tie.

I also understood siblings as important parts of my emotional, social, and material world. I cried when they argued and rejoiced when they included me in their teenage activities. Seven years younger than my closest sibling and twenty years younger than my eldest sibling, I could have easily become a sort of pseudo-niece to many of them, but instead I was fully incorporated into their existing sibling culture from the beginning. Considering that our parents allowed my sisters and brothers to choose my name via democratic election, it should not be surprising that they felt at least somewhat responsible for me. They bought me gifts, included me in road trips (really, who takes a four-year-old on a road trip?), shared a bed with me, read stories to me, included me in their more grown-up entertainments, and they taught me. When I pause to think of it, the scope of what they taught me when I was a young child is staggering. Between them they taught me: how to tell right from left how to sweep a floor, the value of integrity, the importance of table manners, how to dribble a basketball, hit a softball, and throw a football, how to tie my shoes, how to write my name and say my ABCs, how to pronounce 'Tchaikovsky', how to make a make-believe cow udder out of a latex glove, how to treat animals, how to tease (and be teased), and how to make myself heard. None of us knew it, but in many ways we were engaged in a family culture much more like the Georgian families described in these pages than like twentieth- and twenty-first-century families. The parallels are not exact, but I cannot imagine ever having embarked on this project if my own experiences had not inspired me to ask questions about families in the past.

Since that vocabulary-expanding summer, my understanding of sibling relationships has expanded beyond my brothers and sisters to include in-laws, nieces, nephews, and numerous encounters with siblings today and in the past on both sides of the Atlantic. I have benefited, in particular, from the growth of historical sibling studies. My understanding has also expanded through my encounter with genealogical, historical, anthropological, and sociological scholarship on families, women, kinship and gender. In that journey countless people have helped, guided, supported, and cheered me. The following list is by no means comprehensive, but at the cost of unending acknowledgements, it will have to do.

I have been blessed with a lifetime of exposure to superior teachers. Though they may be surprised to find their names here I must begin with three early teachers who inspired much of my intellectual development: Carol Stoker, Launa Costley, and Shirlene DeHart, who taught me to think and write creatively; to read and collect extensively; and to write and read critically, respectively. As an undergraduate and graduate student I continued to be the recipient of long-lasting mentoring. David Pratt, George Ryksamp, and Paul Pixton offered unwavering and enduring support and encouragement of this project. At American University Deborah Cohen, Vanessa Schwartz, Pamela Nadell, and Karin Wulf expected and inspired my best work – including the genesis of this book. Dissertation advisors and mentors at Berkeley had an enormous impact upon my work. I am deeply grateful to Tom Laqueur, Paula Fass, Barrie Thorne, Carla Hesse, Tom Barnes, David Lieberman, and James Vernon. And of course, no one gets a graduate degree in history at Berkeley without a debt of gratitude to Mabel Lee.

The line between friend, mentor, and colleague is not always clear and I have enjoyed a group which has consistently and happily blurred that line. I can't imagine enjoying life in Washington, DC, as much as I did without the friendship of Aleisa Fishman and Tina Gessler-Belanger. And Lisa Kaborycha's insight and erudition shaped much of my thinking and her Florentine hospitality provided a sunny break from the rain. Since joining the faculty at Brigham Young University I have enjoyed the fictive sibling relationship with my cohort: Karen Carter, Rebecca de Schweinitz, and Aaron Skabelund. Lee Chambers, Jill Crandell, Kathryn Daynes, Amy Froide, Mary Hartman, Gerald Haslam, Dallett Hemphill, Paul Kerry, Anu Lahtinen, Julie Radle, Mary Stovall Richards, Lisa Wilson, and colleagues at Brigham Young University have all provided years of support as I have worked through this project.

Research for this project would not have happened without the cheerful and long-lasting assistance of the Gloucestershire Archives staff, particularly Victoria Thorpe and Paul Evans, and the staff at Chester Archives and Local Studies. My research was greatly enriched by the generosity of F.E.B. Witts, Geoffrey Castle, Carolyn Greet, and the Earl of Wemyss. Abigail Armistead at the Yale Center for British Art was always patient and helpful. In England I enjoyed the friendship of Sherry Avinou, who did more than her fair share of driving through Cotswold villages and lived to tell the tale of my driving. Dawn and Brent Fulwood and Reed and Erin Jones and their utterly charming children made being far from home more enjoyable than I could have anticipated.

Writing is a torturous experience at its best (at its worst it is indescribable in polite company) and I benefited from several colleagues who read chapters. In addition to departmental and university writing groups, I want to thank the thoughtful reading of Megan Sanborn-Jones and Todd Goodsell. Karen Carter and Don Harreld are the only people, other than my mother, who read a complete draft of the book without any hope of financial compensation. I also owe thanks to John Gillis, who read some truly dreadful early chapter drafts. The anonymous readers and the editing team, particularly Emma Brennan and Lianne Slavin at Manchester University Press and the freelance copy-editor, Fiona Little, provided valuable insight for which I am incredibly grateful. I am also grateful to Roderick Phillips and the *Journal of Family History* for agreeing to allow publication of Chapter 5, which is a later, expanded version of the article 'That fierce edge': sibling conflict and politics in Georgian England' in *Journal of Family History* 37:2 (April 2012).

I have been the thankful recipient of financial support from various sources over the years. I would like to thank the entities and donors who so generously supported this research. At Berkeley: the Allan Sharlin Memorial Fellowship (for which I hope Chapter 5 proves a worthy honor), the Sather Memorial Fellowship, the Mellon Consortia Conference held at the University of California, Berkeley, and the Summer Institute for Preparing Future Faculty, particularly Sabrina Soracco and Linda van Hoene. At Brigham Young University:

the Center for Family History and Genealogy, the Women's Research Institute, the Kennedy Center for International Studies, the Family Studies Center, the History Department, and the College of Family, Home, and Social Sciences. I hope the product makes your investments worthwhile.

Over the years I have enjoyed associations with talented and dedicated research assistants. Worthy of particular note was the help of MaLese Moeller, Melissa Chapman Johnson, Debbie Gurtler, Cassie Loyd, Betsy Crane, Katie Ledbetter, and Sarah Schow. Additionally, it is impossible to exaggerate the inestimable help of Rachel Belk Moyar and Katy Naef in the final revisions of the manuscript. Special thanks also go to Josie Ammon, who was always willing to lend a hand.

Good friends Lindseay Brown, Karen Carter, Suzanne Earnshaw, Kari Hutchinson, and Jenny Ostermiller have all listened to far more conversations about sibling dynamics than anyone should be required to endure. For that, and for so many other reasons, I am deeply grateful.

And to my siblings who have coloured every aspect of this project and continue to be the best personal cheering squad a person could hope for. For all their love, affection, hard work, dedication and sacrifice for me they deserve far more than their names in print, but it will have to do: Alan, Lewis, Susan, David, Leslie, Peter, Shelley, and Barbara Harris, Deborah and Fred Ewer, and Betsy and Tom Focareto. And to Naomi Ewer, Holly Focareto, and Shelliece, Samantha, and Anne Harris; David and Joseph Ewer, Connor Focareto, Caleb, Joshua, Matthew, Spencer, Taylor, and Zachary Harris: my nieces and nephews who, unwittingly, provoked thoughts on the generational aspects of sibling relationships and the bonds between cousins, and not-so-unwittingly provided me with endless entertainment, love, and affection.

All of this rambling about siblings may leave the impression that parents were minor figures in our family. That could not be further from the truth. We all understand that the exceptionally rewarding and supportive sibling network we enjoy is due to our truly exceptional parents. My father's and mother's faith in God and belief in me have inspired and sustained me throughout my life. My father did not live to see the end of this project; his decline and death overlapped with the final stages of preparing the manuscript for publication. Experiencing that grief together with my siblings deepened my appreciation for the depth and breadth of siblinghood and the power and comfort found in sharing and sharing alike.

Explanatory note on dates, ages, and names

For the sake of simplicity, all Old Style dates have been converted to the New Style calendar. Throughout the book, individuals' ages are given based on the following guidelines. In some records, particularly the Old Bailey Proceedings, individuals' ages were provided in the original record. For most records, however, ages were calculated. When a specific birth date was known the person's age was calculated from her or his last birthday. Therefore, someone born in November 1750 would be described as nineteen years old in a discussion of the summer of 1770. For those for whom only a baptism date or birth year was known the age was calculated by the year. Therefore, someone baptized or born in 1750 would be described as twenty years old in a discussion about events in 1770.

Because many of the women referred to in these pages had the same name I adopted the following standard for distinguishing between them. When the narrative makes it explicit which person is being discussed, only the first name is used. When the discussion involves several people of the same name, or when one of these women is introduced, her full name is given. If the woman was married at the time being described, both her maiden name and married name are provided. This is less cumbersome than consistently using 'née' to refer to maiden names and clarifies when several people in the same family have the same name. For example, in the Tracy-Travell family women of three generations used the name Anne: Anne Atkyns Tracy (1583–1761), Anne Tracy Travell (1705–1763), and Anne Travell (1737–1826). In Chapter 1 Anne Tracy Travell is referred to simply as Anne Tracy, to highlight her pre-marriage family connections. After that she is referred to by her full name to distinguish her from her mother and daughter. Other women are consistently referred to by both their maiden and married names to emphasize the overlapping obligations to both natal and conjugal families.

Introduction

> There is nothing simple about it. The interior of the family is a scene of multi-layered relationships folded over on each other like geological strata. In no other institution are relationships so extended in time, so intensive in contact, so dense in their interweaving of economics, motion, power and resistance.
>
> R. W. Connell, *Gender and Power*, 1987[1]

On 14–15 November 1768 the genteel, single Anne Travell made a typical entry in her daybook: 'I rec'd from my Br the remainder of what he ow'd Agnes to last midsum, £6.10.0. £3. I had paid her before, & other part £3.10.0 is to go to Chelt. Housekeeping for to pay her ... but Kitty has borrowed it & now owes Chelt. House purse £3.10.0.'[2] Anne was thirty-one when she noted the money her younger sister Kitty (Catherine) and elder brother Francis owed to the household account. Anne, Catherine, and another sister, Agnes, lived together in Cheltenham, but Francis lived in their childhood home – the respectable Swerford House in western Oxfordshire, some thirty miles distant. Forty-year-old Francis, despite having his own income and household, had borrowed from twenty-year-old Agnes, then returned the money to Anne, who distributed it to Agnes after deducting what Agnes owed to the common household funds shared by the sisters. Before it could rest in the communal coffer, however, Kitty borrowed it and now she owed the remaining sum. This brief entry hints at an untold story about English families in the past. There has been virtually no accounting for the Travell siblings' domestic and financial interaction in historical scholarship until recently. Most scholarship on early modern families begins with married couples or with parents and children. It is possible to tell the story of the Travell family from that perspective. That starting point would not be Anne, Catherine, and Francis in 1768, but first their parents and then perhaps Agnes, who married Edward Witts in 1776.

The Witts story is recognizable to anyone familiar with the historiography of English families. A wealth of documentary evidence reveals the tension between affection and practicality experienced by couples and parents in eighteenth-century England. Agnes's clear preference for her son, Francis Edward, over his brothers, Edward's and Agnes's labour to provide their sons with education, occupations, and marriage prospects, Agnes's and Edward's genuine love and affection, Edward's relief that Agnes inherited enough money to remove financial worries from his courtship prospects, Agnes's grief over the loss of two sons and, later, Edward's and Agnes's approval of their daughter-in-law and grandchildren all readily appear in the diaries, letters, and wills left by the family. Looking for more detail reveals the financial support that Agnes's brother, Ferdinando gave to the Wittses and Edward's involvement in the disastrous – and short-lived – marriage of his sister, Apphia. However, from this couple- and parent-based perspective, Ferdinando's financial support of Agnes and Edward becomes merely a footnote to the couple's money difficulties and the strain this put upon them.[3] Because it involves another couple, the story of Apphia Witts's marriage to the rapacious Lord Lyttelton becomes disconnected from Agnes and Edward's story and becomes a story about troubled marriages and their dissolutions.[4] But through it all Agnes and Edward, or Apphia and Lord Lyttelton, the married couples, remain the focus, the actors on stage. Even R.W. Connell, whose insightful depiction of families heads this introduction, recognized that families are 'internally complex', but still tended to reduce families to an adult man and woman with their dependent children.

Siblinghood and Social Relations proposes to shift focus to a different set of actors, not because married couples with children were unimportant, but to suggest that couples and parents had other important and demanding family relations, relations they had to negotiate and combine with spousal and parental duties. In particular, what follows draws attention to the sibling relationships that supported, supplemented, and even supplanted marital and parental relations. By shifting the focus to siblings, Ferdinando's financial support becomes not a footnote to the Wittses' story, but its own story about family relations, family economics, and family power – all older and longer-lasting than Agnes's marriage to Edward or her years as a parent. A sibling focus also brings Anne's, Catherine's and Francis's financial transactions into sharper relief. These transactions underscore the connections between sibling households and the unique gender and power relationships between sisters and brothers. Shifting attention to sibling relations reveals the essential labour of and contribution of siblings to early modern family economics and politics. Eighteenth-century marriage and parenting were, by definition, hierarchical.

Men and adults had more power than women and children. That was just the way things were. Siblings, however, were not that way. Yes, they encountered hierarchical understandings of their relationship that emphasized birth order and male privilege, but they also encountered powerful reminders that they were equals – that they should share and share alike. In that tension between hierarchy and equality, sibling relationships offer not only new ways of understanding Georgian families, but also insight into eighteenth-century ideas of social and political governance

Since its inception English family history has detected something special about the long eighteenth century, and more specifically the Georgian period. Whether tracing affective individualism, the cult of motherhood, or the ascendance of the conjugal family form, historians have pinpointed the eighteenth century as a transition phase to 'modern' families, even if they disagree on precisely what constitutes modernity or families. During the eighteenth and early nineteenth centuries a tight focus on children and the parents who raised them, romantic love, and the exclusionary nuclear family gradually replaced the long-standing and important communal and neighbourly connections between families. While older ideas of household and family that extended to servants and non-resident kin retained their significance throughout the Georgian period, by Victoria's reign the 'family' had disconnected from these broader connections and narrowed to mean a nuclear, private, and domestic entity focused on a conjugal couple and their offspring. Whether the impetus came from industrialization, the Enlightenment, or Romanticism it is clear that families underwent significant changes between the Restoration and the Regency. The nature of siblings' place within this historical trajectory and transition is problematic. They were both the vestiges of a previous nuclear family and lifelong contributors to new nuclear families. Their contribution and position, however, went unremarked upon at the time and in most historical scholarship.

For social scientists, like historians, the importance of siblings has paled in comparison with the impact of marriage and parenting, but unlike historians, social scientists have paid consistent attention to sibling relations. In fact we owe the term 'sibling' to early twentieth-century anthropology. Like anthropology, the disciplines of sociology, family therapy, psychology, and their popular versions have an enormous literature about siblings. Earlier scholars spent much of their time understanding birth-order dynamics and the role of parents in rearing young siblings. Recently the literature has increased its coverage of inter-sibling relations throughout the life course and social scientists have discussed the impact that sibling death has on children and adults.[5] They have explored the impact of sibling interaction on childhood and adolescence and its connections to the development of self and individuality and how to improve the quality of sibling relations. They have recognized the tugs and pulls between friendship and rivalry and the ever-shifting power dynamics between siblings.[6] They have also recognized the particularities of sibling conversation and sibling inequities.[7] They have focused intently on the origins of and solutions to sibling conflict within families, but they have also raised important questions for historical consideration. Social scientific interest in how the deaths of siblings affected childhood and children's relationships with their parents and their perceptions of self offers insight into how high childhood mortality rates affected early modern siblinghood and how this dovetailed with developing eighteenth-century attitudes about the individual and the self. Social scientists' recognition of differences in parental treatment of children and the lifelong repercussions this had on their children's relationships with each other is central to understanding much about Georgian siblings. The current research on contemporary siblings throughout the life course – with special salience in childhood and old age – underscores the importance of understanding historical siblinghood rooted in childhood and lasting a lifetime.

Though family historians have been slow to analyse sibling relationships, a study of brothers and sisters benefits from fifty years of scholarship on early modern and modern English families. Since spousal and child–parent relationships have undergone enormous changes, are subject to weighty legal and religious control, and exert a powerful influence on our cultural imagination, the emphasis on marriage and parents and children has generated a rich and deep historiography. Demographers and social historians of the 1960s, 1970s, and 1980s worked to understand the structures and meanings of early modern family – the 'only viable unit of study', according to Lawrence Stone.[8] The twentieth-century effort grew from an intellectual engagement with and an intense scholarly study of questions posed by eighteenth and nineteenth-century observers of the economic and demographic shifts of their day, writers such as Smith, Engels, and, of course, Malthus and Marx.[9] Driving this work, both demographic and historical, was the race for the real prize: the key to unlocking 'modernity'. Whether their definition of modernity was tied up with notions of economic change brought about by industrialization and capitalization or with a modernity defined by the creation of an independent self who shuffled off the confining coils of communal and familial identity to become that great invention of modern life – the individual – these scholars turned to families to find the roots of modernity.[10] Demographers' early conflation of 'family' with 'household', and the centrality of the small nuclear family, sent historians scrambling for the archives to find evidence to prove or disprove the statistical analysis of population reconstruction. If small nuclear family life and the centralization of property ownership through primogeniture were what allowed England to industrialize, and therefore modernize, then proving the prevalence of such a system would not only explain historical shifts in families, but also provide the framework for explaining modern economic, political, and social systems. Lawrence Stone's resounding *The Family, Sex and Marriage in England, 1500–1800* argued for major changes in family life between the sixteenth and eighteenth centuries – changes that brought forth not only new family forms, but the essence of modern life itself. His sweeping narrative generated massive debate as historians argued for a longer historical trajectory for the rise of individualism, nuclear families, and affection.[11] As these historians found roots of modern families as early as the Middle Ages and as historians of women, gender, and children disputed and dismantled arguments about the rise or creation of family affection, scholars came to accept that there were long continuities in English family life and that the nuclear family structure was much older than the cultural shift in attitudes about that family – shifts clearly visible in the eighteenth and nineteenth centuries.[12]

Despite efforts to find long continuities in English family history – a school of thought espoused by Alan Macfarlane, Barbara Hanawalt, Linda Pollock, and Ralph Houlbrooke – and similar efforts to emphasize changes in family life dating to the medieval or early modern period – associated with Lawrence Stone, Randolph Trumbach, and John Gillis – both schools were firmly anchored in ideas of modernity. In all this effort to look for the seeds of modernity (whether medieval or eighteenth-century) there was a tendency to pass over family relations less prone to change, less prone to state interference, and less prone to generate advice and prescriptive literature solely targeted to them than marriage and child-rearing were. Marriage with its tension between the patriarchal and the companionate and parenthood's tension between affection and control were grounded in the ancient hierarchies of gender and age and on the obedience of women to men and children to adults.[13] Siblinghood, however, sits uneasily with these configurations because brothers and sisters were peers – in daily practice and law in a way never imagined for married couples or parents and children – and yet were treated unequally according to gender and age.[14] By setting aside family relations beyond the vertical husband–wife and parent–child relations, researchers missed other important and dynamic elements of family life, family economy, and family politics. The interest in modernity in family structure uncovered the importance of family to social, political, and religious developments, but it also simultaneously narrowed the analytical attention granted to the family on its own terms.

The interest in finding connections between modernity and families made family history a growth industry in the 1970s and 1980s. Though those heady days faded, the flourishing of gender and women's history brought new questions and new perspectives to the study of English families. Since Leonore Davidoff and Catherine Hall's seminal *Family Fortunes*, women's and gender history has played an increasing role in interpretations of Georgian families. For the purposes of this study, Davidoff and Hall's key contribution was in signalling how families were implicated in the creation of class and gender norms and how gender informed family power structures.[15]

Though Davidoff and Hall recognized the salience of sibling relations, most gender and women's history sees family ties through a life-cycle lens. Because women were often defined by and confined to their family roles, this approach has concentrated on discussions of what the limits and possibilities were of being a daughter, wife, mother, or widow. The problem with life-cycle-based analysis is that it often depicts men and, especially women as moving from one family niche to the next without any connection between stages.[16] In this depiction of men's and women's lives they move from category to category without careful attention to the overlapping of those experiences. At any one time an individual woman could be a daughter, a wife, a mother, a sister, an aunt, a niece, a cousin, and so on while also participating in larger social and communal activities. Similarly, a man, though he might also fulfil a variety of public, non-familial duties, would also have the obligations of being a son, husband, father, brother, and so on. Attention to overlapping family and extra-familial obligations reveals the untidy nature of early modern family life. Despite didactic prescriptions that neatly ordered the differences between men and women and their respective roles, their lived experiences were much more complicated.

Since the 1990s a burgeoning interest in marital status, in children and childhood, in women's property, and in the meaning and language of kinship has served to enrich historiography of Georgian families. Influenced by feminist and gender historiography, legal history, and the cultural turn, this work has offered multiple ways of understanding family relations. Some women's and legal historians have noted that many of the changes of modern families actually led to a decrease in women's, particularly wives and widows', power over land, business, and kinship.[17] Others, however, have argued for women's control over property, especially in the case of daughters and unmarried women.[18] Historians of childhood and age have recognized the influence of gender and family relations upon children and the elderly.[19] Cultural historians, such as Naomi Tadmor, have analysed the important overlaps between household, family, and friends in eighteenth-century familial and financial relations.[20] Tadmor's work has been particularly important because it has focused on eighteenth-century understandings of kinship instead of trying to explain the origins of nineteenth-century kinship. Taken together these various strands of historical scholarship have revealed the richness and complexity of early modern and Georgian family relationships.

Scholarship on Georgian families has emphasized a shift from loosely allied extended kin networks to the emotionally intense married couple and nuclear family. Emotions among family members, particularly spouses and parents and children, have been key to much family historiography.[21] Since Lawrence Stone bequeathed the phrase 'affective individualism' to subsequent generations, historians have grappled with changes in familial emotions and their impact on marriage and individuality. Stone highlighted the seventeenth- and eighteenth-century origins of the affective family – a family isolated from kin and neighbour and focused on fostering love and individuality among its members, particularly romantic love fulfilled by successful marriages. More recently Ruth Perry has suggested that the late eighteenth and early nineteenth centuries saw the rise of the 'conjugal' family in both culture and practice. The conjugal family resembles much of Stone's affective individual family – the married couple became the centerpiece, and the consanguineal family subsequently lost its importance. Perry's analysis reveals that the cost of this shift rested disproportionately on the shoulders of women, in some ways echoing Gillis's and Davidoff and Hall's classic analyses of the cost, often to women, of creating enterprising, middle-class families in the Georgian and early Victorian periods.[22] Taken together these works posit a coherent picture of Georgian families increasingly ignoring or reducing the impact of family relations beyond those between spouses and between parent and child. However, taken together they also form an awkward fit with Naomi Tadmor's elucidation of eighteenth-century kinship and friendship, Davidoff's more recent research on Victorian siblings, and Adam Kuper's recent assertions about the importance of cousin marriage to middle-class Victorians. These scholars have demonstrated that nineteenth-century families still reaped enormous rewards from relationships well outside the boundary of the conjugal or parental. In essence what is missing from the earlier works is not astute analysis of families, but a lingering, if often subtle, insistence that the Romantic and Victorian notion that often equated married couples with family is not a historically contingent notion, but a given. A study of sibling relations brings these various strands together. It is clear that attitudes about family life did undergo an enormous change between the Tudor and Victorian periods, and this undoubtedly affected many aspects of family life and the records of family life. By beginning with siblings and studying them over the life course, it is possible to see both the cultural importance of both marriage and the continued importance of other kin, both within the family and in social interactions. Siblinghood offered women and men a mixed-sex relationship during a time of increasingly romanticized and sexualized ideas of marriage and a peer relationship among a litany of hierarchical connections. As models of family life and governance shifted from one of order and obedience in the seventeenth century to one of affection and love in the eighteenth and nineteenth centuries, siblings felt the rub keenly in their own relationships.

This increasingly rich understanding of eighteenth-century families, however, has not prevented older historiographic claims, particularly that family power moved vertically only and that co-resident siblings did not constitute a family, from influencing how many view early modern and Georgian families.[23] This has had the unfortunate outcome of a continued equation of marriage with family.[24] The conflation of marriage and family is old in both the historiography and our contemporary imagination, but it forgets that people have families of origin, even if they never marry or have children. In a time like the eighteenth century, when kin were essential to one's social and financial credit, reducing family to the married couple reduces our understanding of both kinship and social relations. In essence, what emerges in a discussion of siblinghood is a picture of early modern family life more complicated than that offered by earlier generations of family historians. If, as is suggested by the structure and content of many histories of the family, marriage and parenting are the organizing principles of early modern family life, then family life and family duties occupy a vertical axis that puts families in a strict age and gender hierarchy. While this is undoubtedly true for certain aspects of family life, it misses the lifelong horizontal nexus of siblings' contribution to their families. As Amy Froide has asserted, 'we may have overestimated the relative significance of spouses and children in early modern England'.[25] While marriage carried heavy normative weight, most families were combinations of nuclear units connected to single, widowed, and married kin.[26]

Though family history has become heavily influenced by gender history and the cultural and literary turn, the debate about 'modern' families as being built on conjugal couples and early modern families as being connected to kin and friends continues to inform much of the scholarship on eighteenth-century English families, particularly the recent work on siblings. Ruth Perry's work represents a strain of scholarship invested in tracing the origins of

Victorian nuclear domesticity. In Perry's *Novel Relations* Stone's thesis receives a reinvigorated analysis. Though she is careful to distinguish her argument from Stone's 'affective individualism', Perry argues that in the latter half of the eighteenth century and the beginning of the nineteenth the conjugal family replaced the consanguineal family. Tying together fiction, law, and, to a lesser degree, practice, she makes the case that as inheritance law narrowed the pool of appropriate heirs, writers of fiction developed plots centred on the happy reunion not of romantic, conjugal couples, but of consanguineal family members – parents, siblings, aunts, uncles, cousins, nieces, and nephews. Perry sees a nostalgic celebration of these relations just as conjugal families competed with and then slowly superseded consanguineal families. This idea works particularly well when one is interested in the end point – Victorian domesticity and the assumption that families consist of men with wives and dependent children. However, as in many family histories interested in explaining how English culture arrived at nineteenth-century middle-class domesticity and private, nuclear families, the period just before is not fully appreciated on its own terms. Even if Gillis is right that 'young people ceased to be sons and daughters long before they became husbands and wives' he still misses the fact that siblings were there all along – in the natal home, after work and education separated them physically and death took their parents, and still there when they entered marriage.[27] Sibling relationships were the only relationships that literally lasted a lifetime, spanning the other stages of family life. The conjugal is an important family stage more than it is an important family type, and this was true from the Middle Ages through to the early nineteenth century. While fiction may have come to isolate the conjugal unit increasingly from the consanguineal unit and while primogeniture, entail, and other inheritance practices may have come to privilege the conjugal, most families (particularly those without large enough estates to consider the complications of strict settlement) relied on siblings. And siblings, of course, spent parts or all of childhood together – even in times that prized conjugal families.

Perry's two excellent chapters on sisters and brothers raise important issues and open the gate for further and full exploration of the sibling connection. They also leave unexplored several aspects of sibling relationships. Much of Perry's evidence for the diminished importance of consanguineal ties comes from recognizing the changing nature of families and family relationships implied in changing inheritance and enclosure practices. The difficulty with property relations as a starting point is that a lateral, lifelong relationship like siblinghood does not fit easily within them. Siblings were on the ground and had to be grappled with before any potential spouse (and generational inheritance scheme) entered the picture, and they had to deal with the remnants of previous inheritance practices.[28] While Perry recognized the importance of marriage in generating conflict between sisters and sisters-in-law, this reinforces the idea that real families began with marriage and ignores the dynamic between siblings (particularly brothers) before, during, and after marriage. The evidence of property relationships also reifies families as centred on vertical ties to descendants only – forgetting that conflict, negotiation, and compromises occurred not just over material survival, but also over emotional and social concerns. Perry recognizes that the twentieth-century preoccupation with nuclear families led to earlier inaccurate or incomplete interpretations, but even her brilliant analysis allows the end point (Victorian domesticity) to pull the analysis along. Her great chapters on siblings still focus on siblings through the lens of married couples. The chapter about sisters is really about sisters' conflict with their brothers' wives – the married brother being at the centre of the tug of war. The chapter on brothers centres on brotherly protection only until the sister married. Putting these patterns in isolation from the other aspects of siblinghood – its roots in childhood, its persistence even after marriage, its internal dynamics, paradoxes, and possibilities – forces a framework on siblinghood that limits our understanding of sibling ties and their importance to individuals, families, kinship, and even political imagination. Perry ends by reifying the married couple as coterminous with 'family' even as she fights against that analytical trajectory.

Perry's intriguing work signals the growth of sibling studies covering the eighteenth and nineteenth century and highlights some of the work that remains to be done. The nineteenth century did not only see the rise of the conjugal family; it saw a flourishing and sentimentalizing of the sibling tie. Perry's work and scholarship on nineteenth-century siblings, however, provide no framework for understanding the valorization and idolization of sibling relations that developed in the latter half of the eighteenth century and fully flowered in the middle of the nineteenth.[29] The most recent work on siblings, *Sibling Relations and the Transformation of European Kinship*, a volume edited by Christopher Johnson and David Sabean, suggests an answer at odds with Perry's conclusions.[30] Johnson and Sabean assert that 'a wholesale transformation in the structure and practice of kinship in which vertical patrilineages gave way to horizontally organized consanguineal kindred occurred during the century surrounding the age of the French Revolution'.[31] In this way they connect with assertions by scholars as varied as Randolph Trumbach, Steven Ruggles, Mary Hartman and Amanda Vickery, who have all hinted that as the language of certain forms of kinship narrowed in the eighteenth and nineteenth centuries, sibling relations actually strengthened.[32] Even in the nineteenth century, when kinship terms completely lost their earlier expansive definitions, siblings 'thickened' kinship within households.³³ Johnson and Sabean are building on a decade's worth of scholarship about siblings that is just now fully flowering. Articles and edited books have uncovered the power and reach of siblinghood from the Middle Ages to the nineteenth century and throughout the Western world.³⁴ This holds true for Georgian England, where accounts of siblings saturate the pages of diaries, letters, wills, and account books. Other than in Johnson and Sabean's introduction, however, this work has yet to be synthesized into a larger narrative. Johnson and Sabean's introduction gives that larger narrative, but because it covers 600 years and all of Europe it is by definition not an in-depth analysis of siblinghood in a particular context. Forthcoming books on early modern and modern siblings in America and nineteenth-century siblings in England are about to take sibling studies to a new level.³⁵

The nascent sibling literature has recognized the material and social connections of siblinghood and siblings' influence on gender relations.³⁶ This study builds on this literature and brings childhood into the discussion. As described in Lynne Bowdon's account of medieval kinship, Georgian siblings engaged in intricate patterns of symbolic and material support.³⁷ Additionally the book's analysis picks up some of the threads with social and political ideas hinted at by Leonore Davidoff.³⁸ Davidoff recognized the importance of siblings over the life course; she noted their connections to the development of the self, to ideas of social and political fictive siblings, and to the tension between love and conflict, and between equality and hierarchy. Davidoff has only hinted at siblinghood's earlier origins. It is in the eighteenth century, however, that the real tension is exposed as a language of equality began to lose its all-male connotations, and when older patterns of social and financial support from kin were still essential. *Siblinghood and Social Relations* outlines the contours of Georgian siblinghood in an attempt to understand its specific advantages and disadvantages because it was in the Georgian period that lived siblinghood began to lose the public recognition of its meaning and function while fictive siblinghood increased its abstract reach.

Social and political thought

Benedict Anderson has described the rise of nationalism as an imagined experience of parallel lives – in the 'idiom of sibling'.³⁹ This intriguing use of sibling language raises questions about whether national models built on fictive fraternal and sororal ties found such resonance because men and women were already accustomed to thinking of themselves as part of a peer group accustomed to considering their common cause. As Mary Hartman has argued for early modern families, 'before equality was widely touted in what historians have isolated prematurely as the "public realm," there was grounding in daily experience to make that abstraction meaningful and to encourage its application to political rhetoric and action'.[40] Much of the tension in eighteenth-century siblinghood resulted from a long-standing tradition of sibling equality, combined with eighteenth-century ideas of social and political equality, grating against ancient practices that privileged elder siblings, brothers, and married siblings. Georgian siblings enjoyed more equality, more familiarity, and more similarities than were available in any other mixed-sex relationship. However, that equality was situated within a broader framework that ordered families, societies, and nations along hierarchical lines.[41] Common law preferred lateral kin like siblings, but eighteenth-century practices often privileged elder brothers over sisters and younger siblings. If medieval and early modern women 'were never offered anything like equality with men within the family economy', they simultaneously benefited from an inheritance scheme that adapted and moderated their subordination.[42] Marriage was idealized as a partnership, but simultaneously rested on shared ideas about the 'indispensable virtue' of obedience and hierarchy.[43]

Current scholarship has recognized the importance of family and kinship to political and social imagination. Naomi Tadmor has noted the importance of friendship to social order; Rachel Weil, Richard Price, and Richard Grassby, among others, have realized the intricate connections between political, economic, and familial relations.[44] Jonathan Barry, in work about voluntary associations, notes that such organizations contained a 'mixture of hierarchy contained within a subscriber democracy'.[45] Despite occasional references to siblinghood there has been little recognition of the fact that the increased use of fictive siblinghood had implications for families and for social and political order. Much of this scholarship has emphasized parent–child and marital relations and conflict, not sibling co-operation.[46] However, contemporaries often drew on siblinghood as a model for social and political governance. The seventeenth and eighteenth centuries saw a flourishing of new ideas about social organization and governance. Consistently using the language of family and home, early modern and Enlightenment thinkers began a re-evaluation of who should govern the state, the church, and the home. The political-religious conflicts of the seventeenth century had heightened this discussion and eighteenth-century debates about women, slavery, justice, and equality further complicated it. Gradually, a new model of political organization emerged, a process further spurred by the American and French Revolutions.[47] This model replaced the hierarchal Leviathan model with an equality-driven model of *fraternité*.⁴⁸ The inklings of the sisterhood of feminism are also visible in the late eighteenth century.⁴⁹ The use of brotherhood as a template for social organization was not an eighteenth-century invention; monasteries, convents, guilds, and even inheritance practices had long used a sibling-based notion of communal co-operation and support.⁵⁰ The wholesale importation of brotherhood (and the unspoken complication of sisterhood) into political and religious models, however, was just beginning to lose the radical association with religious and political dissidents that it had held in the seventeenth century.⁵¹ While much has been written about the shifts in early modern religious and political organization that valorized the equality of brotherhood, and occasionally sisterhood, there has been little discussion of the experiences of real brothers and sisters. Understanding real sibling relations highlights the difficulties in using a sibling political or social model in the eighteenth century. Though a language of siblinghood was meant to conjure notions of equality, real and fictive sibling relations were infused with hierarchy. Political thinkers often dwelt on the justice and equality of brotherhood, but still saw it as subject to rules of patriarchal and paternal rights, and of course any incorporation of women, who were by definition unequal to men, complicated matters even further.⁵²

Chronology and sources

The Georgian period is ideal for studying sibling relationships.⁵³ The period came after the late seventeenth-century changes in inheritance law, which put most brothers and sisters on more equal ground while simultaneously increasing their inequalities as husbands and wives. The later eighteenth-century interest in women's rights increased authors' attention to sisterly and sister–brother relationships. The American and French Revolutions and their explicit use of sibling language influenced how sibling relations were perceived in England. The end of the Georgian period – 1830 – is also a useful end point for this story. Industrialization, the expansion of state control of poor relief, and the development of extra-familial credit networks all led to a diminution of siblings' material and practical support – or at least a diminution of the recognition of such support. As the practical aspects of siblinghood decreased in the face of corporations and the state, its emotional and sentimental expectations increased. As equality, even with its detractors, solidified its assault on hierarchy as the central social organizing principle in England, the tensions between hierarchy and equality found in sibling relationships lost some of their immediacy.

Linguistically, the eighteenth century saw siblings as inhabiting two worlds – one flexible and informal and the other rigid and hierarchical. In the Georgian era sibling terminology followed a pattern of less rigid boundaries on labelling affective ties. The terms 'brother' and 'sister' meant more than one's biological siblings to eighteenth-century families. If technical or legal definitions were required, a person might distinguish between siblings by blood and siblings by law or marriage, but in daily usage people referred to their biological siblings, half-siblings, step-siblings, siblings-in-law, and even illegitimate siblings all simply as 'sister' or 'brother'. The law recognized differences between these different grades of sibling: siblings-in-law did not have the same claims to an inheritance from a parent, nor were step- and half-siblings and illegitimate siblings considered as having the same obligations and benefits of full biological siblings. This suggests that despite legal and cultural expectations, real brothers and sisters worked with a much more flexible notion of siblinghood. Ideal siblings-in-law came from the same social stratum and even from the same extended family, thus facilitating their incorporation into the sibling network. Though they had no legal status as equals with siblings, siblings-in-law took on the sibling network of their spouses and were expected to behave accordingly.

Eighteenth-century hierarchies replicated themselves in sibling social address. Eldest brothers kept their surname with their fraternal designation. Younger sisters and brothers were labelled only with their forenames. In correspondence and diaries the Travell sisters always referred to their eldest brother as 'my Brother Travell' and their other brother as 'my Brother Ferdinand'. The title 'Sister Travell', ideally reserved for the eldest brother's wife, was also used by the eldest single sister. The Sharp family of Northumberland, Durham, and London followed similar patterns and referred to their sisters-in-law as 'my sister James' or 'my sister John'. The formality and the strict adherence that families paid to such forms of address conflicted with the familiarity afforded by siblings' use of nicknames. While letters might open formally, references within the letters were often decidedly informal. The Travell sisters referred to one another as Fanny, Kitty, and Nanny, suggesting that the formality demanded by genteel letter-writing did not reflect the familiarity that siblings enjoyed in face-to-face interactions.[54] This type of labelling was common in eighteenth-century family correspondence and provides another example of the tension between equality in daily face-to-face association and the socially recognized system of ranked titles.

Sibling relations were indissoluble and more durable than any other relations: relatively late marriage ages and high mortality rates, a proportion of the population who never married, and people left without spouses due to death meant that siblinghood was the only lifelong aspect of kinship.[55] The demographic transition of the eighteenth century set the stage for such a lifelong relationship. The population declines of the sixteenth and seventeenth centuries, largely due to diseases such as the plague and the poor harvests of the mid-seventeenth century, were slowly reversed as the eighteenth century progressed. The temperature warmed, harvests became more reliable, and towards the end of the century better hygiene and the introduction of inoculation against illnesses such as smallpox allowed people to live longer and healthier lives. Simultaneously, marriage ages decreased, meaning that women had more children than in the previous century. Demographers have postulated that during the eighteenth century a thirty-year-old adult had on average two surviving siblings of each gender.[56] Though co-resident siblings never made up more than 3 per cent of households before 1821, siblings, whether co-resident or not, constituted between 18 and 22 per cent of relatives during the same period.[57] If in-laws are taken into account, a married adult would also interact with her or his spouse's siblings, not to mention the spouses of her or his own siblings. Taking into account half- and step-siblings, biological siblings, and siblings-in-law, it was a rare individual who went a lifetime without sibling ties. And even with relatively high mortality rates, having multiple siblings of both sexes meant that the death of one or more siblings rarely left a person bereft of all sibling ties. In the context of eighteenth-century demography, financial practices, and understandings of family and friends, sisters' and brothers' economic transactions were necessary to their family's financial and social survival. The mortality rate of parents, late marriage ages, and high numbers of people who spent a significant portion of their adult life single, all established a family structure that favoured sibling economic networks because siblinghood began early in one's life, was legally unbreakable, and lasted longer than any other family relationship.[58]

Families did not, and do not, live by neat chronologies, nor do their experiences often suggest neat beginning and ending points, especially for siblings whose relationships were largely unbounded by legal statute. This study is primarily concerned with relationships and how they changed over both familial and historical time. Therefore, personal accounts, probate records, and court testimony have been privileged over demographic analysis. The evidence comes from a selection of gentry families for whom extensive and varied materials were available. The most detailed accounts are for seven families where it was possible to trace several generations and use numerous sources. For each of these families it was possible to find many, if not all, of the following sources: large correspondence collections, one or more diaries, land and probate records, marriage settlements, account books, memorabilia, parish registers, and portraits. These families' stories will appear repeatedly in the pages that follow. Not all of their experiences were identical to those of other families, but the patterns demonstrated in the sources were evident throughout the data on other families. These families are the Tracys and Travells, covering three generations between 1700 and the 1820s; the Wittses, covering two generations between the 1750s and 1820s; the Sharps, covering three generations between 1700 and 1830s; the Edwards and Freeman family, covering two generations between the 1710s and 1750s; the Sheridans, covering three generations between the 1720s and 1820s; the Cumberland brothers, in their correspondence between 1771 and 1784; and the Jacksons, covering three generations between 1690s and 1770s. The Tracys and Travells originally came from Oxfordshire and Gloucestershire and retained strong ties there as well as in London; the Wittses were almost exclusively in Oxfordshire; the Sharps were based in Northumberland, Durham, Northamptonshire, and London (their records are stored in Gloucester because of descendants' residence there); the Edwardses and Freemans were in London and Oxford; the Sheridans shuttled between Dublin and London; the Cumberlands lived in London, attended Cambridge University, and worked in the north, and one member of the family eventually settled in Gloucestershire. The Jacksons were the most tied to Gloucestershire and the family estate outside Bristol, but military service and cousins in London took them from home often. In the next group are some twenty-five families for whom there are smaller collections of information, usually comprising only one or two source types. For each of these families there exists only one collection of letters, or one diary, or a brief biography or autobiography, complemented perhaps by a probate document or two. Additionally, eighteenth-century portraits, predominantly from these families and from the Yale Center for British Art, and prescriptive literature were explored for the light they shed on both relationships and their normative presentation.

These families' records tend to preserve evidence of the positive aspects of siblinghood, if for no other reason than that their descendants preserved them over centuries and had opportunities to edit or remove unflattering items. In order to broaden the social groups represented in the analysis and to find places where sibling relations broke down, probate and court records have been used. These were drawn principally from manuscript records from the Gloucester Consistory Court and the Chester Consistory Court, the Gloucestershire Poor Law records, and transcripts from the Old Bailey. They contain a wealth of information about all sorts of family and economic relationships among a segment of English society which are not available from any other source. Where possible, the probate records were connected to parish registers in an attempt to sketch the generational, age, and gender aspects of family life. These sources demonstrate both smooth-running sibling relations and siblings collapsing under resentment, anger, and disappointment. Information about the families of the very poor is notoriously difficult to find, but the limited information from the Gloucestershire Poor Law records, as well as that gleaned from published primary materials (such as Linda Pollock's work) and secondary literature, has been used to provide as broad a picture of Georgian sibling relations as possible.[59] Overall the records cover most social groups from across England. Both 'prescriptive' and 'descriptive' families appear in these pages.[60] The 'prescriptive' families are used to show patterns of expectation, but it is the 'descriptive' families who are at the heart of this analysis.

The Travell family records figure prominently throughout the book. The records left by Anne Tracy, John Travell, and their children cover the years 1723–1826 – conveniently nestled within and spanning the majority of the Georgian period. Their records – letters, diaries, wills, and account books – offer an opportunity to contrast the specifics of one family with the more general pattern. Additionally, this approach highlights the lifelong nature of sibling ties and the way family and kinship patterns often moved at their own pace and not according to other historical chronologies. In particular, the records written and preserved by Anne Travell (1737–1826) – multiple volumes of a daybook, letters, recipes, a commonplace book, and probate records – underscore the possibilities and responsibilities of siblinghood. While Anne's long life makes her an ideal vehicle for studying Georgian families, her story is highlighted for additional reasons. Though the eighteenth century saw an increase in female literacy and literary production in the West, historical artefacts made and preserved by men still outnumber any surviving sources left by women. Anne's accounts offer more than just the chance to have a woman speaking for herself.[61] Siblings were important to all families – as both children and adults – but the lifelong relationships available with siblings had special salience for never-married people, childless people and particularly women. Understanding lives like Anne Travell's is impossible without understanding sibling relationships. While Anne cannot be a generic icon of a sister, a never-married sister like her was embedded in sibling relationships and explicitly acknowledged this. For married women or married men other family relationships crowded in and overlapped with sibling ties. Anne's life offers the chance to see the sibling relationship in the foreground. This approach emphasizes sibling relationships and simultaneously recognizes that those relationships co-existed with numerous other familial and social relations. For Anne, a never-married woman, orphaned well before her thirtieth birthday, siblings were the cornerstone and foundation of her family and kin connections. Her records bring the labour and benefits of siblinghood into sharp relief. If traditional, vertical, conjugal, and parental approaches to family history are used to analyse Anne's life she is reduced, at best, to a footnote in her parents' and married siblings' stories. At worst she becomes an 'ancient maiden' to be ignored or pitied as a burden to her family.[62]

The chapters that follow are organized thematically, but with attention to family and historical time. Chapter 1, 'Learning to be a sibling', considers siblings as children and how they learned the role of sibling in both familial and social settings. Historians of children emphasize childhood as important to the development of class and gender identities. Historians of family and gender emphasize the role that parents and other adults played in those developments. This chapter argues that children's impact on each other – particularly their siblings, with whom they spent the bulk of their early years – has been underestimated. Siblings knew that their financial, social, and material futures were interlocked. Even if schooling took some brothers away from their sisters, and even if training took sisters and brothers from home, childhood interaction had already established family rituals and patterns of family power that shaped their adult behaviours. Current literature depicts English adolescence as characterized by separation from parents, as a space for individuality and creation of class and gender behaviour. Chapter 1 posits instead that children and youths carried sibling relations with them, as bridges to adulthood and as necessary supports for lifelong social, financial, and material success.

Chapter 2, 'Ties that bound', explores injunctions about friendship, affection, and love between siblings. Other than passing references to the fact that sisters were particularly close or that brother–sister ties were strong, little has been written about sibling emotional attachments. Using prescriptive literature and personal accounts, Chapter 2 reveals that for siblings, love, affection, and friendship meant ideas of unity, solidarity, and unwavering support. Others have recognized that early modern friendship often meant instrumental help, often arranged between those of unequal position. Sibling friendship, however, demanded not only instrumental exchanges, but a disregard for duty, obligation, or patronage in such exchanges. From this concept of sibling friendship, fictive siblinghood drew its meaning and function.

Chapter 3, 'Ties that cut', links with the previous one to survey social and cultural fears about sibling relations gone awry. Prescriptive literature declaimed siblings to be natural friends, but warned parents to avoid treating children unequally, thereby allowing discontent and rivalry to develop. Previous scholarship has reduced sibling acrimony to property conflicts between the eldest son and his younger brothers. This chapter exposes the more mundane and corrosive disappointments and jealousies that stalked sibling relations. All siblings, no matter what their birth order or gender, were keenly aware of any differences between one another's experiences and treatment. Sibling acrimony developed when brothers and sisters proved unable to live up to the lofty expectations of sibling love and support. The chapter also touches on eighteenth-century fears of incest.

Chapters 4 and 5, 'Sibling economics' and 'Sibling politics', analyse how childhood patterns of adult friendship and resentment affected household management, relationships, and power. No other family relationship (or non-familial relationship) faced the kind of contradictory tension between natural enemies and natural friends that siblinghood did. Other family relationships, including marriage, contained a recognized element of conflict, but they did not assume that the relationship was based upon both a natural tendency to rivalry and a natural tendency to love. Entering family life from the point of view of siblinghood reveals a family relationship that had to balance other relations carefully and was composed of a unique power structure. Old debates about the role of parental influence on marriage choice, for example, are given new perspectives when it is realized that sisters and brothers also exacted an influence over marriage partners, sometimes as a negotiator for their siblings and sometimes as a buffer between differing paternal and fraternal desires. Property relationships, though technically governed by the custom of primogeniture, take on new meanings when siblings' participation is factored in. And within the sibling networks themselves, brothers and sisters confronted internal and external power lines that tangled with gender, marital status, and birth order.

'Sibling economics' focuses on the familial, material, social, and financial work done by siblings, particularly within and between households. Much current scholarship emphasizes patriarchal and conjugal households. However, the success of households was grounded in careful work by siblings in conjunction with each other and with spouses. The material and emotional functions of sisters and brothers show how an imagined household could be just as significant as any physical household. Siblings imagined themselves as equal participants in a household that could reach across time and space. Sibling economics were the conduit through which affection, love, friendship, rivalry, discord, and discontent flowed and ebbed. In this way, attention to siblings brings together literature on families, marriage, and the unmarried to show them working together in households – both real and fictive.

Chapter 5, 'Sibling politics', uses analysis of probate disputes between siblings and returns to the Travell family in order to trace the long-term effects of childhood, sibling friendship, rivalry, and economics on family power dynamics. Sibling dynamics had to take female forms of power seriously, but they also fostered a type of male domestic power unparalleled in other familial relationships. Siblings had the most equal of mixed-sex relations in early modern England, even when not strictly equitable. Legally brothers had no statutory rights over their sisters or their sisters' property, unlike their sisters' fathers and husbands. There were numerous inequalities between men and women both inside and outside the family, but there was no established legal preference for brothers and their interests in their status as siblings. Within the family, siblings had to negotiate several layers of complex gender and age hierarchies that cannot simply be categorized by gender or marriage relationship. Unlike marital or parent–child politics, sibling power dynamics were built on the complicated connections between gender, birth order, and marital status. Authors of prescriptive literature imagined a simplified sibling power structure – one where brothers were always older and sisters always in need of their protection, at least until a husband came along. The reality of eighteenth-century demographics meant that siblings had to negotiate a more convoluted reality. The further relations diverged most sharply from ideas of equality (excluding the eldest son's right to claim the patrimony), the sharper and more contentious the power struggles between siblings became.

The experience of siblings reveals how incomplete our understanding of early modern English family life has sometimes become. The neglect of horizontal familial relations such as those between siblings and cousins, or even attenuated hierarchal relations such as those with aunts and uncles, has skewed our understanding of gender and power in the family, the influence of property and inheritance on family relations, and the connections between families and other social relations. *Siblinghood and Social Relations* does not utterly dispute these strains of family and gender history, but it disrupts them by exposing another layer of historical experience and historical analysis. Siblings confronted cultural expectations that painted them as natural-born friends and/or natural-born enemies. The tension between those competing labels was further complicated by the heavy material expectations placed upon brothers and sisters and their negotiation with familial power structures. 'To share and share alike' was more than a legal phrase enjoining siblings to divide property equally: it neatly summarized the expectations placed upon them by eighteenth-century English culture and by their own families.

Notes

1. R.W. Connell, *Gender and Power: Society, the Person, and Sexual Politics* (Palo Alto, 1987), p. 121.
2. Anne Travell, daybook, 14–15 November 1768, Bowly Family of Cirencester Collection, GA, D4582/4/17/4.
3. John Gillis, *For Better, for Worse: British Marriages, 1600 to the Present* (New York and Oxford, 1985).
4. Thomas Frost, *The Wicked Lord Lyttelton* (Stroud, Gloucestershire, 1876, repr. 2006); Joanne Bailey, *Unquiet Lives: Marriage and Marriage Breakdown in England, 1660–1800* (Cambridge, 2003); Elizabeth Foyster, *Marital Violence: An English Family History, 1660–1857* (Cambridge, 2005).
5. Elizabeth DeVita-Raeburn, *The Empty Room: Surviving the Loss of a Brother or Sister at Any Age* (New York, 2004).
6. Rand D. Conger et al., eds., *Continuity and Change in Family Relations: Theory, Methods, and Empirical Findings* (Mahwah, NJ, and London, 2004), pp. 293–382; Rosalind Edwards et al., *Sibling Identity and Relationships: Sisters and Brothers* (London and New York, 2006); Dorothy Rowe, *My Dearest Enemy, my Dangerous Friends: Making and Breaking Sibling Bonds* (London and New York, 2007); Douglas W. Mock, *More than Kin and Less than Kind: The Evolution of Family Conflict* (Cambridge, MA, and London, 2004); Peter Goldenthal, *Why Can't We Get Along? Healing Adult Sibling Relationships* (New York, 2002).
7. Deborah Tannen, *You were Always Mom's Favorite! Sisters in Conversation throughout their Lives* (New York: Random House, 2009); Dalton Conley, *The Pecking Order: Which Siblings Succeed and Why* (New York: Pantheon Books, 2004); Frank J. Sulloway, *Born to Rebel: Birth Order, Family Dynamics, and Creative Lives* (New York, 1996).
8. Lawrence Stone, *The Family, Sex and Marriage in England, 1500–1800* (New York, 1977), p. 19; Peter Laslett, *The World we have Lost: Further Explored* (London, 1983) and *Household and Family in Past Time* (Cambridge, 1972); E. Anthony Wrigley and Roger Schofield, *The Population History of England, 1541–1871: A Reconstruction* (Cambridge, 1989).
9. Keith Wrightson, *Earthly Necessities: Economic Lives in Early Modern Britain* (New Haven, 2000).
10. Amanda Vickery, *The Gentleman's Daughter: Women's Lives in Georgian England* (New Haven and London, 1998), p. 4; Alan Macfarlane, *The Origins of English Individualism: The Family, Property and Social Transition* (Cambridge and New York, 1978); John Demos, *A Little Commonwealth: Family Life in Plymouth Colony*, 30th anniversary edn, (Oxford, 1999); Philip Greven, *The Protestant Temperament: Patterns of Child-Rearing, Religious Experience, and the Self in Early America* (Chicago, 1977).
11. Alan Macfarlane, 'Review of *The Family, Sex and Marriage in England 1500–1800*, by Lawrence Stone', *History and Theory*, 18:1 (February 1979), 103–26.

12 Mary S. Hartman, *The Household and the Making of History: A Subversive View of the Western Past* (Cambridge, 2004).
13 Gillis, *For Better, for Worse*, p. 82; Macfarlane, 'Review of *The Family, Sex and Marriage*'.
14 Tom Arkell, Nesta Evans, and Nigel Goose, eds., *When Death Do Us Part: Understanding and Interpreting the Probate Records of Early Modern England* (Oxford, 2000), pp. 19–22.
15 Themes to which Davidoff later returned in an essay on Victorian siblings. See Leonore Davidoff, 'Kinship as a Categorical Concept: A Case Study of Nineteenth Century Siblings', *Journal of Social History*, 39:2 (Winter 2005), 411–28.
16 Olwen Hufton, *The Prospect before Her: A History of Women in Western Europe* (New York, 1995).
17 Leonore Davidoff and Catherine Hall, *Family Fortunes: Men and Women of the English Middle Class, 1780–1850* (Chicago, 1987), pp. 319–22, 415–26; Eileen Spring, 'The Strict Settlement: Its Role in Family History', *Economic History Review*, 41:3 (August 1988), 454–60; Eileen Spring, *Law, Land and Family: Aristocratic Inheritance in England, 1300 to 1800* (Chapel Hill and London, 1993); Ruth Perry, *Novel Relations: The Transformation of Kinship in English Literature and Culture 1748–1818* (Cambridge, 2004).
18 Amy Louise Erickson, *Women and Property in Early Modern England* (London and New York, 1993); Bridget Hill, *Women Alone: Spinsters in England 1660–1850* (London and New Haven, 2001); Amy Froide, *Never Married: Singlewomen in Early Modern England* (Oxford, 2004).
19 Anthony Fletcher, *Gender, Sex and Subordination in England 1500–1800* (New Haven and London, 1995); Anthony Fletcher, *Growing Up in England: The Experience of Childhood, 1600–1914* (New Haven and London, 2008); Patricia Crawford, *Parents of Poor Children in England, 1580–1800* (Oxford, 2010); Susanna Ottaway, *The Decline of Life: Old Age in Eighteenth-Century England* (Cambridge, 2004).
20 Naomi Tadmor, *Family and Friends in Eighteenth-Century England: Household, Kinship, and Patronage* (Cambridge, 2001).
21 Carol Z. Stearns, 'Introducing the History of Emotion', *The Psychohistory Review*, 18:3 (1990), 263–91.
22 John Gillis, *A World of their Own Making: Myth, Ritual and the Quest for Family Values* (Cambridge, MA, 1997).
23 Leonore Davidoff, *Worlds Between: Historical Perspectives on Gender and Class* (Cambridge, 1995), pp. 50–3. Anthony Fletcher has recently quoted and repeated this sentiment; see his *Growing Up in England*, p. 47; Peter Laslett, *Family Life and Illicit Love in Earlier Generations* (Cambridge, 1977), p. 96. Lawrence Stone's depiction of affective individualism and the rise of affectionate family forms has been particularly long-lasting in its influence not only on scholars, but on popular notions of past families. See Steven Ozment, *Ancestors: The Loving Family in Old Europe* (Cambridge and London, 2001), p. 110; Wendy Moore, 'Love and

Marriage in 18th-Century Britain', *Historically Speaking: The Bulletin of the Historical Society*, 10:3 (June 2009), 8–10.

24 Susan Dwyer Amussen, *An Ordered Society: Gender and Class in Early Modern England*, (New York, 1988); Patricia Crawford, *Blood, Bodies and Families in Early Modern England* (Harlow, 2004), pp. 3, 231.

25 Froide, *Never Married*, p. 45.

26 Carol B. Stack and Linda M. Burton, 'Kinscripts: Reflections on Family, Generation, and Culture', in Evelyn Nakano Glenn, Grace Chang, and Linda Rennie Forcey, eds., *Mothering: Ideology, Experience, and Agency* (New York and London, 1994), pp. 33–44.

27 Gillis, *For Better, for Worse*, p. 35.

28 Erickson, *Women and Property*, pp. 68–78.

29 Valerie Sanders, *The Brother–Sister Culture in Nineteenth-Century Literature* (Houndmills, Hampshire, 2002); Michael Cohen. 'First Sisters in the British Novel', in JoAnna Stephens Mink and Janet Doubler Ward, eds., *The Significance of Sibling Relationships in Literature* (Bowling Green, OH, 1993).

30 Christopher H. Johnson and David Warren Sabean, eds., *Sibling Relations and the Transformation of European Kinship, 1300–1900* (New York and Oxford, 2011).

31 Ibid., p. 9.

32 Randolph Trumbach, *The Rise of the Egalitarian Family: Aristocratic Kinship and Domestic Relations in Eighteenth-Century England* (New York, 1978); Steven Ruggles, *Prolonged Connections: The Rise of the Extended Family in Nineteenth Century England and America* (Madison, WI, 1987); Hartman, *The Household and the Making of History*; Amanda Vickery, *Behind Closed Doors: At Home in Georgian England* (New Haven and London, 2009).

33 John Tosh, *A Man's Place: Masculinity and the Middle-Class Home in Victorian England* (New Haven and London, 1999), p. 21.

34 Naomi Miller and Naomi Yavneh, *Sibling Relations and Gender in the Early Modern World: Sisters, Brothers, and Others* (Aldershot, Hampshire, and Burlington, VT, 2006), p. 1; Lorri Glover, *All Our Relations: Ties and Emotional Bonds among the Early South Carolina Gentry* (Baltimore and London, 2000); Annett Atkins, *We Grew Up Together: Brothers and Sisters in Nineteenth-Century America* (Urbana and Chicago, 2001); Sarah Pearsall, *Atlantic Families: Lives and Letters in the later Eighteenth Century* (New York and Oxford, 2008); Anu Lahtinen, *Anpassning, Förhandling, Motstånd: Kvinnliga Aktörer i Släkten Fleming, 1470–1620* (Stockholm and Helsinki, 2009).

35 C. Dallett Hemphill, *Siblings: Brothers and Sisters in American History* (Oxford, 2011); Leonore Davidoff, *Thicker than Water: Siblings and their Relations, 1780–1920* (Oxford, 2012); Lee Chambers, 'Rocking the Nation like a Cradle': *The Westons Fashion an Antislavery Sisterhood*, unpublished book manuscript, forthcoming.

36 Stella Tillyard, *Aristocrats: Caroline, Emily, Louisa, and Sarah Lennox, 1740–1832* (New York, 1994); Leonore Davidoff. 'Where the Stranger Begins: The

Question of Siblings in Historical Analysis', in Davidoff, *Worlds Between*, pp. 206–26; Patricia Crawford, 'Sibling relationships', in Crawford, *Blood, Bodies and Families in Early Modern England* (Harlow, 2004); Lita-Rose Betcherman, *Court Lady and Country Wife: Two Noble Sisters in Seventeenth-Century England* (New York, 2005); Prophecy Coles, ed., *Sibling Relationships* (London and New York, 2006), pp. 209–38; Stella Tillyard, *A Royal Affair: George III and his Scandalous Siblings* (New York, 2006).

37 Lynne Bowdon, 'Redefining Kinship: Exploring Boundaries of Relatedness in Late Medieval New Romney', *Journal of Family History*, 29:4 (October 2004), 407–20.
38 Davidoff, *Worlds Between*, pp. 218–19.
39 Benedict Anderson, *Imagined Communities: Reflections on the Origin and Spread of Nationalism*, rev. edn (London and New York, 1991), pp. 187–8.
40 Hartman, *The Household and the Making of History*, p. 221.
41 Emmanuel Chukwudi Eze, *Race and the Enlightenment* (Oxford, 1997); Fletcher, *Gender, Sex and Subordination*, pp. 283–96, 407.
42 Judith M. Bennett, 'Medieval Women, Modern Women: Across the Great Divide', in David Aers, ed., *Culture and History, 1350–1600* (Hemel Hempstead, 1992), pp. 151 ff, quoted in Hannah Barker and Elaine Chalus, eds., *Gender in Eighteenth-Century England: Roles, Representations and Responsibilities* (London and New York, 1997), p. 14. See also Judith M. Bennett, *Ale, Beer, and Brewsters in England: Women's Work in a Changing World 1300–1600* (New York and Oxford, 1996), pp. 6–8, 156–7.
43 Vickery, *The Gentleman's Daughter*, pp. 49, 59–60.
44 Richard Price, *British Society, 1680–1880: Dynamism, Containment, and Change* (Cambridge, 1999); Rachel Weil, *Political Passions: Gender, the Family and Political Argument in England, 1680–1714* (Manchester and New York, 1999); Richard Grassby, *Kinship and Capitalism: Marriage, Family, and Business in the English-Speaking World, 1580–1740* (Cambridge, 2001); Susan Kingsley Kent, 'Gender Rules: Law and Politics', in Teresa A. Meade and Merry E. Wiesner-Hanks, eds., *A Companion to Gender History* (Oxford, 2004), pp. 86–109.
45 Jonathan Barry, 'The Making of the Middle Class?', *Past and Present*, 145:1 (November 1994), 201.
46 Jay Fliegelman, *Prodigals and Pilgrims: The American Revolution against Patriarchal Authority, 1750–1800* (Cambridge, 1982); Lynn Hunt, *The Family Romance of the French Revolution* (Berkeley and Los Angeles, 1992); Weil, *Political Passions*; Demos, *A Little Commonwealth*.
47 Holly Brewer, *By Birth or Consent: Children, the Law, and the Anglo-American Revolution in Authority* (Chapel Hill, 2005), pp. 36–9.
48 Hunt, *The Family Romance of the French Revolution*.
49 Karen Offen, *European Feminisms, 1700–1950* (Stanford, 2000), p. 41.
50 Jonathan Barry, 'The Making of the Middle Class?'; Kari Boyd McBride, 'Recusant Sisters: English Catholic Women and the Bonds of Learning', in Miller and Yavneh, eds., *Sibling Relations*, pp. 28–39.

51 David Herlihy, *Women, Family and Society in Medieval Europe* (Providence, RI, 1995), pp. 116–17, 119–120.
52 Weil, *Political Passions*, pp. 51–4.
53 Though the term 'sibling' is a twentieth-century innovation, its roots come from Old English. 'Sib' was not limited to sisters and brothers, merely denoting someone related by blood or descent. By the seventeenth century this use was virtually obsolete, and in the seventeenth and eighteenth centuries 'sib' came to mean anyone to whom one was closely related, allied, or similar.
54 Amy Harris, 'This I Beg my Aunt may not Know: Young Letter-Writers in Eighteenth-Century England, Peer Correspondence in a Hierarchical World', *Journal of the History of Childhood and Youth*, 2:3 (2009), 333–60.
55 Wrigley and Schofield, *The Population History of England, 1541–1871*, pp. 257–65, 421–30.
56 This approximation comes from computerized models of family size developed by the Cambridge Group for the History of Population and Social Structure, Cambridge University, England. My thanks to Jim Oeppen for sharing this information.
57 Richard Wall et al., eds., *Family Forms in Historic Europe* (Cambridge, 1983), p. 500.
58 Wrigley and Schofield, *The Population History of England*, pp. 257–65, 421–30.
59 Linda Pollock, *A Lasting Relationship: Parents and Children over Three Centuries* (Hanover and London, 1987).
60 Rosemary O'Day, *The Family and Family Relationships, 1500–1900: England, France, and the United States of America* (New York, 1994).
61 Mary Jo Maynes, 'Age as a Category of Historical Analysis: History, Agency, and Narratives of Childhood', *Journal of the History of Childhood and Youth*, 1:1 (Winter 2008), 117.
62 Georgina Galbraith, ed., *The Journal of the Rev. William Bagshaw Stevens* (Oxford, 1965), p. 304. Rev. Bagshaw encountered Francis, Anne, and Catherine Travell in Bath in 1795 and described the sisters as 'ancient Maidens both Inhabitants of Cheltenham'. At the time Francis would have been sixty-seven, Anne fifty-eight, and Catherine fifty-three.

1

Learning to be a sibling

> Children of the same family... have some means of enjoyment... no subsequent connections can supply.
>
> Jane Austen, *Mansfield Park*, 1814[1]
>
> The Colours of life in youth and age appear different as the face of nature in spring and winter.
>
> Samuel Johnson, *The Prince of Abissinia*, 1759, extracted by Anne Travell, c.1780s[2]

As the slanting autumn light shone across the gardens and through the windows of Stanway House, nineteen-year-old Anne Tracy 'spent the greatest part of the day contriving and packing up things for my Brothers' journey'. Two weeks later she 'help'd to pack up some things' to send to her eighteen-year-old brother, Robert, recently departed for Oxford. For Anne a phase of her life was drawing to a close; though she could not know it, within two years she would be married. The departure of 'Robin' and his twin 'Jack' (John) in November 1724 signalled the beginning of the dissolution of her childhood family. Education would open opportunities for her brothers that she could not imagine, and marriage would remove her from her parents' authority and siblings' daily association and place her under her husband's governance. She would leave the fine manor house in eastern Gloucestershire for her own household and a new future. No more would she enjoy evenings 'pleasantly' while 'Jacky' read to her and their siblings. Her future would require managing servants, organizing social gatherings, and producing and rearing children. The family and home of her childhood would be left behind.[3]

Or so we have been told. Life-cycle depictions of families, children, and women have emphasized the vulnerability and 'fragility' experienced by adolescents when they departed their childhood homes and began to acquire the trappings of adulthood.[4] But Anne's packing 'some things' for her 'Br Robin' was not about jettisoning old patterns and relationships in preparation for the future. Instead that package, the letters from Robin and Jack that preceded it, and the letter Anne wrote the same day were the material manifestations of old patterns being reshaped for the new world of adulthood, upon the threshold of which Anne and her brothers stood. If age and kinship, as has been recently argued, can be their own categories of analysis, then sibling childhood relations offer new ways of understanding not only the experience of children, but the development of gender and family power.[5] Anne did not leave one family behind as she started the next, any more than Robin and Jack abandoned their family by beginning their university education. Though they stood on the threshold of adulthood, streaming behind them were nearly two decades of established behaviours and experiences that they would carry with them the rest of their lives. Their relationships with one another and their younger siblings had already shaped their childhood and would continue to influence them as adults. Letters, packages, holidays, and visits would keep them connected even as education and marriage decreased their daily interaction. Like other siblings in Georgian England, the Tracy brothers and sisters were essential to one another's financial, emotional, social, and material success – something that their shared childhood had already taught them and that their shared adult success would depend upon.

To date, depictions of parental and adult influence on childhood have dominated the secondary literature.[6] Children, particularly siblings, however, played important roles in one another's lives and development. Focusing on siblings does not render parental influence irrelevant, but instead points to ways in which siblings' power sometimes mitigated, sometimes ignored, and sometimes reinforced parents' power. Parental advice literature and parents' own accounts demonstrate that mothers and fathers were expected to teach morals and class- and gender-specific behaviour and to treat their children fairly.[7] Except in the case of certain established gender and age privileges that influenced inheritance and education practices, parents encountered numerous messages to the effect that having a favourite or 'little darling' was pernicious and guaranteed to render the child, at best, useless and at worst, a tyrant.[8] Prescriptive literature enjoined, and children expected, equal affection from parents to help them foster the unity, equality, and solidarity expected of siblinghood. In the contradictory space between sharing equally their parents' affections and being destined for decidedly unequal futures, young siblings had to learn both their social and their familial niche.

Siblings worked out this contradiction throughout their life course, but as children they established patterns and shared a history that could colour perceptions much later in life. As young children, brothers and sisters spent the majority of every day in one another's company, eating the same food, enjoying the same entertainments, praying the same prayers, learning the same lessons. They also cared for one another when ill and mourned the loss of a brother or sister – sometimes for a lifetime. In work and play they learned to garner adult approval when they practised gendered, age, and class behaviour. Simultaneously sisters and brothers established daily patterns that defied some of these teachings. Despite this differentiation, sisters and brothers built and maintained connections with each other even as they became adolescents and as they slowly worked into adult roles. Schooling, apprenticeships, work, and marriage took children from home; parents and older kin aged and died; but siblings journeyed throughout the life course together. A constant during childhood and much of adolescence, siblings formed the bridge into adulthood for one another.

Parents and family hierarchy

Most prescriptive authors agreed that love was the natural state between siblings – if parents fostered it. Any careless or ambivalent treatment was not seen as normal family friction, but as unnatural or savage, and the parents' role was to remove any unnatural aberrations from their children. 'Should the parents, instead of discouraging these civil broils and unnatural contests in their families give ear to a little darling, a favourite, whom they give a manifest preference to, even to the prejudice of the rest, there is no saying what may be the consequence', the pseudonymous Palinurus cautioned.[9] Simultaneously, children were admonished to maintain amicable relations with their siblings. Any sibling conflict not only cankered family relations, but spoke of degenerate humanity. Palinurus went on to describe the consequences of sibling discord – consequences that spiralled down into a barbarous collapse of the family, complete with wicked Pharaohs and vengeful Amazons. And Sir Herbert Croft wrote that so much as a 'wry word or a wrinkled look, a captious observation or a short reply' between a person and 'one who is marked, perhaps, by the same set of features; who sleeps under the same roof, drinks out of the same tumbler, and is descended from the same dear father and same dear mother, and has hanged at the very self same nipple – the bare possibility of such a thing is a reflection upon humanity'.[10] Ideal sibling relations grew from just and equitable parental guidance. As a character in Sarah Fielding's *The Governess* described her relation with her siblings: 'We played together, and passed our time much in the common way: sometimes we quarrelled, and sometimes agreed, just as accident would have it. Our parents had no partiality to any of us; so we had no cause to envy one another on that account; and we lived tolerably well together.'[11]

Siblings enjoyed equal access to love and affection rarely granted in parent–child relations. Prescriptive literature enjoined children to obey and submit to parents, but rarely instructed the young to love their parents. Instead, there was recognition that parents naturally had greater affection for children than the reverse.[12] Children were to direct their love and affection to their siblings, and then to neighbours and friends, who were often described as fictive siblings (that is, all were children of God).[13] 'Honour and obey your Parents and Teachers', Isaac Watts recommended to children, and 'Love your Brothers and Sisters.'[14] 'To their Brothers and Sisters', children 'owe not only a tender but an unalterable affection'; obedience and duty were due only to parents and other adults.[15] Obedience to and respect for parents could elicit love, but the inequality of their positions kept them from sharing like siblings did. Siblings, 'they who join in Blood', so the reasoning went, 'Should live in Unity and Peace.'[16]

Despite counsel to treat children equally, from their birth Georgian parents taught their children important social hierarchies, particularly those associated with age, class, and gender. Learning proper conduct involved social, moral, and religious training and the explanation of how their children would fill specific social niches.[17] Historical scholarship has discovered much about the expectations of parenthood and the teaching of children. We know parents in early modern and Georgian England wanted children of both sexes, they worried and fretted about their health, their development, their learning, and their happiness, and they invested considerable resources to the tasks of child-rearing.[18] Parents like Jane Johnson made flash cards that taught her children not just reading skills, but the importance of social literacy. Parents like Ferdinando and Martha Travell taught their children the importance and style of letter-writing. And parents such as John Taylor, despite sometimes feeling 'sincerely troubled' that they had 'done no better', strived to lovingly teach their children to work, to avoid sin, to read, and to pray.[19]

In the process of rearing children parents recognized three stages of pre-adult development. During the first five or six years of life children spent the bulk of their time in the company of their mothers and each other. As they reached the end of this period they slowly gained more responsibility that might find them helping with household, workshop, or field tasks, as five-year-old Nathaniel King did when he helped his sister dry the family's clothing.[20] This phase of life went remarkably undifferentiated by gender; infants and younger children were dressed the same regardless of sex, and parents did not fret if their children did not immediately act according to gender norms. Gender became increasingly important in the next phase, which covered the years from the age of five or six until the early teens. The importance of gender to this stage was often signalled by the 'breeching' of boys – clothing them in breeches and distinguishing them from the dress of both infancy and femininity. From that point gender formed a central aspect of much parental teaching. Boys avoided becoming domesticated by spending less time solely in the company of the women who had dominated their infancy – an ideal perpetuated in print and art.[21] Siblings recognized that the change in boys' clothing symbolically settled them on different gendered paths. Annabella Wentworth, when an adult, remarked to her brother that she would have 'been happy enough to wear Breeches instead of Petticoats and been your Brother instead of your Sister'.[22] Once early childhood ended, boys, no matter what their social standing, had more opportunities of formal training and education than their sisters. Fanny Burney read the Old Testament to her seven-year-old son, but was unsure of its appropriateness for girls, because translators were incapable of 'guarding it from terms and expressions impossible – at least utterly improper to explain'.[23] Girls had more training in domestic and household management than their brothers. Both girls and young women like Anne Tracy and her daughter Anne Travell and their brothers learned to keep daily financial accounts, but it was the girls who concentrated on the household management.[24]

As siblings grew into adolescence, their formal education and training began and parents began to expect early signs of class-specific adult responsibility in their children. Lord Chesterfield told his eight-year-old son that his ninth birthday would make him a 'youth' and that as a youth he must 'commence a different course of life, a different course of studies'.[25] Youth was a long and vaguely defined period that covered the years until marriage and/or the early twenties, when education and apprenticeships ended and employment began. Parents, teachers, masters, employers, and nurses had a recognized influence on this development, but young siblings also recognized that their elder and younger sisters and brothers experienced different daily routines, enjoyed different rewards, and suffered different punishments.[26] The teenaged Anne Tracy visited the nursery, but both she and her younger siblings would have recognized that she was not under the power of the nurse and that she spent the bulk of her day in the company of older family members. A little sister who visited her apprenticed brother at his master's also would have marked the difference that age and gender made to their daily experiences.[27] Like the children depicted in *The Marlborough Family* by Reynolds, eldest sons were positioned to assume patriarchal duties, and eldest daughters stood as surrogate matriarchs – guarding younger siblings from teasing one another or as the object of younger siblings' desire for attention and recognition.[28]

Teaching and preparing their children for their proper social roles, while laborious, was straightforward, but when teaching their children about their familial roles parents faced a more ambiguous project. Manuals for children and child-rearing emphasized social niches – superior and inferior – but siblings were rarely included with either group. There was 'nothing more reasonable', one author enjoined, 'than a considerable Difference between the Children of inferior People, and those of Rank'.[29] 'Brothers and Sisters', however, were recommended 'to love one another mutually, like Fellow Members of the same Community, whose social Interests are united by those Ties of Nature, or of Providence, jointly to pursue them, and not seek each his own alone, but each other's Welfare, as Opportunity will frequently occur'.[30] On the one hand parents were to love their children equally, and on the other they were to ensure that their children learned their place in the gender and birth order hierarchy. In other words, they were to be 'just'. Natural law dictated that children should be equals 'without distinctions of sex or age', but human law required an 'unequal division between equals' to guarantee orderly succession.[31] Repeatedly parents and the advice literature emphasized that they, like William King, held their children in 'equal esteem regard and affection'.[32] Yet their children had to learn to combine the expectations of equal parental affection and the reality of very different forms of parental teaching and investment. It has been argued that children 'were drilled to defer not only to parents but also to older siblings'.[33] 'Drilled' overstates the case; the occasional injunction for younger children to 'revere' older siblings, even older sisters, was tempered with reminders that parents' common affections made all siblings 'closely united'.[34] Some argued that it was 'perfectly right' that younger noble and gentry sons should have to pursue careers instead of receiving an inheritance. All of a gentleman's sons should receive the same education, but the eldest son 'must be graced with every Ornament'.[35] Parents invested more land in elder sons than in younger sons, and they invested more resources in all older children, regardless of sex. Some agonized over these decisions, but others, like Heneage Dering, thought it unremarkable that their older children should inherit £50 each and the younger children should go unnamed in a relative's will.[36]

Family portraiture illuminates the ambiguity generated when age and gender hierarchies were contrasted with representations of equal and peer relations. In her discussion of eighteenth-century portraiture, Kate Retford noticed a fashion for painting the elder son with his father alone or in a family group to distinguish him from his younger siblings.[37] However, concentrating on the relationship between the children depicted in these paintings reveals an alternative interpretation. Portraits show siblings of all ages and both genders interacting with each other, either to the exclusion of the adults in the paintings or in paintings solely of children. Sisters and brothers play cards and cricket, play make-believe with toys and pets, pick flowers, ride hobby horses, enjoy outdoor parties, grow flowers, and play soldiers.[38] Gainsborough's *Heneage Lloyd and his Sister* shows a strong alliance between young children close in age and enjoying the same pursuit (the sister holds the arrow, the brother the bow). The title of the painting makes the brother the central figure, but the painting itself does not emphasize his gendered power, instead showing them with linked arms and, because he is leaning, standing at almost the same height (see Figure 1). The blurring of equality and hierarchy was standard in Georgian portraits of young siblings. They were sometimes depicted as equals (painted in the same plane, participating in the same

1 Thomas Gainsborough (1727–88), *Heneage Lloyd and his Sister* [*Lucy*], c.1750 (oil on canvas). With permission from the Fitzwilliam Museum, University of Cambridge, UK. The Bridgeman Art Library International

activities) and sometimes arranged hierarchically (in separate gender and age groups), making sibling age and gender privileges ambiguous.

Despite the ambiguity of their position of being, and not being, equals, siblings seemed accepting of certain externally imposed hierarchies; they understood that eldest brothers had family and social obligations that required more resources, but that this unbalanced distribution should be made fair and younger siblings given other supports.[39] Anne Tracy's siblings reportedly supported John's efforts to inherit their maternal grandfather's estate without any hint that they should receive something from the estate.[40] The eldest son may have been the usual heir of real estate, but daughters and younger sons were often more likely to receive monetary remuneration from their parents and other kin. Also, women were more likely than men to receive legacies from other female kin. Inheritance practices tried to enforce a type of justice that, while not strictly equal, encouraged brothers and sisters to 'share and share alike'.[41] This pattern is discernible among Anne Tracy Travell's children by studying their father's will of 1762. The eldest son (first John and later Francis) stood to inherit the land and house in Swerford, Oxfordshire (in addition to receiving the university education he had already completed). The younger son (Ferdinando) received a university education and an inheritance from his grandfather. The daughters received their various portions of the £5,000 granted to their father's 'younger children' in his marriage settlement. The girls, however, did not receive equal portions. Instead, their birth order determined the amounts given to them: their father bequeathed Frances Mary £1,400, Anne £1,300, Catherine £1,200, and Agnes £1,100. If parents, unlike the Travells, left goods and money to their children in equal measure it was still standard to list all sons first, in order of age, then all of the daughters. The hierarchical thinking was so ingrained that it seemed 'perfectly right'.[42]

Even if it was 'perfectly right' for the eldest son to be set apart from his siblings and for younger siblings to grant respect to, and receive less than, older siblings, birth order was not the stable entity that prescriptive authors imagined it to be. In historical scholarship, birth order is often reduced to a discussion of elder sons and everyone else, but siblings encountered multiple and ever-shifting family dynamics based on birth order.[43] Demographers have demonstrated that somewhere between a quarter and a third of children did not survive to their tenth birthday.[44] In matters of land, parents and grandparents compensated for this volatility by designating long lists of potential heirs and through the mechanisms of entail and strict settlement. Families without land still used birth order to determine who received particular types of education, training, or apprenticeships or who inherited the tools of a trade or the best set of bedding. For young siblings, however, that volatility meant that they could not predict their future position within the family or how this would affect their educational, occupational, and marital prospects.

A detailed discussion of the Tracy and Travell families reveals siblings' experience of death and birth order behind the demographic facts. Before her birth in 1705 Anne Tracy's parents had already had and lost one son, but concerns over having sons to inherit the house at Stanway were short-lived, with the twins Robert and John being born in 1706. They were followed in rapid succession by an additional six brothers and three sisters, all before Anne's twentieth birthday; one final daughter joined the family in 1729. The Tracys had extraordinarily good chances of surviving childhood. Other than the first son, only two children did not see their tenth birthdays. Edward died at fourteen in 1723 and Ferdinando (Nando) died at twenty-two in 1729. It is not known how the deaths affected Anne's younger siblings – particularly her younger sisters, who remained at home (three never married, and one did not marry until 1762 when she was in her thirties).[45] Unlike the Tracy family, John Travell's sibling set was subject to higher rates of mortality. John Travell, born in 1699, was the eldest of six children, but the loss of two siblings as children and an additional adolescent brother in 1722 meant that he, his sister Jane (three years his junior), and his brother William (five years his junior) had lost half of their cohort before they became adults.[46]

Though Anne Tracy and John Travell's natal families had experienced the unpredictability of infant and childhood mortality, both families had the good fortune to have elder sons who enjoyed a lifetime of grooming for their responsibilities and who fulfilled those responsibilities by marrying well and having sons. Their own children faced a very different reality. Anne and John married in 1725 and had thirteen children between 1726 and 1748. The deaths of six children all before the age of five between 1734 and 1745 were not unusually high; they meant that the surviving children's relative birth order was in constant flux during those eleven years.[47] Clustered together in the centre of the sibling cohort were Frances Mary, born in 1736, Anne, born in 1737, Ferdinando, born in 1739, and Catherine, born in 1742. At either end were John, born in 1726, Francis, born in 1728, and Agnes, born in 1748. At the time of Agnes's birth, the sibling niches associated with birth order and gender would have appeared to be set: John, aged twenty-three, training for the law and heir-apparent, twenty-year-old Francis established at Oxford, four daughters (Agnes, six-year-old Catherine, eleven-year-old Anne, and twelve-year-old Frances Mary), and ten-year-old Ferdinando having survived the most dangerous years of childhood. When John the younger died in 1749 his established privileges passed to the twenty-one-year-old Francis. However, Francis had never been prepared for the role of eldest brother and he proved singularly ill suited to the task. Still, everything seemed fine until his parents died during the autumn and winter of 1762–63. He resigned his army commission, returned from the war, and assumed ownership of his childhood home. His inability to find a suitable wife, his two illegitimate sons with a local woman (who later married someone else), and his poor financial skills indicated that he would not successfully fulfil the role imagined for eldest sons. Francis had not become the eldest son until he was over twenty, meaning that all of his childhood and adolescent training – including how he related to his siblings – had already been shaped by ideas that he would not assume the role of family leader.[48] He also faced a common critique of eldest sons; eighteenth-century publications bemoaned the fate of younger sons whose talent for family governance were ignored or underdeveloped because of primogeniture and the focus on their elder brothers.[49] Though the Travells appreciated Ferdinando's financial and social success and support, the fact remained that John's death had made the less-gifted Francis the heir. While referring to someone as 'a younger brother' referenced the unfair advantages given elder brothers, the Travell siblings' unstable relative positions made 'an older brother' out of a previously younger one and thereby destabilized the siblings' roles and relationships.[50]

The impact of birth order and mortality's shifting sands on adult sibling relations will be discussed in subsequent chapters, but its impact on children and childhood was two-fold. First, as death reshaped birth-order dynamics it reshaped children's daily interactions. For the Travell siblings, death had carved an island in the middle of the overall birth order. Frances Mary, Anne, Ferdinando, and Catherine were separated by only six years and had a close association as children and adolescents. Ferdinando may have had older brothers, but he spent more time and had closer relations with his sisters – particularly those with whom he had shared the nursery and schoolroom. He went to Oxford in 1757, seemingly causing a break in his childhood relations with his siblings. But by 1757 his two older sisters were over twenty and Catherine was fifteen, meaning that these four siblings had years of close contact and interaction as they grew and were educated. They learned, in an intimate setting, the characteristics of their sibling and family culture. Therefore, when their parents died in 1762 and 1763, and despite the absence of Ferdinando at university, the four middle siblings had already laid a foundation for their lifelong relationship – a relationship that further isolated Francis as the eldest and Agnes, who was only nine when Ferdinando left for university, as the youngest.

Second, infant and childhood mortality meant that most children experienced the loss of siblings repeatedly, even as mortality declined after the middle of the eighteenth century. We know a great deal about parents' experience of grief in the past but very little about how childhood demographic volatility affected young siblings.[51] As grief and mourning became more familial than communal affairs in the eighteenth century, young siblings acted as pallbearers, read funeral rites over deceased brothers and sisters, and kept mementoes like locks of hair of the dead sibling.[52] Unfortunately, very few first-hand accounts of children's experience of a sibling's death survive, but glimpses can be garnered from parents' accounts and from adult siblings' recollections. Children clearly knew the rituals of death and mourning, sometimes ceremonially burying their dolls, duplicating adult mourning rituals, but how they experienced the loss of their closest family peers is difficult to determine.[53]

The constant threat that illness and death could take a brother or sister shaped childhood as much as it shaped parenthood.[54] Anne Tracy's anxiety about her young siblings and her parents' health permeates much of the diary she kept between late 1723 and early 1725. She fretted over baby Charles's birth and health in the autumn when her brothers went to Oxford. She worried when Nando fell or had a toothache and when Nanty (Anthony) or Betty felt ill. Jack's poor health in July 1724 made her 'uneasy'.[55] During her mother's recovery from Charles's birth Anne assumed much of the household, social, and family duties. Almost a hundred years later, the experience of Maria Capel similarly blurred the line between sororal and maternal duties. When she wrote to her grandmother of her infant sister's death, Maria described the specifics of 'our dear little Baby' and her last hours. Maria sat up that night holding the hand of the sister she 'loved ... so much'.[56] After breeching, brothers had a less direct presence in the care of younger siblings, but may have read the funeral services over a sibling, as Arthur Young did in 1797.[57] Little survives of children's own accounts of mourning a sibling, but a seventeenth-century example suggests that young children could feel the loss of one of their number keenly. Houlbrooke recounts that a 'Lancashire minister recorded that his [three-year-old] daughter Mary ... "seemed utterly to despise life" after the death of her younger brother ... and "would frequently talke of heaven and being buried by him".[58] Anne Tracy remarked on the death of her younger brother Edward (Neddy) over a year after his passing. 'Made very melancholy', she wrote, 'by contemplating a picture ... for my D[ea]r Br Neddy whose endearing behaviour is never to be forgotten.'[59] How the other siblings responded to Neddy's death or the melancholy associated with gazing on a picture of someone never to be met again is unknown. What children thought when they saw depictions of deceased siblings in stone and sculpture in churches and churchyards or paintings of deceased siblings is also unknown, but for the young who lost siblings the impact could last a lifetime. When he wrote his will in 1792, the sixty-three-year-old Francis Travell requested burial beside his 'ever blessed elder brother'. The 'ever-blessed' John Travell had died when he was twenty-three, over four decades before Francis wrote his will.[60] John and Francis were only two years apart, and the death of their three closest younger siblings before either of them turned ten isolated the brothers at one end of their sibling birth order. The loss of his childhood companion just as they both entered adulthood made an indelible impact on Francis.

Another aspect of childhood mortality's impact on children that was rarely remarked upon was the habit of naming younger children after deceased elder siblings. In early modern England nearly two-thirds of children born after the death of a sibling of the same sex were given the same Christian name as the deceased child.[61] In a rural Gloucestershire parish, Hannah Margrate lost her two 'infant sisters with the smallpox' within two weeks of each other during May 1752. She was not quite six, but would have had memories of these girls – Mary and Hester – memories that may have persisted after her parents baptized another daughter Esther when Hannah was nearly thirteen.[62] Anne and Frances Mary Travell received the reused names of an earlier Anne and Frances. Frances Mary replaced a sister who had not survived infancy, but Anne received the name of a sister who had survived to her fifth birthday. Many historians have remarked on parental grief being greater when children died at greater ages, but the memories of the older Anne's personality must have influenced how Anne (the mother) and John viewed and treated the new Anne. It is not unreasonable to think that Anne's older brothers, John and Francis, who were nine and six respectively when the older Anne died, may have confused memories of their two little sisters named Anne. In the Gibbon family, the name Edward, unusually, was shared by several brothers simultaneously. The famous historian noted that his father had hit upon this strategy because he was concerned that the first Edward's health was so frail and hoped the name would still 'be perpetuated in the family'.[63] The pattern of reusing children's names continued until the middle of the nineteenth century, at which point declining mortality and changing sentiments about children seem to have rendered it unacceptable.[64] Experiences like this abounded, and they raise questions about how children thought of their own individuality – that hallmark of eighteenth-century thought – when their names, both last and first, were not markers of individuality, but of family or lineage. One's name was not entirely one's own unless one was born last or had survived to adulthood, thereby ensuring that no subsequent siblings would inherit one's name.

Parental death also influenced sibling relations. Older sisters and brothers raised younger siblings when parents died, as Anne Tracy Travell's children did when she and her husband died during the autumn and winter of 1762–63, and as the ten-year-old John Whitting's sister did for him and his brothers when their parents died.[65] Parish and city officials recognized the importance of both parent and sibling relationships even among the poor when they allowed orphaned poor children to stay together until older siblings could be put into apprenticeships.[66] Though Poor Law officials recognized the sibling ties of young children, there was no guarantee that older siblings from such families would have the means or inclination to take in their young brothers and sisters, as the ten-year-old orphaned Mary Atkinson discovered when parish officials sent her to live with her thirty-year-old sister, a servant in London. The sister, probably lacking any other option, put Mary 'into lodgings'.[67]

Power, education, and play

In addition to confronting adult attitudes towards gender and birth order and death's role in reshaping those factors, siblings experimented with convention and developed their own internal power arrangements. Parental efforts to treat and love children equally, social expectations that they would be equals, and the fluctuation of siblings' relative positions meant that Georgian siblings learned at an early age that not all hierarchies were straightforward. Notwithstanding assertions that 'Gendered parenting ... produced gendered children', siblings played an important role in teaching each other gender-based behaviours.[68] Adult siblings recalled receiving instruction in reading and games from elder siblings, and occasionally prescriptive authors considered it 'a very happy expedient ... to make children instructors to each other' of moral and religious lessons.[69] This time together allowed siblings to establish their own routines and to test their own power.[70] In caring for one another, in education, and in play, siblings used childhood to learn external social hierarchies and to test the limits of equality prescribed to them.[71] An unusual mid-eighteenth-century painting depicts how young siblings could play by their own rules behind the backs of unknowing adults. In the painting, showing an unnamed family, the brother teases his sister by upending the tea set she has carefully arranged around her doll. The painting captures the moment at which the brother tips the table over and his sister reaches out to stop him. Their father continues fishing with the help of another sister (see Figure 2). Why a family would choose to memorialize this petty childhood

2 Unknown British artist, eighteenth century (formerly attributed to William Hogarth, 1697–1764), *A Family Group Called 'The Stafford Family'*, c.1730. Yale Center for British Art, Paul Mellon Collection

squabble is indecipherable, but it hints that Georgian adults recognized that their children often negotiated their own relationships without parental oversight. They realized that birth order was not just about elder sons inheriting property or a greater share of goods – an eventuality in the distant future – and they slowly learned just how different their experiences would be as a result of their gender. Small children gradually learned extra-familial social roles and hierarchy, but first survival and thriving in family culture meant knowing their position and acting accordingly.

Parents were to teach gendered norms, but siblings taught, reinforced, and resisted those norms. Anne Tracy worked with her sisters at sewing and letter-writing, cared for ailing parents and siblings, and managed the household while her mother recovered from childbirth. She demonstrated to her younger siblings what appropriate female behaviour was while their mother was incapacitated. Similarly Jack, Robin, and Nando went riding and hunting with their father and learned social customs from one another. The siblings also often engaged in mixed-sex activities. They played cards together, visited relatives together, and celebrated birthdays together, and Anne even hunted with her father and brothers on occasion.[72] At times Anne uncomplicatedly accepted gendered expectations; at other times she chafed at their impositions. Though there was 'a great deal of laughter' some days, Anne usually described a day full of 'work'. She, her mother, and sometimes a sister or two were usually 'employed' or 'engaged' in writing, sewing, and other domestic duties. Anne contrasted this with her father's and brothers' activities. Anne and the women worked, but her brothers and father spent the days 'pursuing their sports'.[73] Whatever work her father and brothers did was completely invisible to Anne's observation because they did not participate in the female work that consumed a portion of each of her days. On the eve of beginning her own life as wife and mother, she found household management exhausting and thankless. As her mother recovered from the birth of her thirteenth child at the end of 1724 Anne commented that she 'thought it a terrible thing to be mistress of a family'.[74] It is no accident that these things are evident in Anne's writing when she was eighteen and her brothers seventeen and fifteen. The similar trappings and daily routines of infancy and early childhood were gone. The siblings' clothing, games, and daily activities became increasingly different and gendered. Although they spent an enormous amount of time together at prayer, on visits, and dining, important daily activities were separate, thus teaching a gendered lesson. This lesson sometimes irritated Anne, especially when it was contrasted with earlier experiences. It would not stop her from replicating similar differences among her own children, nor a general acceptance of her brothers' inheritance privileges, but already she felt the tension between a past of equality and a hierarchical future.

Like Anne Tracy Travell reading and hunting with her brothers, young siblings were important fixtures in one another's educational and recreational lives. Existing historical scholarship unintentionally overflows with examples of young siblings teaching one another.[75] Older siblings taught younger brothers and sisters to read and encouraged lifelong literacy by discussing and exchanging reading materials.[76] Young brothers and sisters were often educated together at home, at catechism, at grammar school, and, in the case of brothers, at university.[77] Jane and Cassandra Austen went to Abbey School in Reading together, Charlotte Papendiek kept her daughters together as 'day scholars', the Tracy brothers went to university together, the Wynne sisters sat at lessons together, and the Sharp siblings discussed and exchanged opinions on politics.[78]

Scholars have recognized that sisters in the eighteenth century were perhaps particularly close because they received all of their education in company with one another.[79] Anne Tracy's teaching her little sisters to play games and sew was replicated by her own daughters, and by countless others. The Jackson sisters and their cousins the Martins learned together and visited family together. The Wynne sisters received French and music tuition together. Hannah More's sisters were also her teachers. The Treby sisters learned to draw together. John and Harriet Carr went on the Grand Tour together when they were in their early twenties.[80] Spending the majority of their time together was no guarantee of sisterly love, however. Alicia and Betsy Sheridan were always together, even as their care and education bounced from their parents to their eldest brother and then to a 'French elderly maiden'. This did not prevent Alicia, fifty years after the fact, from recognizing and resenting the fact that her 'father's affections were fix'd' on her younger sister.[81] In the same way as shared learning kept sisters close or provided fodder for envy, schooling could solidify or canker bonds between brothers. Genteel families like the Tracys and Travells had traditions of sending sons to the same college at Oxford or Cambridge, and this was replicated in choices of school. The Pearson and Forster brothers, for example, attended Crewkerne School in Somerset together and went to Oxford together, the Pearsons attending the same college.[82] Residential public schooling for boys could be brutal in its inculcation of manly virtues, and there was no guarantee that the experience would bring boys together. In a school environment where boys 'learnt endurance and self-reliance ... in an unregulated and competitive environment', and where, as one boy reported in 1803 a 'system of bullying seemed to have banished humanity' from the older boys, sharing the experience with a brother may not have always been an advantage.[83] Additionally, because boys' education was more formal and expensive, differences between brothers' training could rankle some siblings. When John Edwards complained that his 'Father neglected to give me any Education, altho' at that Time, it was in his Power', his primary grievance was that his father's 'chief Care was, for my eldest Brother Thomas, who he maintain'd at School'.[84] For those who attended day schools together or trained together like the Tracy, Sharp, Pearson, and Forster brothers, however, education could forge lifelong bonds. William and Samuel Jones, for example, were trained under the same scientific instrument-maker and then later established their own instrument-making business.[85] Not all siblings were gender-segregated while learning. In labouring and trades families, sisters and brothers learned their catechism and basic reading skills together in parish and dame schools and at home.[86] And brothers, via letters and visits, shared with their sisters the lessons they had learned in supposedly male-only fields of endeavour.[87]

Play was another important site for sibling interaction. Children's play was not merely for entertainment purposes; they also tested the limits of their power with one another (as described in the discussion above of Figure 2). Hence in 1721, the seven-year-old Ralph Verney's delight in 'the book and the top and other diversions' was increased when 'he please[d] himself with imagination of his brother's being copped up in a little house while he has the liberty of ranging the garden and the fields'. That on 'church-days [Ralph] has the sole ringing of the bell, and the whole property of the newspapers', highlights the fact that getting such sole ownership was an unexpected treat when he typically shared all amusements with his older brother.[88] Competition could turn to co-operation when siblings used play as an alliance-building activity. The Blundell sisters planned and executed a funeral for their doll – something that amused their father, but which undoubtedly required much solemn joint planning on the part of the five-year-old Frances and seven-year-old Margaret.[89] Sibling childhood alliances were sometimes formed in opposition to parents and their high-minded instruction. The Sewell sisters charmed a toy shop owner into allowing them to purchase 'little tin and lead plates' for their 'baby-house' despite lacking sufficient funds. They knew they did not have enough money with them, but '[t]emptation was very strong, and we asked if the man could trust us till we came again and paid him.' They obtained the small toys they wanted, but they were 'unwilling to trust any one with our disgraceful secret'. Eventually, though Mary could not recall the details of restitution, the sisters' 'consciences obtained peace'.[90]

The quotation from Samuel Johnson at the beginning of this chapter was prefaced by the sentiment (not copied by Anne Travell) that 'the opinions of children and parents, of the young and the old, are naturally opposite'.[91] Children might replicate adult behaviours, but young siblings also colluded in opposing or experimenting with adult expectations. At the end of the eighteenth century the Wynne sisters grew up in a home with much laughter – their parents often cross-dressing for entertainment – and took special pleasure in playing tricks on their tutor. The highlight of one entry of their shared diary was the attempt to put a hedgehog in his bed.[92] The Sharp siblings' common letters, written when the younger siblings were still in their teens, purposely ignored the standards explained in letter-writing manuals. Instead the letters were full of inside jokes, puns, and humorous drawings. Despite their children's thumbing their collective noses at many social conventions, the Sharp parents approved of the letters as important for their children's sibling relations.[93] Even when not in opposition to parents' teaching, young siblings' 'great game of romps' could encourage parents to 'escape' and leave their children to their own high-spirited culture.[94] Play allowed young siblings to collude or compete and created a child-centred space within the adult-controlled world. Moreover, childhood alliances could lead to adult alliances against parents, as in the case of the Beale sisters, who waged a protracted probate battle against their mother at the turn of the nineteenth century.[95] Or the pattern might manifest itself if one sibling died without a spouse or children to inherit and the siblings were thereby induced to claim rights to inheritance over their parents, as Edward Stock did in 1744.[96]

Separations and connections

Siblings' patterns of interaction, of envy and friendship, of alliance building and competition, persisted even after they left home. As children entered adolescence and their daily routines increasingly took them away from one another they found other ways to maintain their connections. Too often this period of life is used to show how weak kinship ties were and to equate separation from parents with separation from all kin. Scholars emphasize the 'vulnerability' and isolated nature of English adolescence.[97] Historians have recognized that ties between fictional siblings in eighteenth-century literature were important to educational and occupational success, but have missed the way in which real siblings were essential bridges between childhood and adulthood.[98] Some have even argued that prosperous families produced children, specifically girls, who were even less prepared than girls in labouring or trade families for the family separations of adulthood because they stayed longer in their natal home.[99] These interpretations place too much emphasis on separate living arrangements and not enough on how young siblings maintained connections across households. Letters, holidays, and visits kept brothers and sisters connected in their adolescence and early adulthood. Games and shared daily routines diminished, but siblings replaced them with jests, inside jokes, and exchanges of gifts, news, and letters. As mentioned, many brothers and sisters followed older siblings to the same school; additionally others followed one another to the same town, the same master, or the same occupation. When fifteen-year-old Granville Sharp moved from northern England to begin his apprenticeship with a London draper, he joined his two brothers – of whom one had recently completed his apprenticeship, and the other was still in training. Their father brought 'Greeny' down to London and took great pains to report to their mother and sisters that Granville's older brothers were well situated to help him. William met Granville's master and dined with Granville as he settled into his new life, and James had purchased a work apron for Granville. The three boys lived at walking distances from one another's accommodations, triangulated in a pattern that comforted their father.[100] John Holder took a similar strategy with his sons. While the eldest son was apprenticed in Cheltenham, some thirty miles from home, he placed his two younger sons in London – one at Covent Garden and one in the Strand, less than a mile apart.[101]

Less prosperous families might not always be able to maintain physical proximity and might lack the resources for extended correspondence or visits. However, incidental information from Old Bailey transcripts hints that even for labouring London families, young siblings could continue to have regular contact after one of them left home. Fourteen-year-old Thomas Smith fetched 'his [brother's] linen home of a Saturday night', much as fifteen-year-old William Armstrong did when he was accused of stealing a saddle. An erstwhile thief, fourteen-year-old John Rowe, and his master took it as matter of course that John's younger sister would visit during his apprenticeship. At eighteen, Thomas Hallard lived a largely independent life as a bargeman during winter and as a fisherman during the summer. When he was out of work, however, he returned to his parents' home and shared a bed with his ten-year-old sister.[102] Thirteen-year-old George Wolfe traded on his brother's good reputation to procure employment, and fifteen-year-old Mary Wright was checked on and taken home by an older sister when she struggled to fulfil an employer's expectations. For most families leaving home did not mean the end of sibling ties; adolescent siblings borrowed money from, ran errands for, shared beds with, and exchanged regular visits with sisters and brothers after leaving home for work or apprenticeships.[103]

Little literature was published to help siblings negotiate turning siblinghood into the bridge between childhood and adulthood. But the material objects best suited to build that bridge – letters – had established models for young siblings to follow.[104] Letter-writing manuals offered plenty of examples of how brothers and sisters setting out into the world should correspond with one another. Sibling letters demonstrated support of socially acceptable behaviour, occupations, and marriage partners. They also established a language of sibling equality and affection. Formulaic salutations and signatures promised duty and obedience to parents and affection and love to siblings. Manuals and actual letters agreed that siblings were due affection, not deference or duty.[105] When eighteen-year-old Richard Dennison Cumberland went to Cambridge for education or to Leeds for employment he wrote regularly to both his mother and his seventeen-year-old brother George, who was employed at the Royal Exchange in London. The letters came to George at work with the expectation that at least some of their content would remain private between the brothers. George constantly sent gossip and news of home, kin, and friends along with packages of clothing and books. The brothers' correspondence began after their father's death when occupation and education separated them, and it continued as they progressed in their professions, considered whom to marry, and dealt with their mother's declining vitality and health.[106] Letters also kept mixed-sex siblings tied to one another. The Jackson siblings immediately began their correspondence in their teens when the oldest brother, Robert, departed for military training at fifteen. Robert corresponded primarily with Catherine-Anne, the eldest sister in the family, and through her with their parents and younger siblings. The letters continued throughout their lives, Robert transferring his correspondence to his surviving sister, Mary, when Catherine-Anne died.[107] It was not just the landed or educated elite who enjoyed adolescent correspondence, especially later in the Georgian period as literacy and communication expanded and improved. Though the one-time potter Charles Holford (later a sailor and then a convict) left home 'when very young' in the 1770s, he exchanged 'several letters' over the years with his sister Sarah.[108]

Conclusion

Georgian siblings spent the majority of their early childhood in the company of one another. Unlike modern children, who are separated by age into non-kin groups in school and in child care, early modern children of all classes often spent the first seven years of life mixing with children of both sexes and various ages. The timing of children's departure from home depended on the social standing of the family. Some children started apprenticeships as young as seven, and some like the Tracy and Travell brothers did not leave home until their late teens. Most siblings, however, stayed at home or close to it until formal education or employment started them on the path to adulthood – typically in their mid-teens. During these first seven to fifteen years of life, siblings learned their familial and social responsibilities both from parents and from one another.

Obedience to parents was axiomatic, no matter what a child's social standing, but working with siblings was a more ambiguous arrangement. Prescriptive literature about parenting emphasized the equal treatment of children. However, once they left infancy children were treated differently according to their gender and birth order, even though death made hierarchies based on birth order fluid. From their earliest years siblings sat between injunctions that they should be equals and the reality that equality did not mean identical treatment or opportunities. Death, birth order, and gender influenced sisters and brothers' familial position and sculpted their interactions. Siblings studied, prayed, and played together, thereby establishing patterns, for good or ill, that would shape their adulthood. Some have argued that childhood was central to eighteenth-century ideas about the self – that childhood was the 'depths of historicity within individuals'.[109] Siblings were so intertwined that their shared childhood shaped their adulthood and their ideas of selfhood. Whether it was thirty-one-year-old Thomas Huntingford fondly reminiscing with his brother, 'Don't you remember, Henry, the nice thick gruel we used to have?', or twenty-four-year-old Edward Witts telling his brother, 'let Sally [their sister] know I never forget a single Day to think of my sweet little winch in ye nursery', or sixty-three-year-old Alicia Sheridan LeFanu not so fondly remembering her and her brother's childhood – 'neither he nor I were very happy, we were strongly attached to each other' – shared childhood embedded sisters and brothers in one another's lives.[110] Class differences determined the extent of their horizons, but all children and youths would need to take siblings with them on their life's journey to establish and maintain their social, material, and financial credit.

Fourteen years after she gathered items to send to her brothers at university, Anne Tracy Travell, now a thirty-three-year-old married mother of seven children (four living), wrote to her husband about a planned visit to her brother. 'I believe I shall go', she wrote, 'tho' indeed . . . I never heard one word from my Br. . . . or any message that has passed, nor has he ever been to see me.' The brother was probably Anthony, seven years her junior and recently married. Clearly, despite their not having lived under the same roof for thirteen years, Anne expected a continued and strong connection with Anthony. After all, he lived in the neighbouring parish, and it could not have been a great labour to write to or visit his sister. Anne considered it 'a little hard that my Br. should never mention me'.[111] She could remember how 'delight'd with seeing . . . Nando' she was when he returned from a visit with their father, the thrill of hearing stories about Oxford from Jack and Robin, and how carefully she had monitored Nanty's health when he was in his early teens.[112] The Tracy siblings may have enjoyed good sibling relations during their childhood and adolescence, but even then journeying with their siblings into adulthood together was not without its obstacles and disappointments. For better or worse, siblings like Anne anticipated that childhood connections with their brothers and sisters would continue to tie them together in bonds of affection and support. Some managed this and some did not, but all had to confront the expectation of that affectionate connection and the consequences of its collapse.

Notes

1 Jane Austen, *Mansfield Park*, chapter 6.
2 Samuel Johnson, *The Prince of Abissinia*, vol. 2 (London, 1759), p. 3, ECCO; Anne Travell, commonplace book, c.1780s, GA, D4582/4/18.

3 Anne Tracy Travell, diary, 5 February, 4 and 17 November 1724, transcribed by Celandine Tracy, 1911, in private possession of the Earl of Wemyss, STWY.
4 Ilana Krausman Ben-Amos, *Adolescence and Youth in Early Modern England* (New Haven and London, 1994), pp. 156–7; John Gillis, *Youth and History: Tradition and Change in European Age Relations, 1770 – Present*, expanded student edn (Orlando, 1981); Olwen Hufton, *The Prospect Before Her: A History of Women in Western Europe* (New York, 1995); Fletcher, *Growing Up in England*; C. Dallett Hemphill, 'Sibling Relations in Early American Childhoods: A Cross-Cultural Analysis', in James Marten, ed., *Children in Colonial America* (New York, 2007), pp. 77–89.
5 Davidoff, 'Kinship as a Categorical Concept'; Maynes, 'Age as a Category of Historical Analysis'.
6 Philippe Ariès, *Centuries of Childhood: A Social History of Family Life* (New York, 1962); C. John Sommerville, *The Rise and Fall of Childhood*, (Beverly Hills, 1982); I. Pinchbeck and M. Hewitt, *Children in English Society*, 2 vols. (London, 1969); Linda Pollock, *Forgotten Children: Parent–Child Relations from 1500 to 1900* (Cambridge, 1983), pp. 236–60; Fletcher, *Growing Up in England*; Mary Abbott, *Life Cycles in England, 1560–1720* (London and New York, 1996), p. 30.
7 Pollock, *A Lasting Relationship*, pp. 53–90, 165–244; Fletcher, *Growing Up in England*, pp. 1–52; Andrew O'Malley, *The Making of the Modern Child: Children's Literature and Childhood in Late Eighteenth-Century England* (London and New York, 2003).
8 Henry Kames, *Loose Hints upon Education, Chiefly Concerning the Culture of the Heart* (Edinburgh and London, 1781), p. 54, ECCO. See also Fletcher, *Growing Up in England*, p. 45.
9 Palinurus, *Familiar Letters, from and Elder to a Younger Brother, Serving for his Freedom in the Trinity-House, Newcastle-upon-Tyne* (Newcastle, 1785), pp. 19–20. BL, 1455.f.15.
10 Sir Herbert Croft, *A Brother's Advice to his Sisters*, 2nd edn (London, 1776), pp. 196–7, BL, 230.k.52.
11 Sarah Fielding, *The Governess: The Little Female Academy* (Dublin, 1749), p. 64, Project Gutenberg, Ebook 1905, www.gutenberg.com/ebooks/1905 (accessed 10 October 2008).
12 Thomas Secker, *On the Relative Duties between Parents and Children* (Dublin, 1790), pp. 5, 11–12, ECCO. Secker was the Archbishop of Canterbury in 1753–68. Ralph Houlbrooke, *Death, Religion and the Family in England, 1480–1750* (Oxford, 1998), p. 238.
13 George Chapman, *A Treatise on Education* (Edinburgh, 1773), p. 248, ECCO; Isaac Watts, *Prayers Composed for the Use and Imitation of Children, Suited to their Different Ages and their Various Occasions* (London, 1728), p. 8, ECCO.
14 Watts, *Prayers Composed for the Use and Imitation of Children*, p. 102.

15 James Nelson, *An Essay on the Government of Children under Three General Heads, viz. Health, Manners, and Education* (London, 1763), p. 185, ECCO.
16 John Marchant, *Puerilia: or, Amusements for the Young* (London, 1751), pp. 23–4, ECCO.
17 Pollock, *A Lasting Relationship*, pp. 165–245; Fletcher, *Growing Up in England*, pp. 1–52, 196–280; O'Malley, *The Making of the Modern Child*, pp. 1–16, 39–65; Crawford, *Parents of Poor Children*, pp. 112–49; Nelson, *An Essay on the Government of Children*.
18 On the desire for both sons and daughters see Vickery, *The Gentleman's Daughter*, pp. 105, 315 n. 66; Erickson, *Women and Property*, p. 49; Hartman, *The Household and the Making of History*, pp. 91, 96–8. On the investment involved in parenthood and the importance of teaching gendered expectations see Fletcher, *Gender, Sex and Subordination*, pp. 297–321, 364–75, and *Growing Up in England*, pp. 1–52; Vickery, *Behind Closed Doors*, pp. 115–16, 118–19, 126; Pollock, *A Lasting Relationship*, pp. 83, 87.
19 Evelyn Arizpe and Morag Styles, ' "Love to learn your book": Children's Experiences of Text in the Eighteenth Century', *History of Education*, 33:3 (May 2004), 337–52; Martha Rollinson Travell and her daughter Martha Travell, Paris, 12 October 1776, to their sister-in-law and aunt Anne Travell, Cheltenham, GA, D4582/4/5; Adam Taylor, ed., *Memoirs of the Reverend John Taylor* (London, 1820), quoted in Pollock, *A Lasting Relationship*, pp. 176–7; *Lessons for Children, Historical & Practical* (London, 1713), ECCO; Watts, *Prayers Composed for the Use and Imitation of Children*, p. 29.
20 OBP, 7 September 1715, trial of Mary Savage (t17150907-4).
21 Vickery, *The Gentleman's Daughter*, p. 289; Fletcher, *Growing Up in England*, p. 39; Kate Retford, *The Art of Domestic Life: Family Portraiture in Eighteenth-Century England* (New Haven and London, 2006), pp. 128–38.
22 Annabella Wentworth, Paris, to Sir Thomas Brackett, baronet, Wakefield, Yorkshire, 2 December 1778, York Court of Chancery, testamentary cause papers, FHL, British film 1785844, case 1784/5.
23 Fanny Burney, *Diary and Letters of Madame D'Arblay* (London: Hurst and Blackett, 1854), quoted in Pollock, *A Lasting Relationship*, p. 219.
24 O'Malley, *The Making of the Modern Child*, pp. 102–5.
25 Eugenia Stanhope, ed., *Letters Written by the Late Honourable Philip Dormer Stanhope to his Son Philip Stanhope Esq.* (London: J. Dodsley, 1774), quoted in Pollock, *A Lasting Relationship*, p. 149.
26 Harry Hendrick, 'The Child as a Social Actor in Historical Sources: Problems of Identification and Interpretation', in Pia Christensen and Allison James, eds., *Research with Children: Perspectives and Practices* (London and New York, 1999), pp. 36–61.
27 OBP, 9 January 1793, trial of John Rowe and John Martin (t17930109-4). For theoretical discussions of children's peer socialization see Allison James, Chris Jenks, and Alan Prout, *Theorizing Childhood* (Oxford and Cambridge,

1998) and Barrie Thorne, *Gender Play: Girls and Boys in School* (New Brunswick, NJ, 1993).
28 Retford, *The Art of Domestic Life*, pp. 128–38, 215–18.
29 Nelson, *An Essay on the Government of Children*, p. 33.
30 William Willets, *Christian Education of Children* (London, 1750), pp. 45–6, ECCO.
31 Johann Gottlieb Heineccius, *A Methodical System of Universal Law* (London, 1763), p. 224, ECCO.
32 William King, testamentary cause, August 1805–December 1813, Consistory Court of Gloucester, 1807, GA, GDR B4/2/K5; Consistory Court of Gloucester, Court Minutes, August 1805–December 1813, GA, GDR B3/36-44.
33 Abbott, *Life Cycles in England, 1560–1720*, p. 119.
34 Chapman, *A Treatise on Education*, p. 248; Charles Gobinet, *The Instruction of Youth in Christian Piety* (London, 1741), p. 220, ECCO.
35 Nelson, *An Essay on the Government of Children*, p. 303.
36 'Extracts from the life of Dean Dering [Heneage Dering, 1665–1750], made by his Children, and copied by Granville Baker Dec 1870', entry for 1726, included in Elizabeth Sharp Prowse's diary and memorandum book, Lloyd-Baker Family of Hardwicke Court Collection, GA, D3549/14/1/1.
37 Retford, *The Art of Domestic Life*, pp. 128–38.
38 James Christen Steward, *The New Child: British Art and the Origins of Modern Childhood, 1730–1830* (Berkeley, 1995), pp. 34, 39, 41, 49, 61, 63, 69, 77, 86, 88.
39 Sheila Cooper, 'Intergenerational Social Mobility in Late-Seventeenth- and Early-Eighteenth-Century England', *Continuity and Change*, 7:3 (1992), 283–301.
40 Caroline Atkyns to her husband John (Tracy) Atkyns, 18 July 1741, GA, D4582/2/4.
41 Richard Burn, *Ecclesiastical Law*, 2nd edn (London, 1767), vol. 4, pp. 360–1, ECCO; Erickson, *Women and Property in Early Modern England*, pp. 62–3, 72, 204–22.
42 John Travell, original will, 1762, ORO, Flick I/i/4; Gobinet, *The Instruction of Youth in Christian Piety*, p. 220.
43 Gillis, *Youth and History*, p 13; Joan Thirsk, 'Younger sons in the Seventeenth Century', *History*, 54:182 (1969), 359; Stone, *The Family, Sex and Marriage in England*; Spring, 'The Strict settlement'; Miriam Slater, *Family Life in the Seventeenth Century: The Verneys of Claydon House* (Boston and London, 1984); Abbott, *Life Cycles in England*.
44 Laslett, *The World we have Lost*, p. 112.
45 Church of England, Stanway, Gloucestershire, Bishop's Transcripts, 1580–1812, FHL, British film 427778, item 2; Church of England, Lower Swell, Gloucestershire, Bishop's Transcripts, 1605–1812, FHL, British film 427785, item 1.

46 Church of England, Swerford, Oxfordshire, Parish Register Transcript, 1577–1943, FHL, British fiche 6142087; J.M.S. Brooke and A.W.C. Hallen, *The Transcript of the Registers of the United Parishes of St. Mary Woolnoth and St. Mary Woolchurch Haw, in the City of London, from their Commencement 1538 to 1760* (London, 1886), FHL, British book 942.1/L 1 K29; Arthur J. Jewers, ed., *The Registers of the Abbey Church of SS. Peter and Paul, Bath*, vol. 2 (London, 1901).

47 Only 54 per cent of the Travell siblings survived to the age of ten, but the average figure used by Laslett (60–75 per cent) still allows for many families with much higher and much lower mortality rates. Other studies suggest that the baptisms and burials recorded in parish registers (the evidence used by Laslett and other historical demographers) potentially under-recorded infant mortality by 10 per cent; see R.E. Jones, 'Infant Mortality in Rural North Shropshire, 1561–1810', *Population Studies*, 30:2 (July 1976), 305–17.

48 Church of England, Stanway, Gloucestershire, Bishop's Transcripts; Church of England, Swerford, Oxfordshire, Parish Register Transcripts; Church of England, Adlestrop, Gloucestershire, Bishop's Transcripts, 1580–1812, FHL, British film 417099.

49 Zouheir Jamoussi, *Primogeniture and Entail, in England: A Survey of their History and Representation in Literature* (Tunis, 1999), pp. 77–102; John Ray, *A Compleat Collection of English Proverbs* (London, 1737), p. 66, ECCO.

50 John Ray, *A Compleat Collection of English Proverbs* (London, 1737), p. 66, ECCO.

51 For examples of parental grief at the loss of children see Fletcher, *Growing Up in England*, pp. 81–93; Pollock, *A Lasting Relationship*, pp. 93–132; Stone, *The Family, Sex and Marriage in England*, pp. 405–80. There has been some discussion of how parental loss affected children, but not of how peer loss did. See William Saffady, 'The Effects of Childhood Bereavement and Parental Remarriage in Sixteenth-Century England: The Case of Thomas More', *History of Childhood Quarterly*, 1:3 (1973), 310–36; Stephen Collins, 'British Stepfamily Relations, 1500–1800', *Journal of Family History*, 16:4 (1991), 331–44; Ben-Amos, *Adolescence and Youth*, pp. 48–54.

52 Fletcher, *Growing Up in England*, pp. 89–93; David Cressy, *Birth, Marriage and Death: Ritual, Religion and the Life-Cycle in Tudor and Stuart England*, (Oxford, 1997), p. 481; Peter Razzell, 'The Growth of Population in Eighteenth-Century England: A Critical Reappraisal', *Journal of Economic History*, 53:4 (December 1993), 743–71.

53 J.J. Bagley, ed., 'The Great Diurnall of Nicholas Blundell', *Record Society of Lancashire and Cheshire*, 110, 112, 114 (1968–72), quoted in Pollock, *A Lasting Relationship*, p. 148.

54 Hendrick, 'The Child as a Social Actor', p. 44.

55 Anne Tracy Travell, diary, 28 February, 4 May, 2 July, 5 September, and 28–9 October 1724, STWY.

56 The Marquess of Anglesey, ed., *The Capel Letters Being the Correspondence of Lady Caroline Capel and her Daughters with the Dowager of Countess of Uxbridge from Brussels and Switzerland 1814–17* (London, 1955), quoted in Pollock, *A Lasting Relationship*, p. 128.
57 M. Betham-Edwards, ed., *The Autobiography of Arthur Young* (London, 1898), quoted in Pollock, *A Lasting Relationship*, p. 127.
58 Houlbrooke, *Death, Religion and the Family*, p. 239.
59 Anne Tracy Travell, diary, 21 February 1724, STWY.
60 Francis Travell, will, written 20 July 1792, proved 14 July 1801, Prerogative Court of Canterbury, ORO, Flick I/i/5.
61 Razzell, 'Growth of Population in Eighteenth-Century England', p. 753; Cressy, *Birth, Marriage and Death*, p 161.
62 Church of England, Deerhurst, Gloucestershire, Parish Registers, family of Stephen and Hannah Margrate/Maggott/Maget, 1746–64, FHL, British film 991281, GA, P112 IN 1/4.
63 Stone, *The Family, Sex and Marriage*, p. 409.
64 Stone argues that this practice did not survive into the nineteenth century, 'indicating a recognition that names were highly personal and could not be readily transferred from child to child' (ibid., p. 409). However, many families continued the practice well into the Victorian age. Thomas and Martha Browett had two sons named Thomas between 1809 and 1821. Their son, the surviving Thomas, had three daughters (Harriet Rebecca, Isabella Rebecca, and Harriet) born between 1848 and 1858. Society of Friends, Gloucestershire and Wiltshire Quarterly Meeting, Transcripts of Digest Copy of Birth, Marriage, and Death Records, GA, 1340/A1R1; Thomas Browett Household, 1851 England Census, St Paul Street, Cheltenham, Gloucestershire, household 96, fol. 398, p. 28, www.ancestry.co.uk (accessed November 2007); Thomas Browett Household, 1861 England Census, 8 Hanover Street, Cheltenham, Gloucestershire, household 98, fol. 41, p. 20, www.ancestry.co.uk (accessed November 2007).
65 Ben-Amos, *Adolescence and Youth*, pp. 67–8.
66 Family of John and Alice Fowler, Church of England, Haselbury-Plucknett, Somerset, Parish Registers and Poor Law records, 1727–57, FHL, British films 1596988–9; Ben-Amos, *Adolescence and Youth*, p. 59.
67 Fordington, Dorset, Settlement Examinations, Dorset Record Office, OV 5/4, Examination of Mary Atkinson, 1821, Dorset Online Parish Clerk, http://freepages.genealogy.rootsweb.ancestry.com/~fordingtondorset/Files/FordingtonPoorLawRecords.html (accessed October 2010). Atkinson was the examinant's most recent married surname when she was examined in 1821, at the age of seventy. No maiden name or place of birth is mentioned in the examination records.
68 Fletcher, *Growing Up in England*, p. 55.
69 *The Friendly Instructor: or, A Companion for Young Ladies and Young Gentlemen* (London, 1741), p. iv, ECCO.

70 Gillian Avery and Julia Briggs, eds., *Children and their Books: A Celebration of the Work of Iona and Peter Opie* (Oxford, 1989), p. 103.
71 James, Jenks, and Prout, *Theorizing Childhood*, pp. 81–100.
72 Anne Tracy Travell, diary, 19 November, 14 December 1723, 4 April, 9 June, 3, 12 July 1724, STWY.
73 Anne Tracy Travell, diary, 6, 29, 30 December 1723, 23 April, 9, 19 May, 5 August 1724, STWY.
74 Anne Tracy Travell, diary, 1 December 1724, STWY.
75 Fletcher, *Growing Up in England*.
76 Abbott, *Life Cycles in England*, p. 68.
77 Nicholas Hans, *New Trends in Education in the Eighteenth Century* (London, 1951), pp. 70, 76–7, 94, 115, 122–3, 130–1, 145, 195–6, 199, 206, 230.
78 Ibid., p. 199; Vernon Broughton, *Court and Private Life in the Time of Queen Charlotte* (London, 1887), quoted in Pollock, *A Lasting Relationship*, pp. 236–7; Anne Freemantle, ed., *The Wynne Diaries, 1789–1820* (London, New York, and Toronto, 1952); Sharp family, common letters, 1755–63, GA, D3549/14/1/4.
79 Davidoff and Hall, *Family Fortunes*, pp. 351–2; Froide, *Never Married*, pp. 49–60.
80 Jackson and Martin families, correspondence, 1743–63, Jackson family of Sneyd Park, Westbury-on-Trym, Gloucester, Collection, GA, D153; Freemantle, ed., *The Wynne Diaries, 1789–1820*; Caroline Treby, diary, 1808–31, Treby Family of Goodamoor Collection, PWDRO, 1148; A.W. Purdue, 'John and Harriet Carr: A Brother and Sister from the North-East on the Grand Tour', *Northern History*, 30 (1994), 122–38.
81 Alicia Sheridan LeFanu to her sister-in-law Esther Ogle Sheridan, 9 November 1816, KCC, LeFanu 20.
82 Rev. Grosvenor Bartelot, *History of Crewkerne School, 1499–1899* (Crewkerne, 1899), pp. 90–1.
83 Fletcher, *Growing Up in England*, pp. 197, 199.
84 OBP, *Ordinary of Newgate's Account*, 4 May 1741 (OA17410504).
85 Hans, *New Trends in Education*, pp. 151–2.
86 Mary Hilton and Jill Shefrin, eds., *Educating the Child in Enlightenment Britain: Beliefs, Cultures, Practices* (Farnham, Surrey, and Burlington, VT, 2009), pp. 10–11.
87 Patricia Fara, *Pandora's Breeches: Women, Science, and Power in the Enlightenment* (London, 2004), pp. 109–13, 145–66; Fletcher, *Growing Up in England*, pp. 209–10.
88 Margaret Maria, Lady Verney, ed., *Verney Letters of the Eighteenth Century from the MSS at Claydon House* (London, 1930), quoted in Pollock, *A Lasting Relationship*, p. 149.
89 Bagley, ed., 'The Great Diurnall of Nicholas Blundell', quoted in Pollock, *A Lasting Relationship*, p. 148.

90 Mary Sewell, *The Life and Letters of Mrs. Sewell*, 3rd edn (London 1889), quoted in Pollock, *A Lasting Relationship*, p. 145.
91 Johnson, *The Prince of Abissinia*, p. 3.
92 Freemantle, ed., *The Wynne Diaries*, p. 45.
93 Sharp family, common letters, 1755–63, GA, D3549/14/1/4; Harris, 'This I Beg my Aunt may not know'.
94 Cecil Aspinall-Oglander, *Admiral's Wife* (London, 1940), quoted in Pollock, *A Lasting Relationship*, pp. 149–50.
95 William Beale, will, written 31 January 1797, proved 17 April 1798, GA, GDR Wills 1798/53; testamentary cause, July 1802–April 1803, GA, GDR B4/2/B77.
96 Thomas Stock, testamentary cause, July–December 1744, GA, GDR B4/2/S118.
97 Ben-Amos, *Adolescence and Youth*, p. 156.
98 Gillis, *Youth and History*, pp. 22–6.
99 Sara Mendelson and Patricia Crawford, *Women in Early Modern England 1550–1720* (Oxford, 1998), p. 130.
100 Thomas Sharp, London, to his daughter Elizabeth Sharp, 26 April 1750, GA, D3549/14/1/3.
101 John Holder, diary, 25 July 1711, 25 March 1719, 20 July 1722, GA, D1371.
102 *OBP*, 29 May 1793, trial of Thomas Smith and Thomas Edward (t17930529-40); 26 May 1790, trial of William Armstrong (t17900526-71). 9 January 1793, trial of John Rowe (t17930109-4); 15 January 1800, trial of Thomas Hallard (t18000115-71).
103 Clementina Black, ed., *The Cumberland Letters: Being the Correspondence of Richard Dennison Cumberland and George Cumberland between the Years 1771 and 1784* (London, 1912), pp. 28–9, 52, 70–2, 114, 117, 122; OBP, January 1808, trial of William Edis (t18080113-39); February 1800, trial of John Tagg (t18000219-26); September 1794, trial of Joseph Samuel (t17940917-36); *Ordinary of Newgate's Account*, 16 May 1750 (OA17500516).
104 Adult siblings followed this pattern throughout the British Atlantic world. See Pearsall, *Atlantic Families*, p. 55.
105 *The Complete Letter-Writer or Polite English Secretary*, 2nd edn (London, 1756), title page, ECCO; Eve Tavor Bannet, *Empire of Letters: Letter Manuals and Transatlantic Correspondence, 1688–1820* (Cambridge, 2005).
106 Black, ed., *The Cumberland Letters*.
107 Jackson sibling correspondence, 1743–63, GA, D153/64, 69, 95, 124, 131–4, 136–8, 140, 142–4, 146–8, 151, 153–4, 159.
108 Fordington, Dorset, Settlement Examinations, Dorset Record Office, OV 5/4, letters regarding settlement of Charles Holford and family, 5 June–20 November 1790, Dorset Online Parish Clerk, http://freepages.genealogy.rootsweb.ancestry.com/~fordingtondorset.html (accessed October 2010).

109 Adriana Benzaquén, 'Childhood, Identity, and Human Science in the Enlightenment', *History Workshop Journal*, 57:1 (Spring 2004), 36.
110 Thomas Huntingford, autobiography, c.1830s, p. 57, GA, PE98; Edward Witts, Paris, to his brother Richard, London, 2 June 1771, WFP, F255; Alicia Sheridan LeFanu to her sister-in-law Esther Ogle Sheridan, 9 November 1816, KCC, LeFanu 20.
111 Anne Tracy Travell to her husband John Travell, 1738, included with her diary, transcribed by Celandine Tracy, 1911, private collection, STWY.
112 Anne Tracy Travell, diary, 8 November 1724, STWY.

2
Ties that bound

> I, who have no sisters or brothers, look with some degree of innocent envy on those who may be said to be born to friends.
>
> Samuel Johnson, letter to Bennet Langton, 1757[1]

> There is no true happiness in a family, without a most cordial union between brothers and sisters.
>
> M. Berquin, *The Children's Friend*, 1788[2]

Anne Tracy Travell and John Travell died during the autumn and winter of 1762–63, leaving behind six children: Francis, Frances Mary, Anne, Ferdinando, Catherine, and Agnes, who ranged between thirty-four and sixteen years old. Like many families, the Travell siblings then had to forge familial and social behaviours without parental oversight. They had to assume some roles previously fulfilled by their parents, and, as only Ferdinando was married, they did so largely without the input of spouses or parents-in-law. Francis resigned his army commission, returned from the Continent, and assumed ownership of Swerford House. Catherine and Agnes, both aged under twenty-one, had to be provided for until they inherited their £1,200 and £1,100 respectively, and living arrangements had to be determined for Anne and Frances Mary. For much of that time all the sisters shuttled between Swerford and Ferdinando's new residence in Chadlington, Oxfordshire (a distance of just over seven miles). In the summer of 1764 the sisters, under Anne's leadership, began to search for a home of their own. By that point Ferdinando had a young daughter, and Francis had an illegitimate son and an unwillingness to discontinue his relationship with the boy's apparently socially unacceptable mother. Frances Mary and Anne were nearing thirty, and Anne's marriage prospects at least seem to have died the previous January with a letter 'most fatal' to her 'happiness.'[3] The sisters settled in a comfortable house in

Cheltenham, which at the time had not yet gained fame as a spa town, but was still an 'eligible residence for single gentle-women'.[4] Undoubtedly it was more suitable than remaining with Francis and his socially inappropriate fatherhood, and more attractive than remaining in Ferdinando's household, where his wife, Martha, controlled the reins of household governance.

The sisters settled in Cheltenham in the autumn of 1764, but continued to visit their brothers, often for weeks at a time, and their brothers and brothers' children (legitimate and illegitimate) visited them in turn. It is at this juncture, when the siblings were no longer tied together through parental connections and as they began their own households, that sibling ties often go unnoticed by scholars in their efforts to describe the importance of conjugal or nuclear families or the development of the self and individuality.[5] But siblings continued their earlier patterns of visits and letters in order to forge adult identities and bind their new households together. Many, like the Travell sisters, established sibling-based living arrangements. Despite the thirty miles between Chadlington and Cheltenham, and despite the divergence between Anne and Ferdinando's social and economic prosperity and Francis's lack thereof, the three Travell households were bound together by ideas that bound siblings together throughout England. The Travells recognized the advice offered by authors like John Burton that 'sisterly love and affection' were central to developing the 'domestic happiness' that grew out of 'family peace and union'. Burton continued, 'Let no jealousies, envying, or animosities disturb that harmony which should prevail amongst Brothers and Sisters. Be kind and obliging to one another.'[6]

Scholars of English families have attributed special closeness to sister–sister and brother–sister relations. Davidoff and Hall have speculated that 'of all relationships . . . sisters may well have been the closest to each other'. They, like Lawrence Stone, have argued that 'the lives of brothers and sisters remained closely interwoven and seemed to have had a special salience'.[7] Though their evidence was anecdotal, it does appear that sister–sister and brother–sister relations often had a special salience across much of the Western world.[8] Brother–brother ties have received less glowing descriptions – their competition and closeness always being in tension – but brothers also enjoyed close relationships.[9] Siblinghood's special strength grew from siblings' common heritage and the ascribed 'naturalness' of their unity and solidarity in the special version of friendship granted their relationship, no matter what its age and gender hierarchies. As Isaac Watts put it,

> Whatever brawls disturb the street,
> There should be peace at home;

> There sisters dwell and brothers meet,
> Quarrels should never come.[10]

Many versions of eighteenth-century friendship contained elements of inequality, but siblinghood's friendship was meant to be an alliance of equals. Siblinghood presented female friendships and male friendships with a model ostensibly stripped of the patron–client attitude that often typified other eighteenth-century friendships.[11] As Richard Cumberland wrote to his only sibling, George, 'believe me to be ever your unfeigned Friend and loving Brother'.[12] In contrast with other family relations and other forms of friendship, English brothers and sisters had to manage simultaneously the dangerous influence of 'unnatural' envying and strife, something their contemporaries across the Atlantic did not encounter.[13] This aspect of sibling relations will be discussed in the next chapter, but its existence put a unique pressure on siblings to maintain close and loving ties.

Sibling attachments offer another way of studying and understanding male–female relations in the early modern world – a way not clearly determined by the legal privileges granted to men. As women's participation in education, commerce, friendly societies, and political discourse expanded throughout the eighteenth century, notions about sisterhood and sister-brother relationships were implicated in unprecedented ways.[14] When commenting on one set of sisters' friendly and jovial visits to their brother at Oxford, Anthony Fletcher described it as perhaps an exception to 'conventional sibling relations', but the conviviality, the inside jokes, and the relaxed and informal atmosphere he found were more typical than exceptional for eighteenth-century siblings.[15] Ideas about natural unity, love, affection, reciprocity, and friendship made sibling relations places of powerful inclusion. Unlike other early modern forms of homo-social inclusion, siblinghood bore with it the implicit recognition that men and women could be more equal than assumptions about gender otherwise dictated.[16] For example, William and Dorothy Wordsworth were particularly close – to the exclusion of other siblings – and Alicia Sheridan felt especially close to her younger brother Richard.[17]

Unity and solidarity

Eighteenth-century authors emphasized common heritage in their depictions of siblinghood. That shared heritage formed a foundation for the solidarity and unity considered natural between siblings. Sisters and brothers of various backgrounds, religious persuasions, and regions expressed the naturalness of sibling unity and solidarity. Anne Travell, using typical sibling labels, referred to Francis as 'my Br[other]', or 'my Br Travell', to Ferdinando and Martha as 'my Br. and Sis', and to herself and her sisters as 'the Sisterhood'.[18] A Travell family friend, Edward Witts, used similar language when he described himself and his brothers as 'the brethren'. Granville Sharp described his siblings as members of a marching band, each adding their own unique sound to the combined harmony. These people played on ideas of siblinghood as expressing solidarity and unity – of belonging to a group enjoying special privileges among themselves.[19] Like Anne Travell and Edward Witts, Georgian sisters and brothers considered themselves a part of a group built on the exclusive and natural connection between children of common parents. Even unrelated people could be mistaken for sisters or brothers through demonstrating 'unity like two sisters' or by loving someone 'as dearly as his own Brother.'[20] Fictional sisters discussed how they 'lived in peace and tenderness together', and 'shared one bed': 'in heart and mind we have ever been united'.[21] Siblings wrote of their natural unity and asserted that brothers and sisters had a 'much closer tie' and a 'stronger call for preserving sweet unity of spirit' than friends or those sharing common convictions.[22] When the yeoman Morse Hobbs died his brothers, 'being in low Circumstances and having in no wise disobliged or offended him', argued that ''twas natural' for Morse to provide for them in his will.[23] When Samuel Johnson learned that his friend Bennet Langton had been a tutor to his own sisters, he remarked on the 'native union' between siblings – something he envied because he did not have siblings of his own.[24] Parents tried to foster this native union between their children. They might, like the Sharps, encourage epistolary practices between siblings, or, like William King, they might wield the law to enforce equality and unity. William went so far as to destroy his will so that his children would have to divide the inheritance exactly equally. Though he could have left a will specifying the equal treatment of his children, instead William left it to a precedent that made no distinction in inheritance between a son and a daughter. He 'frequently observed and declared that it was an act of Injustice in a parent to make an unequal Division of his Property amongst his Children'. As he held his children in 'equal esteem regard and affection', he saw no need to differentiate between them in a will. When others suggested he should make a will, it made William 'very angry, saying he did not wish or want to make a Will as he intended for all his Children to share alike in his property ... he had no Houses or Lands to settle, and asked what he should make a Will for?'[25]

Authors and siblings alike took siblings' natural unity as a given, also extending it to siblings-in-law. Mary Leigh noted 'that Broth[er]s shou[l]d live in such pleasant unity, I trust, is not uncommon', but then asserted that the extension of that unity to in-laws was unusual. '[T]hat the [brothers'] Wives shou[l]d be as fond of each other, is singular'.[25] Mary's description was not entirely accurate; the incorporation of siblings-in-law into a unified sibling friendship was not so singular. Brothers- and sisters-in-law were rarely, if ever, differentiated by title from consanguineous siblings, and the blurring of friendship and kinship often allowed siblings-in-law to participate equally with siblings. Siblings-in-law could be easily included because spouses often came from families that were already friends, as was the case with the Travell and Witts families when Agnes Travell married Edward Witts. Alicia and Betsy Sheridan cemented their ties by marrying brothers – a double solidarity desired by many families.[27] The Sharp family cemented lateral ties through the marriage of first cousins. Siblings often sought the approval of one another when choosing a spouse for the reason that siblings-in-law should be unified with the siblings, but there was no guarantee. Even if siblings were motivated by eighteenth-century ideas about individuality and the transcendent power of romantic love over other affections, in reality their siblings' opinions of their matches could matter a great deal. Men and women routinely requested their siblings' input on marriage partners and the ability of the sibling to accept another person into the unity shared by the siblings. The Wintle and Cumberland siblings employed one another in romantic entanglements, Alicia Sheridan facilitated her sister's marriage, and the Sharp siblings' tempers, otherwise the picture of amicability, flared when some siblings assumed that one brother was not sufficiently accommodating of their new sister-in-law.[28] Ideally, siblings accepted and befriended one another's spouses and received them with a 'prompt welcome'.[29] The Wittses readily included the Travells as siblings, and in turn the Travells readily included the Rollinson family (Ferdinando's wife's family). All three families had grown up together in western Oxfordshire and therefore shared a common background and history, thus facilitating the marriages between Edward Witts and Agnes Travell and between Ferdinando Travell and Martha Rollinson. This also meant that two people, such as Anne Travell and Apphia Witts, who had no direct affinal or consanguineous relationship, could cement their childhood friendship through the marriage of their siblings and become a sort of sister once removed.

From family concerts to summer sailing trips and the elaborate family crests and pedigrees constructed by Judith and Elizabeth, the Sharps believed in and practised unity. Concerts were a particular highlight, with dancing, the brothers playing woodwind instruments, and the sisters singing in harmony and playing the harpsichord and guitar.[30] In addition to Granville's 'marching band' metaphor for siblinghood, in their descriptions of their 'water schemes' the Sharp siblings often differentiated between 'our party' and everyone else, 'our party' referring exclusively to the siblings, their spouses, and their three nieces. And they emphasized this attitude with the names they chose for their small family fleet of sailing vessels. Three of the smaller boats were named after their nieces Jemima, Mary, and Catherine, and one of the yachts, evocatively, was the *Union*. Perhaps they meant a more political statement with the latter name, but the use of the term coupled with the names of the other vessels is emblematic of Sharp family unity.[31] The 1779–81 portrait by Johan Zoffany depicts the family on board the yacht *Apollo*, clustered around their instruments, the Thames behind them, and the flag bearing William's and James's intertwined crests fluttering protectively overhead (see Figure 3). Outsiders recognized the harmony shared by the Sharp siblings. As one observer

3 Johan Joseph Zoffany, *The Sharp Family*, 1779–81. By courtesy of the National Portrait Gallery, London, and the Lloyd-Baker Trustees

remarked, he knew of no family 'wherein more true brotherly kindness appears, While unenvying each shines in their diff[e]rent spheres'.[32]

The Sharps may have been, as Mary once remarked, 'remarkable for unanimity', and they were definitely remarkable in their abilities, but the patterns of solidarity and unity were not remarkable.[33] The Witts siblings enjoyed affectionate relations, and they appreciated the importance of letter-writing in the demonstration of that affection. Shortly after her doomed marriage to Lord Lyttelton, Apphia Witts stressed the importance of letter-writing in representing brotherly and sisterly love. In a letter to her elder sister Alicia, she wrote:

> I have quitted my company at supper to scribble this hasty proof of my not being able to neglect whenever in my power every attention that can prove the sincerity of the former assurances of the perfect love esteem & Friendship that in all places & circumstances you will possess of my Dear Sister Your affectionate and obliged A. Lyttelton.[34]

While her marriage disintegrated, the siblings assured Apphia of their sincere friendship. Apphia had hastily married Lord Lyttelton during the summer of 1772, professing to relations and acquaintances that it was a love match. Lord Lyttelton professed similar sentiments; his love letters expressed devotion and unyielding attachment, but his rakish habits were hard to break. By the early months of 1773 he was living in Europe with his mistress, and Apphia began separation proceedings. Apphia's siblings helped her manage her affairs, found housing for her, and offered emotional support.[35] During this time Edward concluded most of his letters to Apphia with assurances of his faithful friendship. He assured her that he was always her 'most affectionate Brother and sincere Friend', in contrast to the fickle affection she received from her husband.[36] Apphia recognized that the time spent in writing a letter, with or without affectionate content, was 'proof' of love, esteem, and friendship. Siblings from most walks of life shared letters, visits, gifts, bequests, business concerns, execution of wills, and sorrow at a sibling's illness or death.[37] Mary Jackson sent her brother Nicholas pots of apricot jam; the plasterer John Hogan and his sister Mary exchanged letters with their half-brother in the militia; Lydia Martin, a servant to a watchmaker, was regularly visited by her sister, who also tried to protect her against prosecution for larceny; John Clymer, a shoemaker, spent part of his career in business with his brother.[38] John Care, a prosperous yeoman, left £10 to his brother and sister and an additional £10 to his brother's daughter. The considerably less prosperous yeoman John Little made his preference for his siblings by dictating his 'Desier for my to Brothers to com to my buriell', and his additional 'Desier is not for any the family of the Allinses to com a [nerst] me'. Mary Everett housed and nursed her dying brother, Joseph Wyman, and distributed goods to others who cared for him in his last illness. Similarly, John Crewe, a merchant and the son of a maltster, spent his last days in his brother's house.[39] John and Charles Wesley's sister carefully preserved miniatures of her two brothers, and when Charles died in 1788 John 'broke down crying during a hymn when he came to Charles's words, "My company before is gone"'.[40] Though the phrases 'loving sister' or 'affectionate brother' that appear in letters and wills may have been formulaic, their presence was a reminder to siblings that love and affection were central to sibling relations. One sister even went so far as to claim that the death of her 'affectionate' brother had 'troubled' her so greatly as to lead her to murder.[41]

Unity between siblings also encouraged sisters and brothers to see one another as parts of themselves, thus ensuring familial and social harmony and generating healthy individuals. If, as one observer wrote, friends and near relations formed 'part of ourselves' in the eighteenth century, then siblings had a special role in the development of self and individuality.[42] '[L]et all who have Brethren and Sisters', Richard Allestree wrote, 'look on them as parts of themselves, and then they will never think fit either to quarrel with them or to envy them any advantage, any more than one part of the body does another of the same body, but will strive to advance and help forward the good of each other.'[43] Both conjugal and brotherly love were counted as virtues because the 'concord and union' which existed within them perpetuated families. While both might be based on unity, conjugal love aimed at benevolent family and household governance, while brotherly love 'establish[ed] the power, safety, and preservation of families'. Unified siblings, in this formulation, would 'mutually defend each other in their mutual wants, support each other in misfortune and thus secure their common existence'.[44] In this way siblings could also couch concern about themselves as manifestations of their care for a sister or brother; their unity with a sibling was so close that they could appear as mere extensions of one another. Frances Dickenson went so far as to take sole blame for a theft she committed with her sister so that 'her Sister might be acquitted'.[45] When during a journey to Wales with her brother, eighteen-year-old Catherine Travell wrote to her elder sister Anne, reporting on the journey and its toll upon her, she assured Anne that she shared the details not out of any selfishness, but out of consideration for Anne. 'I know you wont be pleas[e]d without I mention myself', she began; she ended with 'It is only for yourself as knowing you would be kindly anxious for me.'[46] Siblings were attuned to fraternal and sororal support and its connections to their own sense of self. They anxiously sought a brother or sister's approval for decisions as important as marriage and as mundane as clothing. And if they found themselves under condemnation, as Henry Goodiff did, they hoped their siblings would be like his sister, who journeyed from Surrey to London to defend him. Benjamin Mush's sister chased after thieves who had stolen her brother's goods. Isaac Broderick's sister, 'upon hearing the Charge [sodomy] laid upon her Brother', went to the home of the accusers asking them, 'is it fit a Man should loose his Reputation for nothing?'[47] Seventy-seven-year-old Hannah Key from Chester fled to the house of her brother, William, when her niece tried to take advantage of her advanced years and difficulty in hearing, and William Key provided for his sister and defended her rights to her property.[48] If no defence could protect a sibling, at least he or she could hope that siblings in their solidarity would not cast aspersions on an innocent brother or sister. As one convict stated in his confession, 'I hope no one will blame my Sister, for she has been very good to me.'[49]

Affection and friendship

Sibling unity was manifested in loving and affectionate exchanges. Authors and playwrights depicted love and friendship as natural between siblings until differences in parents' treatment or romantic conflicts turned them into rivals.[50] Siblings were to experience, as the Musgrove sisters in *Persuasion* did, 'seemingly perfect good understanding and agreement together... [and] good-humoured mutual affection'.[51] Mutual affection, kindly exchanges, and remembrance of important events in one another's lives were all important aspects of sibling relations. Love could be expressed through a variety of affectionate exchanges, but unfortunately the face-to-face demonstration of that love is lost to us. What remains is the written evidence of affectionate words and deeds. Some siblings expressed their affection in public forums. During the 1780s and 1790s the Tomlins siblings exchanged poems on each other's birthdays. What began as private expressions of love grew by 1797 into a published collection (accompanied by other poems). As the brother, listed as simply, 'E', wrote in his 1784 poem 'To His Sister':

> Affection glows within my breast;
> Firm Friendship there her throne has plac'd
> And Love, which shall for ever last.

E's sister, Sophia, echoed this theme in her 1786 poem, 'To Her Brother':

> And why again awakes my lyre?
> My lyre which never yet could prove,

Affection's force, Affection's fire,
Or warble half a Sister's love?[52]

Not all siblings exchanged poems on their siblings' birthdays as the Tomlins did, but letters and diaries, as well as probate records, contain direct evidence of affectionate terms, nicknames, and physical demonstrations such as hugs and kisses. Letters themselves became a form of affection. Their physical presence demonstrated to the recipient that the writer was thinking of them and was willing to engage in the formalized language of affection. Letters were a source of news and gossip and letter-writers were instructed in formulating their epistles as conversations.[53] The eighteenth-century improvements in transport and communication that allowed more frequent and reliable correspondence increased siblings' demands upon one another's time; distance was no longer an excuse for a lack of intimate knowledge and concern for one another's lives. Additionally, women's increased literacy and the importance of letters to the world of female kinwork gave sisters an increased presence in family correspondence and the historical record.[54]

Eighteenth-century letters between siblings were often group conversations. One sibling might write to other, but then refer to the words and actions of several other siblings and make explicit instructions for additional siblings to read or respond to a particular letter. Brothers and sisters also reported the contents and frequency of letters from one sibling to another. Like Austen's fictional Bertrams, 'the letter was not unproductive. It re-established peace and kindness. Sir Thomas sent friendly advice and professions, Lady Bertram dispatched money and baby-linen, and Mrs. Norris wrote the letters.'[55] Letters were also the means by which siblings expressed their expectations and demanded evidence of affection and support motivated by love. From surviving letters and diaries it is apparent that siblings used every opportunity of expressing their love for one another. Phrases such 'your most affectionate brother' or 'my dearest sister' were more than convention. Such salutations reminded brothers and sisters of the feelings that should and did exist. Requests, and even censure, were softened by couching them amid such warm addresses.

The Sharp siblings participated in ideal affectionate exchanges. For over fifty years the eight surviving siblings constantly visited, wrote letters, dined, danced, sang, and holidayed together. In this way they fulfilled the dreams of their parents and prescriptive authors. Beginning in 1754 the Sharp sisters, living in northern England with their parents, began a correspondence with their older brothers in Northumberland and the three younger brothers in London. These 'common letters' circulated between all eight siblings until the early 1760s. Elizabeth Sharp Prowse remarked on their parents' pleasure at this correspondence: 'My Father and Mother on their death Beds expressed the satisfaction this weekly correspondence had given them, being thereby assured that their Daughters would be protected by their Brothers, and happy with them.'[56] The common letters were full of puns and inside jokes – particularly their enjoyment of using the musical symbol for 'sharp' (♯) as a shorthand for their surname. Many of their jokes appear almost completely incomprehensible to modern readers, and one suspects that such insider talk excluded even their parents. At one point the puns flew so fast, particularly from Granville, that even the rest of the Sharps needed clarification. 'I hear that you had a Report in the North of my having gone into the Army', Granville wrote, 'which I suppose was occasioned by my punning in the Common Letter on admission into the Office of Ordnance.'[57] Not every family had such personalized sibling letters, but any family with the means used letters as conversations between individuals and between all members of the group. Edward Cofield, a member of the Middlesex militia, regularly wrote letters to his half-siblings, John, a plasterer, and Mary Hogan, who then shared them with each other.[58] The Travell siblings exchanged letters that were meant to be read with and to all siblings and siblings-in-law, and the Jackson siblings replied to letters with requests that the recipient would pass the message along, in another letter, to absent siblings. A Wintle sister's account that 'My sister Ann reced. a letter from my brother . . . Informed her he had reced. mine of the 14th' was typical of families' correspondence.[59]

Letters were both manifestations of affection and material representations of friendship. As Anne Travell told her lifelong friend and Agnes's sister-in-law, Apphia Witts, 'I think myself so much oblig[e]d to you for the very kind Letter, that you favor[e]d me with last month, that I will not longer delay returning you my thanks, for it, esteeming it as a fresh mark of your friendship.'[60] Siblings resisted when letters and friendly exchanges seemed motivated by obligation, formality, or necessity. Anne's method of expression was less 'glowing' than Agnes's; Anne was not prone to emotional outbursts or demonstrations and she lacked Agnes's self-proclaimed 'too warm' nature.[61] Agnes fretted that 'It does indeed appear as if all my relations thought I could be as easy without their conntinance as with it . . . all of them try to glose it over & accuse me as if I complain[e]d . . . without reason.'[62] No wonder that every one of Agnes's letters to Anne began with a complaint about the lack of letters from Anne, and no wonder that Agnes concluded a letter with 'at all times am to you both an affectionate sister'. Agnes, especially while living such great distance from her siblings, needed evidence of her siblings' love and affection. The reverse could also be true: when Anne wrote promptly,

Agnes was cheered and felt loved. In October 1795 she was glad to find a letter from Anne waiting for her at her house. '[M]y first & most welcome salute', she wrote, 'it was very kind of you to write so instantly after the receipt of mine'.[63] Though similar patterns and phrases can be found in correspondence between unrelated friends, sibling letters often have a more informal style, often addressing the sibling by her or his first name or as 'dear brother' or 'dear sister'. For example, Anne's letter to Apphia begins with the salutation 'My dear Mrs. Lyttelton'. In sibling epistolary exchanges the relationship, not the social or public title, was emphasized. Among the Wittses this was common practice, as evidenced by their letters and diaries. In a 1771 letter to Apphia, Amelia (Broome's wife) was explicit about the love and friendship that she and her husband shared with his siblings. '[P]resent our affectionate regards to Alicia', she wrote, enlisting Apphia's efforts in tying her siblings together. Amelia then continued by expressing both her and Broome's love for Apphia: 'my Dear Broomes heart is full of tender affection for his Appy, a fruitless unavailing wish & ardent prayer for your Happiness is all that your sister y[ou]r Friend & y[ou]r Emma can offer'.[64] ('Appy' was a nickname for Apphia, and 'Emma' a nickname for Amelia.)

Letters themselves did more than convey friendly or loving content: their very existence bound brothers and sisters together across time and space; and letters provided the means for enforcing and strengthening that bond. Letters could also stand in the place of the physical expressions of affection.[65] In a telling letter of 1771 Edward Witts told his brother Richard about his travels in the Netherlands and then concluded by expressing affection for all of the siblings' with whom Richard could communicate:

> If Stone or Alicia are at Ch[ipping Norton, Oxfordshire]. & you think it worth while to send this to them, pray do with my affectionate Love, & let Sally know I never forget a single Day to think of my sweet little winch in the nursery. I would give a good deal to kiss her this moment Adieu give my Love to Broome and Amelia, & let me hear of them [&] you.[66]

That complex list requires some deciphering to clarify the sibling relations. 'Stone' referred to Edward Stone, the husband of Sarah (Sally), Edward's and Richard's sister. 'Ch.' is most likely a reference to Chipping Norton, Oxfordshire, the Wittses' home town. Edward was in Europe and Richard in London, but apparently Richard was planning a visit to Oxfordshire. Broome was Edward's and Richard's eldest brother, and Amelia was his wife. Within these few lines Edward employed his letter to express his affection in a complex way. First, the time and effort in sending Richard a letter was a form of affection (along with the effort Edward took to send one of Richard's trunks back to

London). Second, Edward enlisted Richard's help in demonstrating his affection for the Stones by granting Richard permission to share the letter with them and by specifically referring to an affectionate kiss between him and Sarah. Third, he requested that Richard verbally express Edward's love for Broome and Amelia, and last, he begged a return of affection in a letter from Richard. Edward's letter reveals the verbal, physical, and written forms of sibling affection and the importance of siblings acting as messengers for one another's affection. Letters also recorded the exchange of gifts and household possessions. George and Richard Cumberland were constantly exchanging clothing, books, and gifts along with gossip and news.[67] Love or fondness was meaningless without these affectionate expressions in deed and in spoken and written word.

Sibling correspondence networks were not limited to one generation. As siblings married and had children they incorporated those children into their sibling networks, allowing the next generation of siblings and cousins to learn the patterns of loving and affectionate horizontal ties. The Sharps trained their children to engage early in letter-writing efforts. In a 1769 letter to John, James wrote, 'Jack has receiv[e]d a Letter from Cousin Jemmima by this poast which has given high delight and he promises to answer it very soon.'[68] Jack was James's four-year-old son, and Jemima was John's six-year-old daughter. James and his family lived in London while John and his lived in Northumberland, and they expected their very young children to reinforce the sibling epistolary network that the Sharps had established. Their efforts proved successful: Jemima and her surviving cousins, Mary and Catherine (Jack died just before his sixth birthday), maintained close relations with each other and with their aunts and uncles. The cousin network developed and enjoyed between the three girls, which continued well into the nineteenth century, replicated the system begun by their parents during the 1760s, this despite the differences in location and age.[69] The Jackson and Martin siblings, who were cousins, also repeated the sibling correspondence begun by their parents. The perpetuation of sibling bonds in the next generation was necessary to family relationships; as Anna Barbauld wrote to her husband, 'our child must love our brother and sister'.[70] In this way sibling correspondence could encourage sibling-like horizontal ties among cousins or across the vertical ties between aunts and uncles and their nieces and nephews.

In addition to expressing fond feelings, siblings performed a vital instrumental role in each other's lives, much as the Wittses did during Apphia's marital problems. That demonstration was encapsulated in friendship; friends helped and served one another in very practical ways. Brothers and sisters 'ought to be the best and dearest of friends', one author noted.[71] Friendship implied a mixture of practical assistance and deep devotion, a 'moral and reciprocal relationship' between friends and family members across the social spectrum.[72] Siblinghood resonated with this definition of friendship. As two generations of the Jackson family were fond of writing, siblings could be both 'affectionate' and 'humble servants'. Sibling friendship, like other forms of eighteenth-century friendship, turned love and affectionate feelings into material and instrumental support. Siblings, however, enjoyed a special version of friendship that assumed instrumental support to be given without thought of return benefits or assumption of one sibling 'owing' duty to another. Siblings were meant to be friends by definition, not by necessity.

Prescriptive authors saw friendship as the natural state among siblings. John Gregory (1724–1773), a Scottish professor, saw the sibling relationship as a natural source of friends. In his advice to his two daughters (and three sons) he wrote:

> If all other circumstances are equal, there are obvious advantages in your making friends of one another [sisters]. The ties of blood, and your being so much united in one common interest, form an additional bond of union to your friendship. If your brothers should have the good fortune to have hearts susceptible of friendship, to possess truth, honour, sense, and delicacy of sentiment, they are the fittest and most unexceptionable confidants.[73]

The expectation of natural friendship inculcated reciprocal bonds. Reciprocity among siblings stemmed from their understanding of unity and equality and implied that sisters and brothers would provide services for one another – services delineated by their relative positions. Thus a single sister could expect housing and board from a married brother or sister. Reciprocally, her sibling could expect child care, household management, and nursing care. Though Morse Hobbs's brothers, neighbours, and friends argued about the validity of his will they seemed to accept that it would 'look shamefull and mean' for him to leave too little to his sisters.[74] When John Tracy argued with his brother's widow over his role in his brother's will, his legal representative emphasized that John's role of brother obliged him to execute Thomas's will, but also entitled him to compensation. 'There is certainly nothing more obvious than Brothers owing to each other reciprocal services according to their particular circumstances.'[75] The Sharp siblings constantly exchanged services. A letter from Granville Sharp to his brother John began with the typical salutation 'Dear Brother', and then proceeded to thank his brother for his advice, discuss his own writing career, and report on financial transactions between the brothers and three other siblings, and concluded with a report about John's daughter and an expression of Granville's love to John's family.

'I am much obliged', he began, 'by the fullness & freedom of your remarks on my several Tracts in your kind & affectionate Letter of the 14th ulto., and I will endeavour to keep the subjects of my writings more distinct in future, agreeable to your good advice.' He then detailed accounts between John and William and Judith. Judith often cared for John's daughter Jemima while taking her on long visits or while living with John's family. His concluding comments, which contain an account of financial as well as emotional exchanges, demonstrate the combination of love, affection, and friendship that intersected in sibling relations.

> [T]here remains a Ballance due to you of £6.6.1¼, which I will either pay to Sister Jud, or, if you think proper (& signify that you agree to this Balance) will carry it on to a fresh accot. . . . or any other commission you may happen to want. Your Daughter is very well & a very good Girl – I remain with affectionate Love to my Sister. Dear Brother, your sincerely affectionate Brother Granville Sharp.[76]

Granville settled accounts with his brother on every possible score: he respected and applied the occupational advice John gave; he served as financial go-between for John, William, Frances, and Judith; he participated in the care of John's daughter; and he expressed his love for John and his wife.

At the cornerstone of many sibling friendships lay the expectation of the granting and receiving of emotional support and advice. This support would be expected in times of disappointment or grief and when facing important decisions and moral questions. Prescriptive literature was clear: siblings were to have a positive moral and emotional influence upon one another. In fact, it is this aspect of sibling relations that is most evident in sermons and advice literature.[77] Brothers were to protect and provide for their siblings, particularly younger ones. Sisters were to refine their brothers socially and encourage them. Brothers were to support one another in friendship and love, and sisters were to be each other's confidantes. These duties merely echoed commonly held beliefs on the roles shared by all women and men.[78] In discussions of siblings' special role, however, they emphasized the naturalness of brotherly and sisterly love based on a lifetime of shared physical space and shared parents. Playwrights and novelists loved to turn these expectations around and to depict siblings deceiving one another, hating one another, and even plotting to kill one another. As Richard Allestree asserted, siblinghood was the closest family relationship during childhood and this gave a unique opportunity for unusual friendship or unusual ability to harm.[79]

Prescriptive authors, whether actually writing to their siblings or not, could build on the theme of sibling advisor by situating themselves as siblings offering brotherly love and advice.[80] Often advice literature repeated the theme that brothers and sisters were natural friends and therefore should always be able and willing to support one another and encourage one another in the pursuit of virtuous attributes and behaviours. Repeatedly authors stressed that brothers and sisters were uniquely positioned and responsible for advising one another; one man wrote (and published) specifically to help his brother learn from his mistakes and avoid their cost. He felt compelled 'to point out to him a proper mode of conduct; which I have done by way of beacon, in order that he may evade those rocks and shoals upon which many have been shipwrecked'.[81] He went on to delineate how siblings should 'be the best and dearest of friends'. He recognized that many were not, but blamed this on their 'careless and indifferent' behaviour towards one another. 'They take no pains to please, and are not cautious enough in saying or doing what will give offence.'[82] Clearly, though natural friends, siblings were to be dedicated to lovingly supporting one another. Being a sibling gave one 'liberty' to candidly 'counsel' one another on moral improvement.[83]

Candid counsel meant to improve his brother was very much on Thomas Edwards's mind in 1746 and 1747. In the early months of 1747 Walter Edwards came into conflict with his father over his choice of bride. He immediately enlisted his brother's help in resolving the conflict, encouraging Thomas to convince their father to approve the match. As Thomas was studying at Oxford at the time (while Walter and their father were in London) this required careful attention to correspondence with both his brother and his father. On 16 January Thomas wrote of his concern about Walter's affairs and his disappointment at not receiving a letter from Walter. He concluded his letter with an assurance that he had 'the utmost sincerity, & concern' for Walter's affairs and a plea for Walter to write him 'as soon as [he] receive[d] it'.[84] Walter's return letter was devoid of any mention of an improvement in his situation, but Thomas still hoped that it would be settled 'to the satisfaction of all Parties'. In addition to expressing his hope and confidence in an eventual reconciliation, Thomas's return letter detailed the bills he paid for Walter, sent his 'duty' to their father, and updated Walter on his social activities. He told Walter that he had recently joined a music society, 'being as you may remember, an Encourager of Harmony'. He continued by drawing a parallel to their family relationship:

> This puts me in mind ... of that greatest of Blessings, which shou[l]d subsist between Dearest Friends, I think I cannot conclude this better than by wishing it to mine in the highest Degree, that is Dear Bror. as subsists between yourself & Your affectionate Bror. Tho Edwards.[85]

Thomas's letter demonstrates the various forms of expressing and proving love, affection, and friendship among siblings. He expressed his love and concern, emphasizing their harmony and unity, and he performed vital tasks for Walter in balancing his financial accounts and mediating in affairs with their father.

Fictive siblinghood

It was not just the Edwards brothers who enjoyed friendly advice and support: siblings in different families and different classes counted on love and its evidence in their daily lives. They worked at, and assumed a level of, each other's emotional lives and needs; they possessed true warm regard and love for one another; and they demonstrated that love through affectionate exchanges and instrumental support. From this lived experience and the expectation that siblings were peers, friends, and allies, fictive siblinghood took its cue. When Thomas Turner referred to his father as one of his closest friends he employed a very intriguing qualifier. In an attempt to define their relationship he referred to him not only as his father, but as 'Friend and Brother'.[86] In so doing he burst the bounds of real and fictive vertical relations and replaced them with fictive horizontal ties. This was a far cry from the family romance fiction of brothers rising up to kill the father. Instead, Turner's formulation hints at Georgian attempts to reduce the tension between hierarchy and equality by rendering everyone – even fathers – as friendly equals.[87] Siblinghood's connotation of lifelong connection also resonated beyond the bounds of consanguineous and affinal siblings. Old acquaintances might hail each other as 'brother' or 'sister'.[88] In a similar way, political theory and social and religious reform combined the language of sorority and fraternity with friendship to conjure the image of long-lasting, equally invested allies, allies whose interests were so connected, so similar, that they were virtually identical. When real sibling ties worked this alliance could appear almost automatic, thereby granting notions of fictive siblinghood a powerful grounding in lived experience.

Fictive siblinghood had been common in religious discourse throughout the period, and had older connections to guilds and religious houses. Even after the Dissolution of the Monasteries ministers of various stripes continued to employ the language of siblinghood. The Ordinary at the Old Bailey instructed his listeners to consider 'How much we are bound to love every Man, and look upon him as our Brother, having the same Heavenly Father and therefore should deal justly and kindly with him at all time'.[89] Conjuring up images of mutually beneficial relations, traditional clergy, evangelicals, Quakers, and Methodists all agreed that all Christians were, by definition, brothers and sisters.[90] Fictive siblinghood was not the sole territory of Christians. When hearing of the extensive travels of a condemned Jewish thief, the

Ordinary at Newgate questioned how 'so young a Boy as he then was, could adventure to pass through so many Regions'. The accused, Abraham Pass, replied that 'the Jews in general whereever dispersed, entertain a good deal of Brotherly Love and Affection towards one another; and when their Youth have a longing Desire to Travel Abroad, their Parents and Relations are not averse to send them, but on the contrary, provide them with Letters of Recommendation to their Correspondants in other Countries'.[91] The growth of friendly and voluntary societies from the late seventeenth century onwards and the Enlightenment political philosophy of the latter half of the eighteenth century expanded the social uses of fictive sibling ties. Those working to end slavery or poverty or to expand citizenship or education made use of sibling language to invoke a common cause with friends who were equally invested. If siblings were unlikely to imprison one another for debt, then no wonder that fictive brotherhood and sisterhood had such a powerful resonance with new ideas about a more equitable social order.[92] The use of such language was not without its detractors. Observing the tumults across the Channel, one author decried claims of natural equality; 'Who need obey an equal?' he moaned.[93] This query recognized the problems arising from reducing a social and political model of obedience and hierarchy to one of negotiation and equality.

Conclusion

Sibling affection expressed in letters established that siblings were the best emotional and instrumental support for each other. In June 1760 Robert and Nicholas Jackson wrote to their sister Mary, following a pattern common to many families. On the eighth, Robert began his letter with gratitude for Mary's letter: 'I am obliged to you for your kind Letter'; he continued by suggesting that Mary send him his clothing with a mutual acquaintance and informed her that he had received a letter from Nicholas, who was 'very well', the previous day. On the twenty-third Nicholas wrote along similar lines. He opened with his 'pleasure' at receiving Mary's previous letters, and wrote of his relief over their mother's health. He gave social and weather news and an update on their Martin cousins (children of their father's sister), reported when he had last heard from Robert, and ended with a common conclusion: 'I desire my Duty to my Mother and am Dear Sister Your Affectionate Brother & Humble Serv[an]t Nich[ola]s Jackson.' The pattern of affectionate gratitude for letters, expressions of filial duty, performance of domestic tasks, reference to other siblings' participation in correspondence, and the assurance of love and friendship appears in nearly every letter the Jackson siblings exchanged. The affectionate exchanges of news, clothing, and horseshoes continued throughout the rest of the year. In July Robert requested that Mary pay a Mr Phelps for a horse; in October Mary sent apricot jam to Nicholas and their cousins (with whom he was staying); and in November Mary solicited Robert's advice on the wisdom of ending Nicholas £100. Robert offered his support for the loan, and even offered to 'stand security' for it.[94] He expressed his hope to see both her and Nicholas and concluded 'most affectionately'. Robert was able to demonstrate his love and support for both siblings by expressing his enthusiasm for the advantage to Nicholas and by offering to ameliorate any inconvenience for Mary. Here, in a neat package contained within a few economical sentences, Robert has captured sibling affection and friendship. He told his siblings that he cared for them through words and demonstrated it through advice and concrete support. As siblinghood as an ideal of social organization spread, it was this easy and natural relationship between lifelong peers that influenced fictive siblinghood.

The story of sibling love, affection, and friendship is the other side of the coin described by Naomi Tadmor in her work on eighteenth-century notions of friendship and family. It has long been recognized that the term 'family' had several definitions in the early modern era that have since fallen into disuse. Tadmor furthered this scholarship by historicizing the expansive definition of friendship during the eighteenth century. In her analysis of Thomas Turner's diary she discovered that he applied the term 'friendship' to a range of related and unrelated friends, signifying both emotional and instrumental support: to 'designate kin, set expectations, negotiate exchanges, and express hardships'.[95] Siblings used 'friendship' in a very similar manner, but only siblings shared the intimacy of a common heritage, a common childhood, shared living space, and mutual lifetime memories. Another difference lay in the unique pressures placed upon sibling relationships. Siblings were expected to be friends, but of course they did not have any choice in the selection of their siblings as they did, at least partially, in that of their friends. Additionally, siblings faced cultural expectations that their lifelong connection would translate into fair and amiable interaction, while friends faced no such expectation that they would remain friends no matter what their circumstances or behaviour. Most importantly, friendship did not carry with it an implicit reference to the forces that could destroy it. Siblings were subjected to expectations of their friendship and fears of their rivalry. In literature and in daily life they confronted rivalrous threats to their friendships. The cultural concern about sibling rivalry informed sibling friendships to a degree never confronted in other friendships. Friends were valuable assets and important parts of life, but their instrumental and emotional exchanges often carried an implied inequality between services received and rendered. Siblings expected to be the 'best of friends', the type that did not keep score, nor expect more service than they rendered. Such high expectations meant that siblinghood was ripe with opportunities for disappointment and resentment.

Notes

1. James Boswell, *The Life of Samuel Johnson* (London, 1799), vol. 1, p. 287.
2. M. Berquin, *The Children's Friend, Being a Selection from the Works of M. Berquin* (London, 1788), p. 51, ECCO.
3. Anne Travell, daybook, 25 January 1764, GA, D4582/4/17/1.
4. David Verey, ed., *The Diary of a Cotswold Parson, Reverend F.E. Witts, 1783–1854*, 2nd edn (Stroud, 2003), p. 45. F.E. Witts, son of Agnes Travell Witts, made this comment about his mother and aunts settling in Cheltenham when he remarked upon the death of his aunt Anne in 1826.
5. Felicity Heal and Clive Holmes, *The Gentry in England and Wales, 1500–1700* (Stanford, 1994), p. 87.
6. John Burton, *Lectures on Female Education and Manners* (Rochester, 1793), vol. 2, pp. 255–6, ECCO.
7. Stone, *The Family, Sex and Marriage*, p. 116; Davidoff and Hall, *Family Fortunes*, pp. 350–1.
8. Glover, *All Our Relations*; Miller and Yavneh, *Sibling Relations*; Anu Lahtinen, *Anpassing, Förhandling, Motstånd: Kvinnliga Aktörer i Släkten Fleming, 1470–1620*, trans. Camilla Frostell (Stockholm and Helsinki, 2009).
9. Linda Pollock, 'Younger Sons in Tudor and Stuart England', *History Today*, 39:6 (June 1989), 23–9.
10. Isaac Watts, *Divine Songs Attempted in Easy Language, for the Use of Children* (London, 1727), pp. 24–5, ECCO.
11. Stuart Curran, 'Dynamics of Female Friendship in the Later Eighteenth Century', *Nineteenth-Century Contexts*, 23:2 (2001), 221–39; Trumbach, *The Rise of the Egalitarian Family*, pp. 61–7; Tadmor, *Family and Friends*, pp. 1–17.
12. Black, ed., *The Cumberland Letters*, p. 49.
13. Glover, *All Our Relations*; Hemphill, *Siblings: Brothers and Sisters in American History*.
14. Rosemary Sweet and Penelope Lane, *Women and Urban Life in Eighteenth-Century England: 'On the Town'* (Aldershot, Hampshire and Burlington, VT, 2003); Richard Price, *British Society, 1680–1880*, pp. 234–63, 292–335.
15. Fletcher, *Growing Up in England*, pp. 209–10.
16. Linda Pollock, 'Childbearing and Female Bonding in Early Modern England', *Social History*, 22:3 (October 1997), 286–306.

17 Kathleen Jones, *A Passionate Sisterhood: Women of the Wordsworth Circle* (New York, 2000); Alicia Sheridan LeFanu to Esther Ogle Sheridan, 9 November 1816, KCC, LeFanu 20.
18 Anne Travell, daybook, 27 September 1764, 29 May, 10 June 1765, GA, D4582/4/17/1 and D4582/4/17/2.
19 Edward Witts, Shropshire, to his sister Alicia Witts, 11 March 1766, WFP F255; Granville Sharp, London, to his sisters, Northumberland, 18 November [1757], GA, D3549/14/1/4.
20 *OBP*, 15 July 1778, trial of Elizabeth Rock (t17780715-86); 27 February 1717, trial of John Sweetbones (t17170227-51).
21 William Dodd, *The Sisters; or the History of Lucy and Caroline Sanson, Entrusted to a False Friend* (London, 1754), p. 96, BL, 012611.e.21.
22 Elizabeth Gurney Fry, *Memoir of the Life of Elizabeth Fry, with Extracts from her Journal and Letters*, ed. Katherine Fry and Rachel Cresswell '(London, 1847), vol. 1, p. 249, in British and Irish Women's Letters and Diaries, Alexander Street Press, http://alexanderstreet.com/products/british-and-irish-womens-letters-and-diaries (accessed March 2011).
23 Morse Hobbs, will, written 11 December 1738, proved 12 December 1738, GA, GDR Wills 1738/217; Morse Hobbs, testamentary cause, 4 May 1739–9 May 1740, GA, GDR B4/2/H123.
24 Boswell, *The Life of Samuel Johnson*, vol. 1, p. 287.
25 William King, administration, 12 June 1803, GA, GDR Wills 1803-25; William King, testamentary cause 1807-13, GA, GDR B4/2/K5, Consistory Court of Gloucester, Court Minutes, 1807-13, GA, GDR B3/35-43.
26 Mary Leigh's history of the Leigh family, 1700s, SBTRO, DR671/77.
27 LeFanu and Sheridan papers KCC, LeFanu 20, 22, 25, 39, 43.
28 Wintle (first name unknown), copy diary, 1783, Palser Family of Wotton-under-Edge Collection, GA, D1559/Z1; Black, ed., *The Cumberland Letters*; William LeFanu, ed., *Betsy Sheridan's Journal: Letters from Sheridan's Sister, 1784-1786 and 1788-1790* (Oxford, 1960); John Sharp, Hartburn, to Judith Sharp, Old Jewry, London, 21 April 1770; John and Mary Sharp, Hartburn, to Judith Sharp, London, 14 May 1770, GA, D3549/16/1/1.
29 Jane Austen, *Persuasion*, 1817, chapter 24, in reference to the Wentworth siblings' acceptance of Anne Elliot.
30 Sharp family, common letters, 1754-63, GA, D3549/7/2/15.
31 Sharp family, documents relating to musical and sailing interests, 1750s-1790s, GA, D3549/12/1/1-11.
32 Poem attributed to a Mr Sprigg, 22 April 1776, Sharp family papers, GA D3549/12/1/6.
33 Mary Sharp to Judith Sharp, 14 May 1770, GA, D3549/16/1/1.
34 Apphia Witts Lyttelton to Alicia Witts, undated letter, c.1772, WFP, F263.

35 Letters to and from Apphia Witts (Lady Lyttelton) about her marriage, 1772–75, WFP, F263.
36 Edward Witts to Apphia Witts, Lady Lyttelton, 1773, WFP, F255.
37 Grassby, *Kinship and Capitalism*, pp. 210–15.
38 Nicholas Jackson, London, to Mary Jackson, Sneyd Park, 17 October 1760, GA, D153/152; *OBP*, 4 December 1793, trial of Edward Coffield otherwise Caufield (t17931204-32); 13 January 1808, trial of Lydia Martin (t18080113-62); 30 November 1796, trial of William Bishop (t17961130-55).
39 John Care, will, written 19 January 1791, proved 14 January 1797, GA, GDR Wills 1797/3; John Little, will, written 1777, proved 2 May 1778, GA, GDR Wills 1778/60; Joseph Wyman, testamentary cause, 13 July 1732, GA, GDR B4/2/W171; Finch Smith, ed., *The Admission Register of the Manchester School with Some Notices of the More Distinguished Scholars*, vol. 2: *1776–1807* (Manchester, 1868), p. 235. For a sampling of other sibling bequests see John Hawkins, will, written 28 February 1740, proved 8 April 1741, GA, GDR Wills 1741/60; Thomas Boulton, will, 27 November 1773, proved 21 October 1774, GA, GDR Wills 1774/172; James Walden, will, written 23 April 1795, proved 25 November 1795, GA, GDR Wills 1795/160.
40 Richard P. Heitzenrater, 'A Tale of Two Brothers', *Christian History*, 20:1 (2001), 10–17.
41 *OBP*, 21 February 1810, trial of Catherine Byrne (t18100221-110).
42 Walter Charleton, *A Natural History of the Passions* (London, 1701), p. 74, ECCO.
43 Richard Allestree, *The Works of the Learned and Pious Author of the Whole Duty of Man* (London and Oxford, 1726), p. 87, BAN, F BV 4500.A43 1726.
44 C.F. Volney, *The Law of Nature, or Principles of Morality, Deduced from the Physical Constitution of Mankind and the Universe* (London, 1796), pp. 129–30, ECCO.
45 *OBP*, 10 October 1716, trial of Elizabeth Dickenson and Frances Dickenson (t17161010-17).
46 Catherine Travell to Anne Travell, undated (c.1760), GA, D4528/4/20.
47 *OBP*, 4 December 1793, trial of Henry Goodiff (t17931204-22); 3 September 1719, trial of Henry Davis (t17190903-7); 13 May 1730, trial of Isaac Broderick (t17300513-27).
48 Key v. Henshaw, property dispute (1713), Court of the Exchequer, TNA, E134/12Anne/Mich19.
49 *OBP, Ordinary of Newgate's Account*, 5 October 1737 (OA17371005).
50 For a sampling of these works see the following: Francis Beaumont and John Fletcher, *The Bloody Brother; or, Rollo. A Tragedy* (London, 1718), BL, 11773.g.6; *The Younger Brother: or the Sham Marquis* (London, 1719), BL, 1175.bbb.15; Henry Mestayer, *The Perfidious Brother*, 2nd edn (London, 1720), BL,162.e.10; *The Brothers or, Treachery Punish'd* (London, 1730), BL, 1459.b.30; *The Brother* (London, 1771), BL, CUP 404. b.16; *The Brother in Law* (Littlebourne, Kent, 1817), BL, 18797.
51 Jane Austen, *Persuasion*, chapter 5.

52 Elizabeth Sophia Tomlins and E. Tomlins, *Tributes of Affection* (London, 1797), pp. 27–30, BL, 11644.cc.21.
53 Rebecca Earle, *Epistolary Selves: Letters and Letter-Writers, 1600–1945* (Aldershot, Hampshire, 1999), pp. 4–5. See also Clare Brant, *Eighteenth-Century Letters and British Culture* (Basingstoke and New York, 2006); Bannet, *Empire of Letters*; Linda C. Mitchell, 'Letter-Writing Instruction Manuals in Seventeenth- and Eighteenth-Century England', in Carol Poster and Linda C. Mitchell, eds., *Letter-Writing Manuals and Instruction from Antiquity to the Present* (Columbia, SC, 2007), pp. 178–99; Gary Schneider, *The Culture of Epistolary: Vernacular Letters and Letter-Writing in Early Modern England 1500–1700* (Newark, DE, 2005); James How, *Epistolary Spaces: English Letter Writing from the Foundation of the Post Office to Richardson's Clarissa* (Aldershot, Hampshire, and Burlington, VT, 2003).
54 Vickery, *The Gentleman's Daughter*, p. 287; Carol B. Stack and Linda M. Burton, 'Kinscripts: Reflections on Family, Generation, and Culture', in Evelyn Nakano Glenn, Grace Chang, and Linda Rennie Forcey, eds., *Mothering: Ideology, Experience, and Agency* (New York and London, 1994), pp. 33–44.
55 Jane Austen, *Mansfield Park*, chapter 2.
56 Elizabeth Sharp Prowse, diary and memorandum book, GA, D3549/14/1/1; Sharp family, common letters, 1754–63, GA, D3549/14/1/4.
57 Granville Sharp, London, to his siblings, Northumberland, 1758 GA, D3549/14/1/4.
58 OBP, 4 December 1793, trial of Edward Coffield otherwise Caufield (t17931204-32).
59 Wintle (unknown first name), copy diary, 28 June 1783, GA, D1559/Z1
60 Anne Travell to Apphia Witts Lyttelton, 23 May 1773, WFP, F256.
61 Agnes Travell Witts to Anne Travell, 28 August 1799, GA, D4582/4/6.
62 Agnes Travell Witts to Anne Travell, 9 August 1795, GA, D4582/4/7.
63 Agnes Travell Witts to Anne Travell, 2 October 1795, GA, D4582/4/7.
64 Amelia Witts to Apphia Witts, 1771, WFP, F255.
65 Elizabeth Gurney Fry, 1780–1845, letter from Elizabeth Gurney Fry to Joseph Fry September 8, 1814, in *Memoir of the Life of Elizabeth Fry*, vol. 1, p. 521; Miss G. Herbert, letter to Lady Louisa Stuart, March, 1782, in *Gleanings from an Old Portfolio Containing Some Correspondence between Lady Louisa Stuart and her Sister, Caroline [Stuart Dawson], Countess of Portarlengton [d.1813]*, ed. Alice Georgina Caroline Strong Clark (Edinburgh, 1895), vol. 1, p. 301, in *British and Irish Women's Letters and Diaries*, Alexander Street Press, http://solomon.bwld.alexanderstreet.com/ (accessed February 2010).
66 Edward Witts to Richard Witts, 2 June 1771, WFP, F255.
67 Black, ed., *The Cumberland Letters*, pp. 28–9, 39, 52.
68 James Sharp to John Sharp, 10 February 1769. GA, D3549/9/1/14.
69 Jemima was born in November 1762 and died in 1816; Catherine (James's daughter) was born in June 1770 and died in 1843; and Mary (William's daughter) was born in April 1778 and died in 1812.

70 Anna Letitia Aikin Barbauld, letter from Anna Letitia Aikin Barbauld, 1775?, in *Memoir, Letters, and a Selection from the Poetry and Prose Writings of Anna Letitia Barbauld*, ed. Grace A. Ellis (Boston, 1874), vol. 1, p. 339, in *British and Irish Women's Letters and Diaries* (accessed February 2010).
71 Palinurus, *Familiar Letters*, p. 19.
72 Tadmor, *Family and Friends*, p. 213; Steve Hindle, *On the Parish? The Micro-Politics of Poor Relief in Rural England, c.1550–1750* (Oxford, 2004), p. 52.
73 John Gregory, *A Father's Legacy to his Daughters* (London: W. Strahan, T. Cadell, and J. Balfour, and Edinburgh: W. Creech, 1774), p. 70, ECCO., p. 32.
74 Morse Hobbs, will, written 11 December 1738, proved 12 December 1738, GA, GDR Wills 1738/217.
75 Mary and Thomas Tracy, property documents, 1750s–1790s, GA, D444/E6.
76 Granville Sharp to John Sharp, 3 January 1777, GA, D3549/13/1/S8.
77 *Advice to the Fair: An Epistolary Essay in Three Parts: On Dress, Converse, and Marriage: Addressed to a Sister*, (London, 1738), BL, 11660. g; Hester Chapone, *Letters on the Improvement of the Mind*, 2 vols. (London, 1773), ECCO; Croft, *A Brother's Advice to his Sisters*; Fordyce, *Addresses to Young Men*, 2nd American edn (Boston, 1795); James Fordyce, *The Character and Conduct of the Female Sex* (London, 1776), BAN, BV 4282 F6 1776.
78 Fordyce, *The Character and Conduct of the Female Sex*; Fordyce, *Addresses to Young Men*.
79 Allestree, *The Whole Duty of Man*, p. 87.
80 For example see *Advice to the Fair;* Croft, *A Brother's Advice to his Sisters*; William Hussey, *Letters from an Elder to a Younger Brother on the Conduct to be Pursued in Life* (London, 1809), BL, 10920.ccc.6.
81 Palinurus, *Familiar Letters*, pp. v–vi.
82 Ibid., p. 19.
83 J. Edwards to his sister, 23 August 1713, GA, D2002/17/1.
84 Thomas Edwards to Walter Edwards Jr., 16 January 1747, GA, D2002/13/4.
85 Thomas Edwards to Walter Edwards Jr., 23 January 1747, GA, D2002/13/4.
86 Tadmor, *Family and Friends*, p. 175.
87 Johnson and Sabean, eds., *Sibling Relations*, p. 9.
88 OBP, 17 October 1744, trial of Edmund Long, Henry Townley, and Charles Savage (t17441017).
89 OBP, *Ordinary of Newgate's Account*, 19 January 1714 (OA17140129).
90 Stephen Addington, *Religious and Prudential Maxims Collected from the Sacred Scriptures and Other Writings* (London, 1768), p. 6, ECCO; Kenneth Hylson-Smith, *Evangelicals in the Church of England, 1734–1984* (Edinburgh, 1988); Fry, *Memoir of the Life of Elizabeth Fry*; John Tomkins, *Piety Promoted, in a Collection of Dying Sayings of Many of the People Call'd Quakers*, 3rd edition (London, 1723), ECCO.
91 OBP, *Ordinary of Newgate's Account*, 21 November 1743 (OA17431121).

92 Grassby, *Kinship and Capitalism*, p. 286, citing P. Mathias, 'Business History and Management Education', *Business History*, 27 (1975), 10–11.
93 Rev. Henry Digby Beste, *The Christian Religion Briefly Defended Against the Philosophers and Republicans of France* (London, 1793), ECCO.
94 Robert Jackson to Mary Jackson, 8 June 1760, GA, D153/147; Robert Jackson to Mary Jackson, 15 June 1760, GA, D153/148; Nicholas Jackson to Mary Jackson, 23 June 1760, GA, D153/149; Robert Jackson to Mary Jackson, 15 November 1760, GA, D153/153.
95 Tadmor, *Family and Friends*, p. 175.

3

Ties that cut

[T]hree wise words from your lips made me think you an inhabitant of another country... you have the art to set me at a distance by three words when I am with you, and to draw me to you at a hundred miles off by the same method.

George Cumberland to his brother Richard Cumberland, 1778[1]

Misery is caused for the most part, not by a heavy crush of disaster, but by the corrosion of less visible evils, which canker enjoyment.

Samuel Johnson, *A Journey to the Western Islands of Scotland*, 1775, extracted by Anne Travell, 1780s[2]

Generally the Travell siblings enjoyed the benefits of loving and friendly relations. However, when friendship was not reciprocated in a manner that both siblings understood, the heavy expectations became complicated and even eroded their felicity. During the summers of 1795 and 1799 Ferdinando made serious errors in his relations with Agnes – errors that spread to the relationship between Anne and Agnes and between Anne and Ferdinando. Despite their having had a lifetime of interaction (they were in their fourties and fifties) and having recently lived in the same village, Ferdinando must have forgotten or ignored that Agnes's 'nature' was 'too warm... to not shrink with disgust from the frigid coldness of others'.[3] At the very least he had not realized how his actions could cause such heartache in Agnes. Ferdinando's great crimes were not writing often enough (1795) and using a brisk, businesslike tone when he did (1799). These habits disappointed Agnes, who expected more 'warmth and affection' in letters from her siblings and required regular reassurance that they were all on 'good terms'.[4] In the 1795 exchange Agnes was incredulous to discover that Ferdinando 'by no means acknowledged himself at variance' with her. Though Ferdinando was supporting and aiding her and her husband during a bankruptcy, he was not a constant correspondent. She could not reconcile the discrepancy between his assurance that they were on good terms and the lack of letters from him.⁵ She 'was very glad to be informed' that Ferdinando 'did all in his power to promote our interest', but she went on to complain that Ferdinando's failure as a correspont might prevent her from accepting 'the extreme warm kindness' of a situation offered by some 'warm friends'. In case Anne or Ferdinando should miss the implied criticism that Ferdinando was not such a warm friend she continued by expressing her gratitude for those friends who 'alone have stood forth in the trial of endeavouring to do or get anything for us, but, of such hearts I doubt there are few'.⁶ In Scotland, and later on the Continent when recovering from their bankruptcy, Agnes and Edward Witts were dependent not only on Ferdinando for financial support, but on their siblings to convey news and to tie them to their routines of social and emotional support. Nearly every letter Agnes wrote to Anne opened with a complaint at the delay in correspondence. A long 'silence' from Edward's sister similarly had Agnes convinced that it would 'preclude almost the hope of ever hearing from her again'.⁷ Even after the immediate crisis of the bankruptcy passed, Agnes preferred an affectionate tone in correspondence. In 1799, after receiving a letter from Ferdinando, she reported to Anne that it 'gave more satisfaction than any rec[eive] d from him since I parted from him'. Her satisfaction was grounded in the letter's being 'occasion[e]d more by inclination than the necessity of business, [and] dictated with much more warmth [and] affection than any former ones had been'.⁸ To Agnes, Ferdinando's love and kindness were more important than any physical support he provided. Having him write from 'inclination' instead of 'necessity' made all the difference to her.

Though she once wrote to Anne that she was 'not hurt at your letters being so much more tardy', Agnes considered an interval of more than three or four weeks between letters a sign that her sister did not love or care for her as she should. '[E]ven now', she wrote upon receiving a letter from Anne in December 1795, 'you appear so much hurried as if writing was a kind of trouble to you'. She then took the opportunity to reprove and remind Anne of the importance of letters to the maintenance of their relationship. 'This I can neither help remarking or rep[eating], for if you felt our absence as tedious as I do no employment could be neither so essential or pleasant as writing to such others, this I make certain on my side by only losing a few hours in thanking you for your last rec[eive]d this morning ... & [but] a variety of employs should intervene I will not go ... till I have answered it.'⁹ Once Agnes and her family returned to England, her complaints about gaps in their correspondence lessened, undoubtedly because of the increased face-to-face interaction between the siblings. In fact, she herself could allow two months to pass before responding to a letter from Anne.¹⁰

Because of her warm nature, Agnes struggled to appreciate pedestrian or infrequent expressions of her siblings' concern. Anne preferred her own self-contained, restrained approach to life. As she remarked on the inside cover of her 1767 daybook: 'What am I the worse if a vain Talkative Person, thinks me reserve[ed]. Or if he, whose frolic levity is his disease, call me dull because I vapor not all my Spirits into Froth!'[11] Agnes's dissatisfaction with the tone of Ferdinando's correspondence, however, was enough to rile the calm and steadfast Anne. Though none of Anne's letters to her siblings survive, there is one scrap of a draft of a letter that was preserved with her daybooks which seems to have been a direct response to Agnes's condemnation of Ferdinando. Anne wrote:

> 'you say very right that it does pain parts of your letter, pain give me real pain & uneasiness, it is hard upon me, to be press'd to answer some parts of your letter, I know not, how to do it to you satisfactorily; I cannot join with you in reservations of my Br. Ferdinand, whom I think [such as you] asked, as a carefull faithfull friend, & not as an enemy, not independent only [as] of the sums he has laid down for your benefit, & incompliance with your earnest wishes, but he has unremittingly exerted himself for you, more than he would for himself, he has pass'd forward things on your account, that has been made him been thought ill of by many.[12]

Though it is undated and it is not clear whether its exact wording was retained in the final version, it is clear that it is a response to Agnes's displeasure with Ferdinando. Whatever Agnes's response was, it has not been preserved in the letters between the sisters. The next surviving letter from Agnes to Anne is dated nearly two months later and contains no mention of the discontent expressed in the earlier letter. The financial support was merely the physical manifestation of a more intricate emotional economics, one that though technically between Agnes, her husband, and Ferdinando, enveloped Anne and required her to carefully offer both support to Agnes and defence of Ferdinando. Anne's laborious efforts to produce just the right letter, despite assumptions that siblings could share a natural and easy correspondence style, reveals the awkward balance that siblings had to strike between their responsibility and desire to defend one sibling and their good relations with other brothers and sisters.

Anger or a fiery response in defence of a sibling against outside attackers was a duty of siblinghood, but conflict between siblings required a more nuanced response. In the space between 'natural' affection and brothers' and sisters' ability to exchange love, friendship, and affection equally there was plenty of room for many such small disappointments, for 'less visible evils' to canker and erode sibling relations. Happy were the families whose woes resembled the Travells' problems – small slights that were sometimes overcome, sometimes ignored. Unhappy were those whose disagreements and disappointments festered into bitterness and hatred. Acrimony among siblings ran the gamut from short-lived frustrations to vicious and lasting resentments, and to murderous rages. The real heart of sibling disappointments was a longing for the natural, uncontrived give and take of loving support. Whether it was Agnes's mild reproof or Anne's defence of her brother (which was rather spirited for her), or two brothers competing over who could handle a scythe more deftly, the injunction to share and share alike as equals hid the reality of siblings' inability to live up to all the expectations placed upon them by all their sisters and brothers and throughout their lifespan.[13]

Unlike any other kin or social relationship, eighteenth-century siblinghood sowed its own seeds of destruction. While other relations could sour, sibling relations were described as inherently containing the potential for rivalry, envy, contempt, and even murderous hatred. Their closeness and familiarity could breed either contempt or conversely, unnatural and incestuous tendencies. These fears were highly gendered in fiction and prescriptive literature: brothers were envious of birth-order privileges, and romantic entanglements and concerns about incest centred exclusively on brother–sister relations (particularly between an older brother and a younger sister). In reality incest, even by the broad eighteenth-century definition, was extremely rare, and siblings of both genders and all birth-order positions had to struggle with competing ideas of ideal friend and fearsome enemy. They had to struggle to maintain amicable relations despite perceptions and experience of parental favouritism and the experience of decidedly different and unequal life circumstances. The equality so praised in written depictions of fraternal and sororal relations, and so valued by real siblings, brought with it a host of unresolved concerns and disappointed aspirations. As the excerpts at the beginning of this chapter reveal, siblings had the power to wound each other and 'canker enjoyment' with a cutting glance or word. When brothers and sisters encountered the hierarchical world they quickly learned that they could not always rely on equal treatment from parents, the law, or even one another.

Recent scholarship has recognized the importance of sibling ties in the late eighteenth-century, but has also targeted the inequality of men and women with regard to property and education as a key tension in brother–sister relations; additionally, scholarship has hinted that in smaller families there was not much impetus for rivalry.[14] The evidence presented here paints a very different picture; it portrays siblings, no matter what their number, struggling to maintain what remained an important social, material, and emotional relationship into the nineteenth century against a range of disintegrating factors. The unequal status of men and women could rankle siblings, but other smaller evils existed – evils which could metastasize into seething resentments and even violence. It was precisely because there was so much discussion of siblings' affectionate, loving, altruistic, and friendly relationships that deviations brought with them such rancour and erupted into such hatred. If good siblings shared and shared alike, then bad relations developed when a sibling competed for or demanded a greater share. Advice literature celebrated the 'union which should ever subsist between brothers and sisters' and simultaneously warned that the familiarity of sibling relations, their 'excess of kind affection', could cause discontent when a sister or brother 'expect[ed] unreasonable concessions'.[15] In prescriptive literature unreasonableness and discontent were said to develop over unequal conditions between brothers or over brother–sister incest. In practice unreasonable expectations could have roots in childhood or could grow from perceptions of unfair distribution of goods, services, and support between siblings.

Contradictorily, prescriptive literature often dwelt on the tension between 'natural' sibling friendship and the 'natural' inclination to 'unnatural' sibling rivalry. Printed works described brothers and sisters as the closest and most natural of friends and simultaneously warned against an unnatural inclination to rivalry and envy. Sibling rivalry had been a recognized concern since at least the sixteenth century, but late seventeenth-century and eighteenth-century observers increasingly emphasized the naturalness of sibling affection and the unnaturalness of sibling conflict. The phrases 'unnatural brother' and 'unnatural sister' appeared rarely in printed texts before 1700. After that date they appeared sporadically until the latter half of the century, with peaks around the times of the American and French Revolutions, and they were apparently on the rise as the nineteenth century dawned. The clustering of references to unnatural sibling behaviour during revolutions that employed fraternal language attacking not only parental authority, but also the privileges associated with internal sibling hierarchies, may be coincidental, but it is striking. Eighteenth-century sibling-based fiction and advice literature that focused on unnatural sibling acrimony usually blamed unequal love or inheritance from parents and/or competition over romantic interests, particularly between brothers (there were no references to unnatural sisters before 1798).[16]

Parental favouritism

Some authors considered it siblings' responsibility to encourage friendship and prevent envy, but most agreed that the real roots lay in parenting.

Fraternal and sororal familiarity could breed love, affection, and friendship, or it could lead to unbridled contempt. '[Brothers and sisters] are careless and indifferent in their behaviour to each other', one author noted. Their constant contact made them thoughtless and 'not cautious enough in saying or doing what will give offence'. 'Their freedoms', he continued, 'border too much on that familiarity which is productive of contempt; neglect soon follows, and then, farewell domestic happiness'. The familiarity was the seed of scorn; parents' role was to prevent it from flowering fully. They could render 'happy reconciliation' between squabbling children through judicious support, but when they 'divested themselves of parental feelings' they destined their family to destruction and created 'the most incurable jealousy' between their children.[17] Parents who so acted, who made 'an improper use of the confidence reposed in them', were responsible for setting the 'whole family ... at variance'.[18] The seventeenth-century author Richard Allestree's advice, which was reproduced repeatedly in the eighteenth century, cautioned that siblings' shared childhoods and equality could be turned against brothers and sisters whose parents did not prevent the poisoning of their children's closeness. '[T]he equality that is among them in respect of birth, often makes them inclinable to envy each other, when one is in any respect advanced above the other', Allestree wrote, encouraging parents to inculcate kindness and love in their children to prevent that envy.[19]

It may not have been, as one author wrote, 'often the Case' that one sibling 'proved to be the Fathers Darling', but it was recognized that parents' behaviour could have a ruinous influence on their children's relationships.[20] This was particularly true in matters of inheritance. Many fictional plots revolved around criticism of elder sons' undeserved domination over their younger brothers.[21] Relationships between brothers such as those found in Beaumont and Fletcher's play *The Bloody Brother* of 1718 disintegrated into hatred over inheritance disagreements. When their father dies, Otto considers that he and his brother are 'co-heirs', but Rollo intends to be the only inheritor of their father's duchy. When Rollo menacingly tells Otto, 'You shall know who I am', Otto responds with the rejoinder, 'I do, my equal', and it is the struggle over what that equality means that forms the crux of the plot.[22] Their father has given each son equal provision, but custom gives Rollo, the eldest, privileges over Otto. When Rollo's advisor, Latorch, persuades Rollo to poison Otto and claim the duchy for himself, he argues that at best the brothers have a 'peic'd patcht Friendship' because 'Law and Nature' have demonstrated that path for Rollo. 'Is not he / Born and bequeath'd your Subject?' Latorch queries.[23] Against Rollo's resistance based on fraternal affinity, Latorch argues for a brotherhood subjugated to rights and claims of power.

> Shall the Name of Brother
> Forbid us to enlarge our State and Powers?
> Or place affects of Blood above our Reason?
> That tells us all things good against another,
> Are good in the same line against a Brother.[24]

The play, like many early modern texts, suggests that primogeniture's privileges should be subject to ideas of equality between brothers.[25] On the other hand, overcompensating for their elder sons' privileges by making a favourite out of younger sons, or a 'plaything' of a youngest 'little tiny' child, could cause just as much conflict.[26] In Joseph Flower's reimagining of the parable of the prodigal son, he positions the elder brother's violent opposition to his younger brother's celebrated return as stemming from their father's preference for the younger. 'Greatly too partial, you have always been', he accuses his father. And then, ranting, he asks the key question: 'What, – shall that Rebel now co equal be, / In all the Blessings that belong to me?' The mere thought increased the 'Fury in my Breast' for this fictional older brother and for many real brothers and sisters.[27]

Advice literature and fiction may have made the outcomes more dramatic, but they did not exaggerate how siblings' perceptions of unequal parental treatment could fester for a lifetime. Richard Whiting, a convicted thief, blamed some of his problems on leaving his home in Somerset for the 'wide World' of London – a decision that led to his crime and that, he claimed, grew from the differing affections of his parents for their children. He had 'been always the Favourite and Darling of his Mother' and after her death had been unable to stay at home, where his father 'had more Affection' for Richard's sister than for him.[28] Twenty-eight-year-old Richard Cooper, who was 'naturally inclin'd to Melancholy', could not abide his 'naughty Brother' and 'unlucky Sister' receiving all of their widowed mother's money; he 'turn'd altogether discontented' and left one employer for another 'where he had the Misfortune to Murther' a girl.[29] Throughout the life course, siblings held fast to memories of parental slight or favouritism, but unlike the sisters described in published writings, real sisters resented unfair treatment from parents. Such bitter memories could be wielded as weapons in sibling disagreements long after parents' deaths, as they did with Alicia Sheridan. The daughter and sister of famous Irish playwrights and theatre operators, and a writer in her own right, Alicia was the linchpin of her sibling network. As the eldest daughter she used her position to negotiate between her elder brothers Charles and Richard and her younger sister Betsy. Charles was difficult at the best of times and had a talent for irritating and alienating his siblings; Richard was mercurial and often insecure; Betsy was the arbitrator with their father, Thomas, but she never appreciated Charles and could experience long periods of coolness with Richard. Their relationships were further complicated by their father's, poor financial health and Charles's control of the purse strings. Alicia somehow maintained at least civil relations with all her siblings during her lifetime. Her letters to Betsy show great tenderness and friendship, and Charles's diary shows that she regularly visited and dined with him and his wife and children; she was genuinely heartbroken at Richard's death. Distance was both a blessing and a curse to the Sheridan siblings. Alicia and Charles were married and living in Dublin, while Richard and his family were in London. Their father and Betsy shuttled between London and Dublin, going from sibling to sibling, according to the treatment they received, but Betsy eventually married Alicia's brother-in-law and returned to Ireland after their father's death.

When Richard died in 1816 his widow, Esther, asked Alicia to share her memories of their common childhood in a collection of his papers and a biography. Alicia's response revealed a lifetime of disappointment – a disappointment based on her father's esteem for Charles and Betsy, to the exclusion of herself and Richard. 'I wish', she wrote, 'I could be of the use you suppose in giving a satisfactory account of the early days of my beloved brother. Of his childhood I have a very faint recollection neither he nor I were very happy, we were strongly attached to each other. We had no one else to love.'[30] Richard was two years Alicia's senior and was sent away to school when he was ten, and therefore the memories Alicia referred to must have been from before she was eight years old. The difference she felt between her father's love for the others and for her and Richard must have been vast for her to remember the associated pain for over fifty years – a pain that endured through the death of both her father and Charles, and through the lifetime of Betsy's affectionate support. She placed full blame on her father: 'Had my mother lived our fate would have been different, for she had a spirit of justice that would have prevented her from showing favour to any of her children, but as they might deserve it.'[31] This may have been true, but it also belies the fact that Alicia's mother died when she was thirteen, and her memories of painful favouritism seem to have predated that time by several years. In any case, Alicia felt she had to compete with her more favoured siblings for attention from their father. Her hurt came from his lack of emotional investment in her, not of any physical support or financial benefit.

Sibling rivalry and discontent

How, then, did siblings manage all these competing notions of their relationship and how did they manage the real inequalities rooted in parental treatment and social niches? Sibling acrimony and discontent often stemmed from the experience or perception of unfair treatment at the hand of a sister or brother. Property and money were major factors in sibling rivalry, but emotional and social disappointments were no less cutting.[32] Competition over family resources from their parents could lead to bitter rivalry, while niggardly accommodations or considerations between adult siblings led to numerous court cases as well as many arguments that never reached court. A head injury may have explained Thomas Nash's ranting, but his complaints grew from the old wound of feeling 'cheated of an Estate by his Brother'.[33] According to the trial transcript, his own vices caused Francis Moulcer's father to leave 'his whole Fortune to his Brother, who was the Eldest of Nine Children, as he was the Youngest, all the rest being dead, and left him only one Shilling'.[34] Francis's brother, who enjoyed greater social and financial stability, later tried to persuade him to work with him at their common occupation of collar making, but Francis refused and continued his promiscuous and, eventually, criminal behaviour. The loss of his mother before his second year left John Edwards, the youngest of seven children, at the whims of a father whose 'chief Care' was for John's eldest brother, Thomas. Their father 'neglected to give me any Education, altho' at that Time, it was in his Power', John asserted, while he was able to send Thomas first to school and then to an apprenticeship with an apothecary. Thomas 'behaved but very Indifferently . . . left his Master, and went to Service'. Their father, thereby, left John 'and the rest of his to sink or swim'.[35] Other parents, anticipating sibling disputes, tried to use their wills to prevent future troubles between their children. Thomas Bright, for example, died in 1805, but in 1818 his sons began arguing about the provisions of the will. Thomas had foreseen this difficulty and tried to prevent it. His two sons Thomas and John were given the bulk of his estate and possessions; he divided most things equally and then offered this telling comment:

> [I]f they my said two sons Thomas and John Bright do not or cannot agree in the partition or Division of the said . . . personal Estate and Effects aforementioned then in order to prevent as far as possible any disputes which shall or may happen to arise between them I order and direct and it is my will that they same shall be sold by publick auction for the most monies arising from the sale thereof I order and direct shall be fairly and equally divided between them . . . share and share alike.[36]

Despite their father's efforts Thomas and John could not agree in the partitioning of their father's estate undoubtedly because they differed on just what 'fairly and equally divided' meant.

The probate dispute files from the Dioceses of Gloucester and Chester record hundreds of siblings who, like the fictional David Simple, thought their siblings' share or handling of their mutual inheritance had only 'the appearance of friendship' and none of its substance.[37] The statistical analysis of these cases and their impact on sibling power will be discussed in greater detail in Chapter 5, but for the purposes of this chapter two key patterns of sibling discontent emerge. First, only a small percentage of the Gloucester cases (6.6 per cent) stemmed from siblings' arguments over the validity of a will. Instead, the majority (75 per cent) involved siblings merely asking the court to cite their sibling to bring the will to court to be officially proved, or in the absence of a will to take out letters of administration, or to make a full inventory of the deceased's goods. An additional group (10.7 per cent) was made up of siblings arguing that they had not received the legacy promised to them in a will or the portion owed to them from the administration of an intestate's estate.[38] Altogether nearly 90 per cent of the Gloucester diocesan sibling probate disputes were not so much about how children viewed their parents' and other siblings' provision for them as much as they were about sibling frustration with one another. Travelling to the court was time-consuming, and a legal dispute was costly. Asking the court to cite a sibling on threat of excommunication was a last-ditch effort to get one's brothers and sisters to share or distribute their inheritance. In other words, no matter what the monetary value of the estate, the dispute was often about siblings' perceptions of unjust treatment at one another's hands. Coupled with the gender breakdown of the disputing parties, this pattern reveals a world of sibling conflict very different from that described in printed literature. Prescriptive literature did not imagine a world where sisters sparred just as vigorously as their brothers.[39]

A second analysis of the incidents, by gender, shows that over a quarter of the incidents involved sisters fighting against their brothers.[40] This is close to the number of conflicts between brothers (though brother–brother conflicts involved more in-laws than sister–brother conflicts).[41] Undoubtedly, some of the predominance of brothers as defendants against frustrated siblings rose from parents' habit of making elder sons their executors and from the patterns of male property privileges.[42] Unsurprisingly, female–female conflict represented a substantially smaller proportion of the disputes.[43] However, the 15 per cent of conflicts between sisters serve as a caution against the historical assumption that sisters' lifelong connections and lack of competitive tools like inheritance and formal education made for uncomplicatedly smooth relations.[44] Additionally, disputes started by brothers against their sisters and sisters-in-law accounted for over a quarter of the total incidents.[45] Taken together this small sampling shows that at least in matters of property (usually personal), people were more likely to be in conflict with a sibling of the opposite sex than with a sibling of the same sex, and that while women's legal efforts against siblings focused on their brothers, men's disputes were divided between their sisters and sisters-in-law. The combination of birth order, gender, and marital status and their impact on sibling power is the focus of Chapter 5, but already it is clear that brother–brother conflict, so often the focus of prescriptive and secondary literature, is only half the story of sibling disagreements. Also, despite the interest in incest's pull on brother–sister and brother–sister-in-law relations, real brothers' interaction with their female siblings was more inclined to dissent than to intimacy.

Disappointment was possible between siblings who failed to live up to the heavy expectations placed upon their emotional, social, and material support. Accusations that brothers and sisters did not reciprocate material help or affectionate expressions fuelled bitterness and resentment and could eventually erode even the strongest underpinnings of love, an erosion visible to others outside the sibling network. Morse Hobbs's friends and neighbours agreed that a will not mentioning his sisters was too 'mean'. And a neighbour criticized John Ruddle when he spent the night drinking while 'his poor brother [was] so ill'.[46] Similarly, Ellen Stock reported that others asked why she did not solicit her lawyer brother's help with her miserable marriage. Was it not his 'duty to protect an only sister from the ill-usage of an unkind unfeeling husband'?[47] Failure to live up to sibling duties sparked many fraternal and sororal disagreements. The innate claim of sibling financial support was what drove Edward, John, William, and Nicholas Hobbs to dispute the will of their brother Morse. Morse died, without spouse or children, in 1738 at the house of Francis James, and James then produced a will that left everything to himself apart from small bequests to the four brothers. The brothers claimed knowledge of an earlier will that left everything to them. As Morse's estate was reported to be worth some £400, this was a substantial difference. They claimed that Morse had left them everything because ''twas natural for him to do he the said Morse Hobbs being a Batchelor and they his said Brothers being in low Circumstances and having in no wise disobliged or offended him'.[48] Similarly Benjamin Kench's brothers could not reconcile themselves to being neglected in his will. They tried to discredit the validity of his will despite the fact that 'for several years before the death of . . . Benjamin . . . there was a great coolness between him and . . . Joseph . . . and so continued 'till the Time of Death'. One deponent stated that she had often heard Benjamin 'declare that . . . Joseph . . . nor any of his Brothers should be a Farthing the better for what he had'.[49] For many years before his death Benjamin had been 'much displeased' with Joseph because he had 'greatly offended him'.[50] When money matters did not cause explicit sibling conflict they still could increase the work placed on brothers and sisters to ameliorate their siblings' financial situation. For example, Anne Travell's nephews George and Francis Edward Witts seemed to have had a very amicable relationship, but George's poor money management often left Francis to negotiate and arbitrate on his behalf and made him the recipient of awkward family correspondence requesting the payment of George's debts and discussions of his 'follies'.[51] Francis always defended and supported his brother, but it required constant effort and work to maintain his role as friendly advocate.

Disappointed dreams of equality could come from inequitable inheritance or treatment from parents and from differing levels of social and financial success. A brother might claim that he had inherited only a 'little fortune' from his father, but his sister's murderous rage at the discrepancy between them was not about the small amount, but the relative inequality between her brother and herself.[52] Brothers like Berkeley and William Seymour had a rocky relationship at least partly because of their differing financial situations. William's supposed drunken, lazy behaviour and fathering of an illegitimate child contrasted with Berkeley's 'steady' life. In January 1742, after selling an ox, Berkeley returned to the home he shared with William. A fight ensued and they came to blows, William shooting Berkeley several times and then robbing him before fleeing the house. Why William was angry is not clear, but it may have concerned the ox, because after killing his brother he stole his money and immediately purchased an ox.[53] After returning from the Seven Years' War, Richard (Dick) Milhil found that his already meagre savings continued to shrink and turned to his brother Robert (Bob) for help. Bob, who was apprenticed as a baker to their father, offered financial support from his own wages and worked at reconciling Dick to their parents. In the end, however, this was not enough to bring Dick back into the family fold. According to a published account, Bob eventually ceased supplying his brother with money, treatment Dick classified as being treated 'very ill', and their argument descended into vicious bullying. Dick threatened Bob that 'he soon would be the butcher of him unless he behaved better to him for the future'.[54] Dick made good on his threat and in a passionate rage stabbed Bob to death, a crime for which he was eventually executed. Discontent over one sibling's financial prosperity rarely took such a drastic turn, but the pattern was repeated, with varying degrees of animosity, in numerous families. Brothers or sisters would proclaim their own poverty as justification for turning to the courts to force a sibling to provide better for them. Like the Hobbs and Kench brothers, other siblings cried poverty and argued that their status as siblings qualified them for a share of the deceased's property.[55]

The snippets of sibling acrimony evident in trial transcripts and probate disputes offer only glimpses of perhaps deeper and long-standing resentments, which would not otherwise be visible, such as when the wife of Abraham Wells 'obliged him to take out a Warrant against her Sister for scolding and beating upon her'.[56] However, court records capture only the latest and most dramatic breaks in sibling relations: arguments over money or employment or inheritance were not the cause of sibling fractiousness, but its most obvious manifestation. Murderous siblings were hardly typical of eighteenth-century families, but the 'terrible work' of sibling conflict echoed in more mundane matters of discontent and rivalry.[57] For families who left written evidence it is possible to trace the long-term roots and consequences. Agnes Travell Witts's complaint about Ferdinando, for example, did not spring from the infrequency of his letters, but grew from wishes for kind and affectionate relations with Ferdinando and the constant worry that he was acting as a benefactor instead of as a brother. The Sheridan siblings' relationship also demonstrates that spiteful, angry exchanges about money between middle-aged siblings had long histories of disappointment and unfulfilled longing. Like Ferdinando Travell, Charles Sheridan, the eldest brother, discovered that occasional material support was not enough to ensure his siblings' good graces. Charles had inherited more money and married better than his siblings and therefore was often appealed to for monetary support, especially by his youngest sister Betsy and by their father, but according to his siblings he never did this in a timely manner or with true compassion. He remarked that it was the 'most natural thing in the world' to help his siblings, but to their minds it appeared anything but natural, and much of their discussion dwelt on his inability to participate in an honest and reciprocal relationship.[58]

Two years after his marriage to the wealthy Letitia Bolton, Charles wrote from Ireland asking his father to leave England (and the company of Dick and Betsy) and stay with Charles and his wife. Betsy wrote to Alicia, who also lived in Ireland, to express her disdain for Charles's offer with the following bitter invective:

> Can anything be more sickening. I confess there is scarce any emetick more powerful to my stomach than an affectation of sensibility where I know the heart to be truly selfish.

Her seemingly hyperbolic response to Charles's invitation was based on years of familiarity with his behaviour, and she recognized that her 'having been so completely *surfeited* with unmeaning professions' may have led her to 'feel the disgust to every thing of the kind more strongly'.[59] Her feelings of disgust for Charles persisted throughout her lifetime. She found him 'callous to every right feeling', even when she depended upon his generosity for financial support. As her relationship with and eventual marriage to Henry LeFanu (her sister's brother-in-law) developed, Betsy hoped for communication from Charles – some sort of indication that he wanted to be affectionate and friendly. 'He has never written one satisfactory line to me', she wrote, 'relative to Harry . . . nor do I expect he will.'[60] Charles never seemed to satisfy any of his siblings' expectations, and in their writings he comes across as a thoroughly disagreeable person who could do nothing more than, to borrow a description from Jane Austen, elicit surprise that anyone would like him well enough to marry him [61] Charles had his own difficulties with a wife who, despite her fortune, was moody and fickle, and possessed a fiery temper. To his siblings, however, this was no excuse for what Betsy and Dick's wife classified as 'surface-ish' – undoubtedly a reference to 'Joseph Surface', the hypocritical character in Dick's 1777 play *A School for Scandal*.[62]

Though it was easy to blame Charles for all of their financial and emotional woes, the Sheridans had other tensions and difficulties. In addition to Alicia's complaints of parental favouritism, Dick regularly disappointed his siblings and their father. His creative and talented personality did not compensate for an underlying insecurity and an inability to follow up good intentions. In a 1789 letter to Alicia, Betsy wrote of her anger with Charles and her ambivalence about Dick's help. The overt anger was not present in her descriptions of Dick and his wife Elizabeth (with whom she resided), but Betsy was far from satisfied with either of them. When a letter of Alicias put Betsy out of spirits, so much so that she lost her enthusiasm for a masquerade she was to attend, Elizabeth could not understand what the difficulty was. Betsy was unwilling to unburden herself entirely to Elizabeth because she considered Elizabeth to be one of those people 'who only hear of difficulties at large, but never feel the want of the comforts or even Elegancies of life it never occurs, that others can be without them'.[63] Betsy's constant financial strain kept her on a strict budget: to her eye Dick and Elizabeth lived beyond their means and lacked her own concern about family finances. Therefore Betsy was also unenthusiastic about receiving additional support from Dick:

> And as to my Brother Richard's promises, I have so many daily instances of his engaging for what he is wholly unable to perform that where one's support is at stake it cannot be look[e]d on as a bright prospect.[64]

Though this passage lacks the fury found in her comments about and to Charles, in some respects its pragmatic disappointment is more heartbreaking. Dick had every intention of being a good brother, but apparently never managed to live up to the expectations placed upon him.

In fact, most letters between the Sheridan siblings show every desire and attempt to have ideal and happy relations and the painful and poignant experience of consistent disappointment of those desires. Betsy wanted to marry Henry LeFanu with both families' agreement. As her sister was married to Joseph, Henry's brother, they had no objection to the personal connection, but their lack of financial prosperity concerned both Henry's father and Charles. Though Betsy and Henry eventually married in July 1789, their courtship was not without obstacles. In a letter written in June, Betsy once again complained that Charles had angered and disappointed her by causing strife among the LeFanus. Her anger at Charles's opposition is understandable, but by quoting his response in her letter to Alicia, and by constantly soliciting Alicia's support against Charles, Betsy placed heavy emotional demands on her sister.[65] Alicia and Charles both lived in Dublin and exchanged social visits. Acting as mediator between her high-spirited and sometimes temperamental siblings left Alicia open to numerous hurts and disappointments. She fulfilled her role by abusing Charles in letters to the others and simultaneously maintaining social and civil relations with him. Yet throughout her entire life she resented the affection and attention their father had shown Charles and Betsy – Charles the person who addressed Alicia as 'dear Lissy', and Betsy the person who addressed her as 'my dear love'. Even with loving intentions and expressions of affection, the failure to perform the supportive and instrumental role of friend could damage sibling relationships beyond their ability to repair. Siblings like the Broadway brothers might have generally 'lived very affectionately together', but could quickly descend into competition and brawling over 'who was master' and who was not.[66] Brothers and sisters might fight, throw things and invectives at one another, but they also made claims that no matter what their disparities, 'we are all brothers'.[67]

Beyond feelings of resentment at parental favours withheld or unfair treatment at the hand of a sibling, sisters and brothers encountered concrete differences in their social and legal positions that influenced their relations – often for the worse, particularly in the case of sister–brother relations. Inheritance practices were ambiguous in how they understood brother–sister equality. The practice of primogeniture had been under attack since the Interregnum, but the simultaneous consolidation of property rights in the patrilineage demonstrates competing understandings of social and landed rights.[68] The late seventeenth century saw changes in inheritance law, especially for intestate cases, that impacted upon ideas of sibling equality. Since 1660 testators had been able to alienate all their land as they saw fit. Most landed testators chose to leave estates, even small ones, in the hands of the eldest surviving sons while providing living allowances to widows, and cash and education for daughters and younger sons. This strengthened men's power over land at the expense of both their widows and their sisters. Amy Erickson argues that fathers, mothers, and the courts agreed that eldest sons should be privileged, although 'not too much', but Eileen Spring sees both daughters' and younger children's portions as having declined in the eighteenth century, even as the expanding empire and state allowed more employment opportunities for younger sons to offset their insufficient inheritance.[69] Countering this landed preference for eldest sons was the democratic impulse embodied in the 1670 Statute of Distribution, which dictated the distribution of personal estate after the death of an intestate person.[70] Children had long enjoyed the tradition of equal shares of all of their widowed mother's personal property and of two-thirds of their deceased father's if his wife remained alive.[71] The statute, combined with the loss of traditional widows' rights to a third of her husband's property for life in York in 1693 and London in 1725, meant that children's equal shares often came at the expense of their mother's property rights. The statute's recognition of siblings' equal shares to the personal property of a childless brother or sister and the fact that most people died without land and without a will meant that in most Georgian families siblings shared their inheritances equally.[72] As spouses or children, men and women might occupy unequal inheriting positions, but as siblings they enjoyed a levelled position.

In the debate about injustices associated with primogeniture and the plight of younger sons philosophers, authors, and a host of the middling sort – mostly males – might decry the privileges of primogeniture, but they did so from a class basis and not in an effort to make sisters equal with their brothers.[73] Prescriptive writings' focus on primogeniture left other expressions of sibling conflict relatively untouched. Representations of sisterly conflict were practically nonexistent until the end of the eighteenth century. As women's educational opportunities expanded and as their occupational outlook shifted with the rise of manufacturing, perhaps authors considered that sisters could now envy one another's very different circumstances. Alternatively, until women were considered capable of individuality and selfhood, it was impossible to imagine the selfishness required for envy and rivalry.[74] One of the few to consider sister-sister conflict, Thomas Gisborne, turned sisterly closeness upside down, claiming that it could breed unusual discord. Gisborne argued that though boys and girls received different types of education, based on their different social roles and genders, their parents were to ensure that 'affinity' between the siblings (and later their siblings' spouses) would continue.[75] He cautioned mothers to be especially aware of competition between sisters, considering the constant contact that sisters had in the home – contact, ironically, which he recommended and encouraged – to be a cause of tension. Brothers, he asserted, 'move on in parallel lines; some with greater, some with less celerity, but never cross each other's course'.[76] He must have known this to be inaccurate, but it illustrated his point about the cause of sibling rivalry: too much contact without mutual affection. Mothers, therefore, were to be aware of this tendency and 'confirm' their children 'in reciprocal love'.[77] While Gisborne recognized that sisters could come into conflict much like brothers, there was still no generally recognized sister–brother rivalry. It was here that the limits of prescriptive equality broke down: the difference between men's and women's status formed, at least in print, too large a barrier to equality and rivalry, for one cannot be a rival of someone inherently inferior or superior.

Half- and step-siblings

The presence of step- and half-siblings further complicated tense relationships.[78] Though the decreasing frequency and number of remarriages and declining death rates meant that there were fewer so-called blended families in the Georgian period than in earlier centuries, they were still not uncommon.[79] Because half- and step- siblings were not always distinguished from their full-blooded brothers and sisters it is not always possible to trace the unique contours of their relationships. For example, when Alexander Tate 'feloniously and wilfully of his malice afore-thought' murdered his brother-in-law it was not clarified whether the deceased was married to Alexander's sister or whether the two men were step-brothers (another meaning of 'brothers-in-law' at the time).[80] Tellingly, there are only eight references to half-sisters and fourteen to half-brothers in the Old Bailey transcripts before 1830.[81] Half-siblings were not always delineated as such and tended to be discussed only when there was conflict. Half-siblings claiming heir-at-law status, for example, had to clarify their relationship and perhaps even prove it against other claimants. Jane Williams twice claimed that her half-brother Benjamin Young had died on board an East India Company ship but had left no living parents or other siblings. Women claiming to be his mother and sister appeared before the court disputing Jane's claims. However, when they were unable to prove their claim, Jane was acquitted and presumably received the £8.17s she claimed as heir-at-law. Dennis Dempsey also tried to claim rights to a deceased half-sibling's estate, but without luck, as he could only prove himself next of kin and not a half-sibling.[82] Even if claimants were not actual half-siblings, they clearly knew that half-siblings could make similar claims to full siblings. Though siblings 'of the half blood' inherited equally from one another's intestate estates, the age gaps often found between two sets of siblings, the potential different treatment from parents, and differences in their inheritances from parents all put step- and half-siblings on unsure footing. Nineteen-year-old William Meers, for example, felt himself particularly 'indifferently' treated by first a step-mother and then her sister, who did not treat him 'as he thought so tender as [she did] her own Sister's Children'. This led to his running away 'and soon after his Father dying, he was left entirely destitute', which in turn led to his criminal behaviour. In a different portion of his account, however, for 'his Misfortunes, he blam'd his Brother, Sister and all his Friends, who always complain'd on him to his Father'.[83] The experience of step- and half-siblings was probably more common outside the landed classes. Tellingly, none of the gentry and landed families considered in these pages had half- or step-families. Even if there had been no cultural pressure to remain unmarried, widows' enjoyment of an estate usually ended with remarriage, and the ability to maintain her previous lifestyle meant that a wealthy widow did not have an overwhelming inducement to marry. In families lower on the socio-economic scale, remarriage – for both men and women – may have been an economic necessity and the only viable way to continue to raise young children, even if those who had young children took longer to remarry than those without.[84]

The case of the Coffield and Hogan siblings demonstrates that small disruptions could ignite old, untold histories of resentment and jealousy among half-siblings. These siblings have been referenced previously because of their practice of sharing letters, but difficulties arose when some siblings believed that they had not benefited from equal shares of that correspondence. The trouble began when thirty-three-year-old Edward Coffield returned for a brief visit after seven or eight months' service in the Middlesex militia in October 1793. During his short time off he visited his father, his wife and child, and his half-brother and half-sister, John and Mary Hogan. While Edward's and John's testimonies differ on the subject of how often Mary met Edward, they all agree that the disagreement between Mary and Edward centred on letters written during his absence. Despite a cordial breakfast with Mary and his wife, later in the day Edward learned from John that John had not received all five of the letters that he had sent to his siblings while he was away. Edward claimed that John said this made Mary a 'deceitful sister', and John conversely claimed that Edward had made the statement. In any case, the siblings and John's future wife, Margaret Marshall, spent the day socializing and sharing drinks.[85] In the evening, when they retired to Mary's home, Edward, agitated and pacing, decided to confront Mary about the letters. Either John or Edward questioned 'Polly' about how many letters she had received from 'Ned'. She claimed that she had received four, of which she passed on two and kept two because she had paid for them. The conversation rapidly disintegrated, Edward calling her a whore and she calling him a thief, and ended in violence when Mary threw a kettle at Edward and then Edward began hitting her. Margaret tried to protect Mary by wrapping her arms around her, but Edward kept coming at her, yelling, 'There is your brother, why don't he take your part?' In the tussle Edward, apparently inadvertently, stabbed Mary with his bayonet. Mary cried out for John, 'Jack! Jack! Here is blood', and John attempted to staunch the blood, but within minutes Mary lay dead. Edward fled from the house, supposedly to get a doctor, but never returned. He seems to have hoped that Mary had survived, because the following morning he sent his son to enquire after his aunt's health. The court determined that he had not intentionally killed his half-sister and found him guilty of manslaughter, sentencing him to only a year in Newgate and a one-shilling fine.[86] Even if the stabbing had been accidental, the extreme response to the number of letters Mary shared hints that the siblings had a history of difficult relations. Whether Edward's vehemently pointing out that John, as Mary's full brother, should defend her was the last instance of a long-standing resentment between him and Mary, or he used it merely as a weapon of the moment to highlight the fact that he was only her half-brother, cannot be known. Either way, the disagreement over the letters seems to have been only a spark to ignite the smouldering embers of older hurts, some of which were seemingly linked to their being half-siblings.

Incest

It was not just the various forms of law interested in property that impacted upon sibling relations; ecclesiastical law (and the printed debate around it) also shaped appropriate sibling relations and the limits of equality between them.[87] Siblinghood, whether by blood, half-blood, or marriage, always fell within the prohibited degrees of marriage. Much as debates over primogeniture highlighted discontent between brothers, fears of sibling incest highlighted worries about brother–sister relations grown too close. Sister–brother relations could be a dangerous substitution for marriage and appropriate social and sexual relationships. If rivalry destroyed or eroded sibling affection, then incest directed sibling affection inwards, where it festered into something monstrous. As the terms 'brother' and 'sister' applied to a host of in-laws and half-, step-, and adopted siblings, this made careful negotiation of appropriate and inappropriate sibling interaction a tough business. Even by the eighteenth-century's broad definition of incest it was a rare occurrence, but fears about it highlight the delicate balance that siblings had to strike between clashing notions of sibling intimacy. Suspicions about incest paralleled the cultural fears of unnatural sibling conflict.[88]

Real incidents of sibling incest are notoriously difficult to discover and track in the eighteenth century.[89] Incest, not criminalized until 1908, was under ecclesiastical authority until 1857 and subject only to penance or excommunication, and had to be visible or frequent enough to attract the attention of witnesses and the church.[90] Because it was itself not a crime, the charge was only secondary to general charges of sexual misconduct such as fornication and adultery. In 1727, when Henry Coulson 'did most wickedly commit the great and abominable Crimes of Incest and Adultery with his own Sister, Alice the wife of Daniel Potter', his penance was typical of others accused of adultery: he was to wear a long white sheet with a piece of paper pinned to him inscribed with the words 'I have been guilty of the Horrid Sins of incest and adultery with my own sister Alice the wife of Daniel Potter pray for me.' He wore these marks of penance while seated at the 'most trafficked entrance' to Holy Trinity Church, Chester, before services on Sunday. After services he had to stand before the congregation, recite the words out loud, and plead for forgiveness.[91] Cases like this between blood siblings were incredibly rare (this was the only such case in either the Diocese of Chester or the Diocese of Gloucester for the entire eighteenth century); incest between affinal siblings was not much more common (there were three additional cases in the Diocese of Chester, none in the Diocese of Gloucester). Definitions of incest (and the related topic of degrees of prohibited marriage) based on Leviticus had been hotly debated throughout northern Europe at least since the Reformation, and by the end of the eighteenth century Continental civil law, not religious law, came to define incest increasingly in terms of consanguinity.[92] The narrowing legal definition of incest to exclude relationships of affinity was, however, not completely abandoned in eighteenth- and nineteenth-century England. The closeness of this mixed-sex relationship and the blurring between consanguineous and affinal kin made brother–sister interaction the focus of intense cultural and social scrutiny.[93] The Ordinary's account for the Old Bailey even went so far as to blame one prisoner's living with his deceased wife's sister as a 'fatal omen of his impending ruin'. The Ordinary included this information '[t]o deter the ignorant and profane transgressors of the laws of God from incestuous pollutions'.[94] As the eighteenth century waned, novels and legal debates increasingly focused on a type of sibling incest created through marriage and death: a man's marriage to his deceased wife's sister.[95] Simultaneously, for the Romantics sibling incest became a central motif of both life and fiction.[96] While Ruth Perry points out that fears about incest increasingly highlighted the longing for a consanguineous family lost to the amplified emphasis on conjugal families, the continued, and intensified, debate over marriage with a deceased wife's sister well into the twentieth century suggests the continued pull of affinity and consanguinity despite increased attention to the conjugal.[97] In the Georgian era that pull could put sisters and brothers in uncomfortable situations when a marriage upset a pre-existing sibling bond, as it did for William and Dorothy Wordsworth.[98]

Fiction overflowed with examples of sibling incest. Incest, particularly sibling incest, formed a key plot device for gothic novels and Romantic writing.[99] Partially titillating, partially moralizing, the plots centred on sibling incest of two sorts: intentional and unintentional. Byron, Shelley, and even Dickens based plots on protagonists' knowing attraction to a sibling – a device even more salacious given the persistent rumours about Byron and his half-sister.[100] Earlier writers, however, focused more on unintentional sibling incest. In other words their novels, plays, and poetry were not so much about siblings violating sexual and social taboos as about the instinctual love between siblings. As sexuality became increasingly important to definitions of family in the late eighteenth century, previous notions of sibling love had to be explained within the newer, sexualized model. Plots often situated a man and a woman meeting as adults and feeling a strong mutual attraction. They assumed that this attraction was romantic, sexual, and/or conjugal until it was revealed, usually to their horror and usually just in time, that it was actually fraternal-sororal. This plot device saved the potentially incestuous siblings from consummating their attraction, but preserved their strong emotional connection.

This common plot device suggests two features of eighteenth-century concepts of siblinghood. First, it demonstrates that as the conjugal concept of family and companionate view of marriage grew in importance, the model for ideal marriages drew its impetus from sibling equality and love.[101] Love between siblings, even when they had not shared a childhood or experiences, was so strong that brothers and sisters instinctively felt the connection and attraction. By revealing their fraternal and sororal connections the plots removed the taint of real incest and left behind the idealized equality of siblinghood to suggest that idealized conjugal love should follow this model, though coupled with the appropriate conjugal and sexual expression that was excluded from sibling relations. The second notion of siblinghood that these plots reveal is a belief that a shared childhood would prevent inappropriate sibling interaction. As Sir Thomas articulates in *Mansfield Park*, having the cousins Fanny and Edmund grow up together would make them like brother and sister and therefore prevent any sexual and marital connection between them.

[D]o not you know that of all things upon earth *that* is the least likely to happen; brought up, as they would be, always together like brothers and sisters? It is morally impossible. . . . It is, in fact, the only sure way of providing against the connection. . . . But breed her up with them from this time, and suppose her even to have the beauty of an angel, and she will never be more to either than a sister.[102]

The reader, apparently, was supposed to ignore the fact that, despite having been brought up as brother and sister, Edmund and Fanny do marry.[103] As cousins they could legitimately marry, but their shared childhood has given them a peer relationship instead of the hierarchical relationship usually imagined for marriage.

The few late eighteenth-century plots that did have intentional sibling incest were most often about sexually predatory brothers and innocent sisters.[104] It was in those plots that sibling closeness festered into conjugal or sexual desire for a sibling instead of the approved search for a sibling-like non-relative. In this way they were patterned after father–daughter incest plots, with the sister often saved or protected by another man (sometimes a potential spouse) – someone who is therefore a better 'brother' than her real brother. The author of *The Monk and his Sister* depicted this type of relationship. When Isabel's older brother, Adolpho, whose 'breast had long been filled with an incestuous passion', attempts to seduce her away from her husband, she is rescued not by her husband, but by his servant.[105] In this way, incest literature demonstrates the uncomfortable connection between conjugal and sibling love. When women and men, no matter what their relationship, 'pass'd sometimes for Man and Wife, and sometimes for Brother and Sister' they unwittingly supported the fear of accidental incest and the problem of thinking of siblinghood as preparation for marriage while simultaneously worrying that siblings would start to think of one another in the same way as they thought of potential spouses.[106] The closeness and equality of siblings could prove corrosive when it was not carefully distinguished from marital affection.

The eighteenth-century discussion of marriage to a deceased wife's sister as constituting incest also exposes a tension between marital and sibling relations. Authors and the courts may have considered relations between a man and his deceased wife's sister a 'fatal Alliance', but early in the century many may have considered marriage with a widowed sibling-in-law not to be a misdeed.[107] Such was the case when George Parker married his brother's widow – on the advice of a curate – in 1708; he did not know it was illegal until 1724, when the vicar informed him.[108] Similarly, a lack of understanding was William Crispin's defence: he had been 'a courtier' to his sister-in-law Mary before she married his brother Joseph, and determined that he could marry her once Joseph left her and married someone else.¹⁰⁹ As the eighteenth century drew to a close, however, there was greater debate about whether marriage between former siblings-in-law should be illegal. The passage of the Marriage Act of 1835, forbidding marriage with a deceased wife's sister, made matters worse by jostling the boundaries between sibling and spouse. This would seem to have been the triumph of conjugal relations over siblinghood, since it was assumed that if marriage to a deceased wife's sister was legal, all men would not be able to imagine their sisters-in-law as sisters, but only as potential spouses. The protracted Parliamentary debate between 'natural' (usually sisterly) and legal arguments for and against marriage to one's deceased wife's sister (and deceased husband's brother), however, signals that the 1835 law merely highlighted the continued tension between sibling and spousal relations.¹¹⁰ The Marriage Act of 1835 tried to fix the problem by making all sisters potential wives, thus removing both the spouse–sibling tension and the problem of imagining brother–sister relations as equal, but husband–wife relations as hierarchical. If all women were potential wives, and not sisters, then real sisters could maintain their subordinate status. While the 1835 law can be classified as celebrating and defending the conjugal over the fraternal, as Ruth Perry has done, it also clearly highlights the fact that contemporaries had not yet resolved the boundaries between the two relationships.¹¹¹

Conclusion

Uncomfortably coupled with ideals of sibling love, affection, and friendship were material and emotional pressures that could dissolve amicable relations and cause the 'terrible consequences which attend envy'.¹¹² Ideally the equality and friendship shared by brothers and sisters would conquer any animosity over their disparate financial or social standing, as long as there was 'no pride on one side, and no envy on the other'.¹¹³ Even in highly amicable families this required intense labour. In families already under stress, the added impetus of seeing one's fortunes decline in comparison with those of one's siblings could be the spark that ignited fraternal battles. It was perhaps a recognition of this that made men like the farrier brother of Thomas Sollars not want Thomas to join his trade, 'not thinking it fit that they should be of the same Trade'.¹¹⁴ These rivalries could turn murderous, as the records of trials at the Old Bailey demonstrate, but more often their 'corrosion' came from 'less visible evils' such as Alicia Sheridan's envy of her brother's and sister's relationship with their father or Anne Tracy's hurt feelings when her brother Anthony did not visit. They could also arise from cultural practices highlighting differences between siblings, such as shaming rituals which could occur when a younger sibling married before an elder sibling.[115] If anyone who 'hateth a brother [was] a murderer', then a fair number of eighteenth-century siblings committed murder in their hearts.[116]

The heavy burdens placed upon siblings meant that it was always a relationship in danger of collapsing under the unfulfilled expectations of equitable friendship. Despite universal expectations of equal and friendly sibling relations, real siblings continued to struggle over parental treatment, perceptions of inequality before the law, and their own disappointing and bitter treatment of one another. As one sister in a property dispute told another, 'they as sisters ought to agree and divide every thing fairly and have no disputes'.[117] In their battles over inheritance, in the arguments, brawls, competition, invectives, and physical and verbal violence, siblings clearly felt the general tension between expectations of equality and experiences of inequality in their specific interactions. Siblings excelled at disobliging and offending one another. When a 'very hard Mouth'd' sister 'fell to Scolding and Quarrelling, in the Language of Billingsgate' or a brother 'having some Words with his Sister... threw a Pot at her, and cut her Nose (almost) off', they demonstrated that being born peers did not guarantee lifelong friendship for all brothers and sisters.[118] The tidy gendering of sibling conflict reflected in prescriptive literature and law, however, was not reflected in practice. Sisters and brothers tussled vigorously over every imaginable offence. Despite fiction's obsession with brother–sister incest, real incest cases between siblings-in-law demonstrate the competing pulls of conjugal and fraternal or sororal ties. Rivalry and discontent could destroy any sibling relationship, but brother–sister relations had to contend with the additional fears about their interaction. Throughout the seventeenth and eighteenth centuries the greatest cultural fear for siblings centred on their possible divisiveness and rivalry, but towards the end of the eighteenth century this fear began to overlap with an increased fear of sibling incest.[119] As the sibling relationship began to be described as a place of special emotional closeness between men and women, the tension between natural friendship and natural rivalry developed into concerns about natural and unnatural love.

The struggle in the eighteenth century between the fraternal and the conjugal parallels the struggle between hierarchal and egalitarian ideas of social organization. If, as Catherine Gallagher asserts, healthy individuals equalled healthy social bodies, then rivalry, and particularly incest, showed the decay of families and social bodies. Classification of siblings as equals did not match with gender and age hierarchies, nor did they sit comfortably with masculine notions of individuality and citizenship. One way to negotiate this conflict was to make their closeness – particularly between brothers and sisters – pathological and deviant, thus expressing fears about that equality. An additional means of resolution was to render the sister a wife substitute, thus making her a better fit for the hierarchy.[120] Worries about rivalry or incest reflected concerns about a polity that was increasingly based on individuality and brotherhood but clung to old hierarchies of age and gender that had made the world a stable place for centuries.

Because siblings were to be material, social, and emotional constants in one another's lives, any deviation from that standard could ignite dispute, disappointment, and bitterness, and sometimes even conscientious effort could not patch over the tears in sibling relations. The weakening of those amicable interactions had an enormous impact on the financial and emotional wellbeing of eighteenth-century brothers and sisters. Siblings like Alicia Sheridan could not afford to separate themselves from their brothers and sisters, no matter how painful the associations could be on occasion. Her father was still a part of her life, no matter how much he disappointed her, and she needed Betsy in her status as the favourite to communicate with him and negotiate between him and their brothers. Betsy and Charles had a tenuous relationship at best (perhaps coloured by a rivalry between the two favourites), and they needed Alicia's steadying influence. So even if Alicia did not always prefer Charles' company, she was Betsy's connection to him, and Betsy, in turn, was Alicia's connection to the London family members, Richard and Thomas. Rivalry was rarely the only element in sibling interactions. For most families even bitter resentment had to be balanced by the recognition that brothers and sisters needed one another for the maintenance of their households, and sometimes for their very survival. They could not afford to remove sources of household support and connection casually.

Notes

1 George Cumberland to Richard Cumberland, 18 October 1778, in Black, ed., *The Cumberland Letters*, p. 214.
2 Samuel Johnson, *A Journey to the Western Islands of Scotland* (London, 1775), p. 146; Anne Travell, commonplace and recipe book, c.1780s, GA, D4582/4/18.
3 Agnes Travell Witts, Weimar, to Anne Travell, Cheltenham, England, 28 August 1799, GA, D4582/4/8.

4 Agnes Travell Witts, North Hanover Street, [Glasgow,] to Anne Travell, Cheltenham, 27 October 1795, GA, D4582/4/7.
5 Ibid.
6 Ibid.
7 Agnes Travell Witts, Weimar, to Anne Travell, Swerford, 22 October 1799, GA, D4582/4/8.
8 Agnes Travell Witts to Anne Travell, 28 August 1799, GA, D4582/4/8.
9 Agnes Travell Witts to Anne Travell, 20 December 1795, GA, D4582/4/7.
10 Agnes Travell Witts to Anne Travell, 5 April 1799, GA, D4582 D4582/4/8.
11 Anne Travell, daybook, 1767, GA, D4582/4/17/3. Anne did not attribute passages she extracted. This quote probably came from *The Ladies Library* (London, 1751), p. 252, ECCO.
12 Anne Travell, copy letter, undated, GA, D4582/4/14.
13 *OBP*, 10 September 1823, trial of George Aldridge (t18230910).
14 Perry, *Novel Relations*, pp. 107–89; Grassby, *Kinship and Capitalism*, pp. 208–10; Davidoff, 'Kinship as a Categorical Concept', pp. 411–28.
15 Finch, *Early Wisdom*, pp. 193–4.
16 The references to unnatural sisters and unnatural brothers were counted using the ECCO and Early English Books Online digital databases. The number of references to unnatural siblings was compared with the overall number of publications included in the database. See Leonard Schwarz, review of ECCO, (review no. 408), www.history.ac.uk/reviews/review/408, September 2004 (accessed 26 June 2010). References in ECCO to unnatural siblings were found in no more than 0.37 per cent of the publications dating from before 1760. In works published between 1760 and 1769 it rose to 0.46 per cent, and it remained at 0.45 per cent between 1770 and 1779. It dropped back down to pre-1760 levels in the 1780s, and then rose to 0.43 per cent in the 1790s and was 0.5 per cent in 1800.
17 Palinurus, *Familiar Letters*, pp. 19–21; *The Case of GR Fitzgerald, Esquire, Impartially Considered* (London 1786), p. 5.
18 Palinurus, *Familiar Letters*, pp. 19–21.
19 Allestree, *The Whole Duty of Man*, p. 87.
20 *The Genuine Account of the Adventures of Mr. Richard Brown, and his Sister* (London, 1750), p. 1, BL, 012611.h.37.
21 Aphra Behn, *The Younger Brother: or, The Amorous Jilt* (London, 1696), BL, 644.g.19; *The Younger Brother: or the Sham Marquis*; *The Fair Adultress: or, the Treacherous Brother* (London, 1743), BL, 1094 e5; *The Brother; Memoirs of a Younger Brother* (London, 1789), BL,10826.aaa.30.
22 Beaumont and Fletcher, *The Bloody Brother*, 1.1.
23 Ibid., 2.1.
24 Ibid., 3.1.
25 Thirsk, 'Younger Sons in the Seventeenth Century', p. 359.
26 Aspinall-Oglander, ed., *Admiral's Wife*, quoted in Pollock, *A Lasting Relationship*, p.169.

27 Joseph Flower, *The Prodigal Son, a Poem*, 2nd edn, (Bath, [1750]), p. 26, BL, 11633.c.21.
28 *OBP, Ordinary of Newgate's Account*, 6 November 1723 (OA17231106).
29 *OBP, Ordinary of Newgate's Account*, 14 May 1731 (OA17310514).
30 Alicia Sheridan LeFanu to Esther Ogle Sheridan, 9 November 1816, KCC, LeFanu 20.
31 Ibid.
32 This appears to have had some precedent in the Middle Ages. In a study of gaol deliveries and manorial disputes from the fourteenth century Barbara Hanawalt discovered that while siblings were less likely than spouses or parents to be involved in homicide they made up the majority of people involved in of manorial disputes (66.6 per cent). Barbara Hanawalt, *Crime and Conflict in English Communities, 1300–1348* (Cambridge, 1979), p. 160.
33 *OBP*, 12 April 1727, trial of Thomas Nash (t17270412-21).
34 *OBP, Ordinary of Newgate's Account*, 7 November 1744 (OA17441107). An inheritance of one shilling could indicate that the person had been cut off with no hope for more inheritance, but it could also indicate that the person had previously received an inheritance and merely needed to be acknowledged in the will.
35 *OBP, Ordinary of Newgate's Account*, 4 May 1741 (OA17410504).
36 Thomas Bright, will, written 20 February 1799, proved 23 June 1805, GA, GDR Wills 1805/104; Thomas Bright, testamentary cause, October 1818–April 1919, GA, GDR B4/2/B127.
37 Sarah Fielding, *The Adventures of David Simple*, ed. with an introduction and notes by Linda Bree (London, 2002), p. 3.
38 For the Diocese of Gloucester there were 122 cases of sibling probate disputes between 1700 and 1838 (120 of them between 1715 and 1836). For ten of the cases not enough information was available to determine why they were arguing. Eight cases were disputes about the validity of the will, thirteen were about unpaid or underpaid legacies and portions, and ninety-one were cases of one sibling asking for a will to be proved, letters of administration granted, or an inventory taken. GA, GDR B4/2.
39 Lloyd Bonfield, 'Testamentary Causes in the Prerogative Court of Canterbury, 1660–1694' in Christopher Brooks and Michael Lobban, eds., *Communities and Court in Britain, 1150–1900* (London, 1997), pp. 133–54.
40 The 122 cases involved 152 separate incidents of sibling conflict (including that between half-siblings and siblings-in-law). Of the 152 incidents, 40 involved sisters disputing against brothers: 30 petitioning the court to have their brothers prove a will, take out letters of administration, or provide an inventory, 1 disputing a will's validity, and 6 petitioning for an unpaid legacy or portion; details of the other 3 are unknown. Four additional cases involved sisters and sisters-in-law against brothers and brothers-in-law.
41 Brother–brother conflicts accounted for 29 incidents, including 22 petitioning for a will, administration, or inventory be proved or made, 2 disputing a will's

validity, and 2 contesting over unpaid legacies (details of the other 3 are unknown). The total grew to 39 when incidents between brothers-in-law were included.
42 Erickson, *Women and Property in Early Modern England*, pp. 229–36.
43 There were 23 incidents of sister and sister-in-law conflict (12 between sisters, and 11 involving in-laws).
44 Froide, *Never Married*, p. 60; Davidoff and Hall, *Family Fortunes*, pp. 351–2.
45 Brother–sister conflicts accounted for 19 incidents, with an additional 23 incidents involving in-laws.
46 *OBP*, 20 February 1793, trial of John Ruddle (t17930220-37).
47 Quoted in Vickery, *The Gentleman's Daughter*, p. 80.
48 Morse Hobbs, will, written 11 December 1738, proved 12 December 1738, GA, GDR Wills 1738/217; Morse Hobbs, testamentary cause, 1738–40, GA, GDR B4/2 H123.
49 Deposition of Mary Bartlett/Bartless, 11 May 1804, in Benjamin Kench, testamentary cause, GA, GDR B4/2/K12.
50 Allegations of proctor, Ricketts, 17 May 1804, in Benjamin Kench, testamentary cause, GA, GDR B4/2/K12.
51 Correspondence with Francis Edward Witts from various family members, 1808–10, WFP, F406–13.
52 Berkeley Seymour to an unidentified correspondent, 26 September and 6 October 1730, Freeman, Freeman-Mitford, Edwards, and Dulverton Family of Batsford Collection, GA, D2002/17/1.
53 A. Baine, *History of Kingswood Forest Including All the Ancient Manors and Villages in the Neighborhood*, (London and Bristol, 1891); H T. Ellacombe, *The History of the Parish of Bitton, in the County of Gloucester* (Exeter, 1881). See also burial records for Berkeley and William Seymour: Church of England, Bitton, Gloucestershire, Parish Registers, FHL, British film 1597036, items 2–9.
54 *A Genuine and Authentic Account of the Trial, Life, Behaviour, and Dying Words of Richard Milhil*, (London, [1767]), p. 12, BL, 1568/9284.
55 For example see Cott v. Wright, Exchequer dispute, 1711, TNA, E134/10Anne/Trin12; Smith and Barnaby v. Saltern and Willet, Exchequer dispute, 1712, TNA, E134/11Anne/Mch24; Aylworth Freeman, will, written 16 February 1732, proved 1 May 1733, GA, GDR Wills 1734/55; Aylworth Freeman, testamentary cause, June 1733–April 1734, GA, GDR B4/2 F43.
56 *OBP, Ordinary of Newgate's Account*, 30 May 1739 (OA17390530).
57 Hannah Butler, deposition, in William Brown testamentary cause, 27 September 1773, GA, GDR B4/2/B145.
58 Charles Francis Sheridan to Alicia Sheridan LeFanu, 19 February [1800], KCC, LeFanu 36.
59 Betsy Sheridan to Alicia Sheridan LeFanu, 4–6 May 1785, 21–3 January 1786, in LeFanu, ed., *Betsy Sheridan's Journal*, pp. 48, 79, 120, 155.
60 Betsy Sheridan to Alicia Sheridan LeFanu, 1 April 1789, in LeFanu, ed., *Betsy Sheridan's Journal*, p. 156.
61 Jane Austen, *Northanger Abbey*, 1814, chapter 1.

62 Betsy Sheridan to Alicia Sheridan LeFanu, 4–6 May 1785, in LeFanu, ed., *Betsy Sheridan's Journal*, pp. 48, 201; Elizabeth Linley Sheridan to Alicia Sheridan LeFanu, 25 June 1783 and autumn 1783, KCC, LeFanu 25.
63 Betsy Sheridan LeFanu to Alicia Sheridan LeFanu, 8–9 June 1789, in LeFanu, ed., *Betsy Sheridan's Journal*, p. 165.
64 Ibid.
65 Betsy Sheridan LeFanu to Alicia Sheridan LeFanu, 17–22 June 1789, in LeFanu, ed., *Betsy Sheridan's Journal*, pp. 171–2.
66 *OBP*, 31 May 1827, trial of William Broadway (t18270531-48). William and John Broadway slept in the same bed and were described as 'very affectionate', but the argument escalated until William accidentally killed John.
67 *OBP*, 29 October 1829, trial of Daniel and George Lewis (t18291029-11); 22 February 1764, trial of Walter Marsh (t17640222-36).
68 Jamoussi, *Primogeniture and Entail in England*; Eileen Spring, *Law, Land and Family*.
69 Erickson, *Women and Property*, p. 77; Perry, *Novel Relations*, pp. 143–89.
70 Bonfield, 'Testamentary Causes in the Prerogative Court of Canterbury, 1660–1694', p. 137.
71 Barbara Hanawalt, *The Wealth of Wives: Women, Law, and Economy in Late Medieval London* (Oxford, 2007), pp. 14–19; Barbara Hanawalt, *Growing Up in Medieval London: The Experience of Childhood in History* (Oxford, 1993); Arkell, Evans, and Goose, eds., *When Death Do Us Part*, pp. 19–22.
72 The statute outlined siblings' rights thus. If a person died without parents, spouse, or children, his or her siblings divided the estate equally. A widow without children received one-half, and the siblings of the deceased the other half. If a married man died, his widow received one-third and the children equally divided the remaining two-thirds. If a widower or widow died their children shared all the property equally.
73 Thirsk, 'Younger sons in the Seventeenth Century'; Spring, 'The Strict Settlement'.
74 Carolyn D. Williams, ' "Another Self in the Case": Gender, Marriage and the Individual in Augustan Literature', in Roy Porter, ed., *Rewriting the Self: Histories from the Renaissance to the Present* (London and New York, 1997), pp. 97–118.
75 Thomas Gisborne, *An Enquiry into the Duties of the Female Sex* (London, 1797), pp. 382–3, 386, 393–5, BAN, HQ 1201.G5.
76 Ibid., p. 387.
77 Ibid., p. 388.
78 Heal and Holmes, *The Gentry in England and Wales*, pp. 44, 83; Trumbach, *The Rise of the Egalitarian Family*, pp. 50–8. For an account of blended families in early modern France see Sylvie Perrier, 'The Blended Family in Ancien Regime France: A Dynamic Family Form', *History of the Family*, 3:4 (1998), 459–71.
79 In the eighteenth century approximately between 15 and 20 per cent of marriages were remarriages; this proportion was declining from its height of around

one-third of marriages in the sixteenth century to its low point of under 12 per cent in the middle of the nineteenth century. Simultaneously, the interval between marriages was lengthening. See Wrigley and Schofield, *The Population History of England*, pp. 258–9, and E. Anthony Wrigley et al., *English Population History from Family Reconstitution, 1580–1837* (Cambridge, 1997), pp. 171–82.
80 *OBP*, 18 October 1775, trial of Alexander Tate (t17751018-1).
81 Between 1831 and 1900 there were thirteen references to half-sisters and thirty-seven to half-brothers, but between 1901 and 1912 there were eleven references to half-sisters and fifteen to half-brothers – indicating the gradual hardening and narrowing in the delineation of kinship.
82 *OBP*, 12 September 1759, trial of Jane Williams (t17590912-47); 8 April 1807, trial of Dennis Dempsey (t18070408-81).
83 *OBP*, *Ordinary of Newgate's Account*, 24 November 1740 (OA17401124).
84 Wrigley et al., *English Population History*, pp. 177–81. For a discussion of the economic struggles of family life after the loss of a spouse see Bailey, *Unquiet Lives*, pp. 168–92.
85 The trial transcripts do not explain Margaret Marshall's connection with the Coffield and Hogan siblings. However, there is a record of a marriage between John Hogan and Margaret Marshall on 28 August 1797 in St George's, Hanover Square, London, which suggests that her inclusion in the siblings' socializing was an indication that they expected eventually to incorporate her into their network. John Chapman, ed., *The Register Book of Marriages Belonging to the Parish of St. George, Hanover Square in the County of Middlesex*, vol. 2: *1788–1809*, Publications of the Harleian Society, 19 (London, 1888), p. 170.
86 *OBP*, 4 December 1793, trial of Edward Coffield otherwise Caufield (t17931204-32).
87 Mary Jean Corbett, *Family Likeness: Sex, Marriage, and Incest from Jane Austen to Virginia Woolf* (Ithaca and New York, 2008).
88 The 'unnaturalness' of 'inappropriate behaviour towards members of one's family' was among the 'most common useages' of the term in early modern England. See Robert Hole, 'Incest, Consanguinity and a Monstrous Birth in Rural England, January 1600', *Social History*, 25:2 (May 2000), 186. It should be noted that all sibling incest was heterosexual; there are no references to homosexual incest between siblings in eighteenth-century literature.
89 Polly Morris, 'Incest or Survival Strategy? Plebian Marriage within the Prohibited Degrees in Somerset, 1730–1835', *Journal of the History of Sexuality*, 2:2 (1991), 235–65.
90 The exception was the 1650 Adultery Act, which made sibling incest a capital felony. It was revoked, however, with the Restoration. Crawford, *Blood, Bodies, and Families in Early Modern England*, p. 212.
91 Consistory Court of Chester, Henry Coulson case, CALS, EDC 5 (1727), no. 10 Chester. Alice Coulson married Daniel Potter in St Oswald's, Chester, in 1709. They had seven sons over the ensuing fourteen years, of whom at least

two did not survive childhood. See Church of England, St Oswald, Chester, Cheshire, Parish Registers, 1580–1720, FHL, British film 2068352; Church of England, St Peter's, Chester, Cheshire, Parish Registers, 1588–1812, FHL, British film 2045912.
92 Már Jónsson, 'Defining Incest by the Word of God: Northern Europe 1520–1740', *History of European Ideas*, 18:6 (1994), 853–67.
93 Consistory Court of Chester, CALS, EDC 5 (1727), no. 10 Chester, EDC 5 (1724), no. 9 Bowden, EDC 5 (1722 and 1731), nos. 4 and 14 Middleton, EDC 5 (1716), no. 13 Exeter.
94 OBP, *Ordinary of Newgate's Account*, 11 July 1764 (OA17640711).
95 Elisabeth Rose Gruner, 'Born and Made: Sisters, Brothers, and the Deceased Wife's Sister Bill', *Signs*, 24:2 (Winter 1999), 423–47; Perry, *Novel Relations*, pp. 374–403.
96 Rudolph Binion, 'Notes on Romanticism', *The Journal of Psychohistory*, 11:1 (1983), 43–64. Much like rivalry, sibling incest did not seem to capture the colonial American imagination as it did the English. See Glover, *All Our Relations*, pp. 48–9.
97 See also Ellen Pollack, 'Introduction', *The Eighteenth Century*, 39:3 (1998), 187–91; Vikki Bell, *Interrogating Incest: Feminism, Foucault and the Law* (London and New York, 1993).
98 Jones, *A Passionate Sisterhood*.
99 Adam Kuper, 'Incest, Cousin Marriage, and the Origin of the Human Sciences in Nineteenth-Century England', *Past and Present*, 174:1 (2002), 158–83; Glenda A. Hudson, *Sibling Love and Incest in Jane Austen's Fiction* (New York, 1992).
100 David Crane, *The Kindness of Sisters: Annabella Milbanke and the Destruction of the Byrons*, (New York, 2002); William Dean Brewer, *The Shelley–Byron Conversation* (Gainesville, FL, 1994).
101 Volney, *The Law of Nature*, pp. 113–14, 119–20; Hudson, *Sibling Love and Incest*, pp. 9–32; Leonore Davidoff, 'Sibling Incest in the English Late 18th- and Early 19th-Century Middle Class', *Homme: Zeitschrift fur feministische Geschichtswissenschaft*, 13:1 (2002), 29–49.
102 Jane Austen, *Mansfield Park*, chapter 2.
103 Though *Mansfield Park* contains the most explicit overlapping of sibling and conjugal ties in Austen's fiction, all of her plots contain elements of this. Hudson, *Sibling Love and Incest*.
104 Politicians continued to think of incest in these terms well into the twentieth century. See Bell, *Interrogating Incest*, pp. 140, 147.
105 *The Monk and his Sister* (London, 1811), p. 30, BL, RB23.a.19675.
106 OBP, 6 December 1727, trial of Richard Bloxam (t17271206-65). See also OBP, 9 April 1746, trial of Sarah Hayes (t17460409-47); 25 February 1789, trial of William Patmore (t17890225-1); 6 June 1810, trial of Sarah Puryer (t18100606-30).

107 *The Illegal Lovers; A True Secret History* (London, 1728), BL, 1079.i.12.(1).
108 Consistory Court of Chester, George Parker case, CALS, EDC 5 (1724), no. 9 Bowden.
109 Consistory Court of Chester, William Crispin case, CALS, EDC 5 (1716), no. 13 Exeter.
110 Gruner, 'Born and Made'.
111 Johnson and Sabean, eds., *Sibling Relations*, pp. 1–30.
112 Fielding, *The Adventures of David Simple*, p. 3.
113 Jane Austen, *Persuasion*, chapter 9.
114 OBP, *Ordinary of Newgate's Account*, 3 August 1709 (OA17090803).
115 Gillis, *For Better, for Worse*, p. 72.
116 OBP, *Ordinary of Newgate's Account*, 20 December 1717 (OA17171220).
117 Forestque v. Thomas, Court of the Exchequer, 1716, TNA, E134/3Geo1/Hil19.
118 OBP, 17 July 1728, trial of Mary Ashley (t17280717-37); 6 September 1732, trial of Peter Buck (t17320906-40).
119 David Warren Sabean, 'The Discourse of Incest from the Baroque to the Romantic', *Inzestdiskurse vom Barock bis zur Romantik*, 13:1 (2002), 7–28.
120 Catherine Gallagher, 'The Body versus the Social Body in the Works of Thomas Malthus and Henry Mayhew', in Thomas Laqueur and Catherine Gallagher, eds., *Making of the Modern Body: Sexuality an d Society in the Nineteenth Century*, (Berkeley, Los Angeles, and London, 1987), pp. 83–106, particularly p. 83, quoted in Sondra M. Archmedes, *Gendered Pathologies: The Female Body and Biomedical Discourse in the Nineteenth-Century English Novel* (New York and London, 2005), pp. 4–5. Archimedes also discusses sibling incest in Dickens's *Hard Times*; see especially *Gendered Pathologies*, pp. 61–72.

4

Sibling economics

> It must be remember'd that life consists not of a series of illustrious actions, or of elegant enjoyments; the greater part of our time passes in complyance with necessities in the performance of daily duties, in the removal of small inconveniences, in the procurement of petty pleasures; & we are ill or well at ease, as the main stream of life glides on smoothly, or is ruffled by small obstacles & frequent [como]tion.
>
> Samuel Johnson, *A Journey to the Western Islands of Scotland*, 1775, extracted by Anne Travell, c.1780s[1]

On a Monday in February 1764 Anne, Frances Mary, and their uncle William Travell dined with the Witts sisters – lifelong family friends. The next day Ferdinando and one Witts sister, Apphia, dined with the Travell sisters at Swerford House. On Friday Anne went to Ferdinando and Martha's house in Chadlington, where she had breakfast and stayed for a twelve-hour visit. Catherine, who had been staying with Ferdinando, came back to Swerford with Anne, and they dropped off Apphia on the way.[2] Paralleling the physical connections to her siblings' households, Anne recorded the monetary expenditures of household management: a watch repair for herself, ribbon for Agnes, and money to Ferdinando's servants. This kind of constant material and physical interaction between the siblings was typical and served to strengthen and deepen the patterns of their relationships. Despite her not having a physical household of her own, Anne's careful accounting of monies received and paid for goods and services established a fictive household shared by all the Travell siblings, no matter what their physical location. The pushes and pulls of love, friendship, rivalry, and resentment formed the language and patterns of sibling expectations, but as siblings aged and lost parents, their material, economic, and social connections to kin rested more heavily on their brothers and sisters and brothers- and sisters-in-law. As siblings and spouses died, aging sisters and brothers continued to care for one another in addition to maintaining relations with the remnants of sibling ties found in nieces and nephews.

When Anne began her 1764 daybook she initially paid scant attention to the details of household management. Since her mother's death the previous January she had moved between Swerford House (where her oldest brother, Francis, lived) and Chadlington, Oxfordshire, to stay with Ferdinando and his wife Martha. By July 1764, however, Anne began earnestly seeking to establish her own household. The daybook was in a pre-printed form where the details of social activities and daily expenditures could be noted, and Anne did not include specific indications of her decision to purchase her own house. The only clue she gave about her motivation was a small annotation on 25 January, when she wrote, 'Rec'd the Letter the most fatal to my happiness.'[3] In all of her writings this is among the most personal and direct statements about her thoughts and feelings. If the reference to the death of happiness was not strong enough, the mere existence of such open emotion from someone not usually inclined to get her 'spirits in a froth' underscores the trauma this letter caused.[4] Though she did not state that the letter referred to some matter of the heart, or at least to some matter of marriage, this is its most likely topic. A letter detailing the death of a family member or the loss of some financial standing would have affected other people as well as Anne, and would have been noted as she regularly noted such things. When she received news that her 'poor Aunt Jane Travell' had died in the small hours of 16 November 1767, Anne noted that she was the '3rd Relations as near as that, that we have lost within ½ year'.[5] The sentiment from January 1764, however, was personal, and was a loss for Anne alone, a deathblow to her happiness alone. It is not coincidental that once her planned spring and summer visits were completed she immediately began searching for her own house. Before that January entry she must have hoped to be mistress of her own household once she married, but the arrival of that unhappy letter spurred a conscious decision to make her own way. That May she turned twenty-seven, and she may have decided that marriage was not in her future. Her eldest brother Francis's illicit relationship with a woman of a lower social standing may have served as a caution to Anne that there were few socially and financially eligible men for her to marry. She could have remained with Ferdinando and Martha, but that July they welcomed their first child and perhaps she worried that she and her three sisters were more than Ferdinando's household in Chadlington could reasonably accommodate; she may not have wanted to conform to the 'rhythms and priorities' of a household not under her own direction.[6] Additionally, Anne's sisters, particularly twenty-one-year-old Catherine and fifteen-year-old Agnes, could still hope to marry well, and the need to establish a household for them may have encouraged Anne to imagine some place more appropriate for unmarried young women than Swerford House, tainted as it was by Francis's sexual and social misconduct.

In any event, as soon as she was able, Anne 'Tramp'd all [over] the town House Hunting'.[7] She hoped to buy a house from a Miss Cox, and over the course of two weeks that summer she repeatedly visited Cheltenham to make final arrangements with her.[8] On 9 August she went with a brother and sister (probably Francis and Frances Mary) to 'take a view of our House at Cheltenham', a home situated on the High Street.[9] Cheltenham was not yet the popular spa town it would become in the 1780s and 1790s, but it was already a respectable place for single gentlewomen to settle, as Anne's nephew later remarked. The balls, dances, public breakfasts, and stream of visitors that Cheltenham afforded expanded the sisters' social world, but it did not diminish the connection to their brothers.[10] Instead it provided a third location for sibling visits and interaction. What emerge from Anne's daybooks are not the details of socializing, though the records of teas, dinners, and visitors are there; instead it is the enjoyment of having the household. For Anne, like other Georgians, 'it is hard to overstate the importance of the ... home to its inhabitants'.[11] The daybook is businesslike and almost terse in its lack of personal detail, but when it came to having her own house she became relatively giddy.[12] On 28 October 1764 she and Ferdinando visited some relatives of their mother's and rode away from 'poor Swerford', the household of her youth, bound for Cheltenham, where her three sisters were already entertaining visitors in their new house. Though obviously sad to leave behind 'poor Swerford', she crammed extra words into the space provided for the day to remark: '[E]xtremely happy with being in a house'. The next day she gloried in Francis's joining the group to celebrate the sisters' 'pretty house at Cheltenham' (see Figure 4).[13] Though Anne and her sisters did not enjoy the rituals associated with married householding, the family gathering and celebration that followed the move to Cheltenham echoed those surrounding a newly married couple's occupation of their first home.[14] Running a household made Anne, in many ways, a fictive wife. Even if the older meaning of 'wife' as one who ran a household was obsolete by her day, later in life she began to receive letters addressed to 'Mrs. Travell', which bestowed on her a type of fictive wifehood or widowhood befitting her status as a householder and adult.[15]

Though Peter Laslett once described co-resident siblings as a 'no family' category of household, more recent scholarship has recognized this connection between families and households and hinted at the importance of siblings within them.[16] Anne Travell shared her 'pretty house' with at least one of her sisters for over sixty years. She managed the servants, the upkeep, and

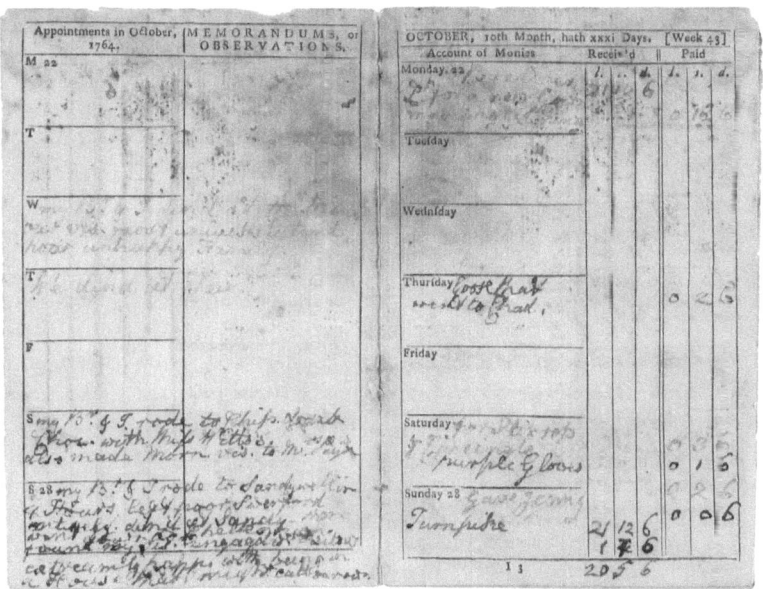

4 Anne Travell's 1764 daybook, entry for Saturday 28 October describing moving to her new house in Cheltenham. Copyright Bowly Family and Gloucestershire Archives, D4582/4/17/1. Used with permission

the social calendar of the household. She housed and entertained her nieces and even her illegitimate nephews. She helped to execute the wills of nearly all her siblings (she was the last one to die). Additionally, Anne maintained a voluminous correspondence with all her siblings, siblings-in-law, cousins, friends, and associates. She continued to buy ribbon for Catherine wrote letters to Agnes when she was away on the Continent, and entertained her brothers when they came for dinner. She also kept meticulous accounts of the health of any siblings, nephews, or nieces who were staying with her. If one fell ill, she kept a note of when they were able to sit up all day, or when they were able to join the family for dinner.[17] As in the Travell family, siblings, even from lower down the social scale, could visit for days or even weeks at a time or might be permanently or seasonally resident.[18] Between 1721 and 1722 George Simpson, a servant, who lived with one sister in Yorkshire, helped her to arrange her finances and plan for her children's future during her husband's declining health. Later he lived with another sister in Sutton.[19] The sister of the pick-pocket Katherine Pember 'kept' her for two years, made sure she 'lived very honestly', and provided her with 'Victuals and Drink'.[20] Anne Travell and other eighteenth-century siblings recognized that Johnson's 'daily duties' were essential to balancing the thrift and 'neighbourliness' of households.[21]

After purchasing a home, Anne's and Catherine's fortunes settled further when they received legacies from deceased relatives. The deaths of Frances Mary and Aunt Jane in 1767, Uncle John Tracy-Atkyns in 1773, and Uncle William Travell in 1775 provided the Travells with increased financial security. It may have been the last that supported the purchase of a new home in Cheltenham, this one closer to the parish church and the social centre of town.[22] Following the cementing of her financial situation and the simplifying of the household with the death of Frances Mary and Agnes's marriage in 1776, Anne recorded fewer and fewer financial and material transactions. While the physical arrangements of her living conditions figured less in her records, the daily effort at maintaining relationships and business transactions continued to be carefully recorded.[23] In the later daybooks, beginning in 1788, Anne began to keep a detailed count of the letters she wrote. For 1788 she noted that in '¾ of a year' she had sent 117 letters.[24] She continued to note her letter-writing count and its increase on previous years. By 1801 she was up to 183 a year.[25] In other words her effort to maintain the symbolic or fictive household through letters and socializing assumed greater significance as the details of financial survival became less pressing.

Because a household's credit flowed through the reputation and financial expenditures of its members, careful control of and accounting for the financial and social resources were key to its smooth running.[26] If nothing else, Anne's daybook – with one page for social exchanges and the other for financial exchanges – is material evidence of this (see Figure 4). Anne also kept a commonplace book. Typically commonplace books recorded snippets of published literature that the owner wanted to remember for future recall and use, but the contents of Anne's commonplace book are littered with the more practical and mundane aspects of life. The above quotation from Johnson is nestled in among a recommendation from a Mrs Hunt to soak new coloured linens in a mixture of 'Fuller's Earth' and water for twenty-four hours, a quotation from a French author about the remembrance of good deeds, and a recipe for curing heartburn from her sister-in-law.[27] This hodgepodge of household details and literary passages underscores the embedded and unheralded performance of daily duties that typified not only Travell sibling economics, but the economics of sibling relationships up and down the social scale. Sibling economics were not 'illustrious actions' or 'elegant enjoyments'; instead they were ordinary and daily – sometimes grindingly so. It is the commonness of siblings' economic labour that has led to its invisibility to both contemporaries and historians, but that labour was essential to family and individual social and material well-being.[28] Their economic transactions were also 'expressions of inner impulses, conflicts, desires and expectations'.[29] Exchanges of goods and services that bound households together in companionable partnership could express instrumental friendship or unravel into arguments over who should govern the household.

Keith Wrightson has argued that 'at the heart' of overlapping social networks was 'an individual household' that required careful control and management – a burden that 'fell most heavily upon the master and mistress'.[30] Perhaps, this is true, but the assessment misses how pre-existing familial obligations and resources trailed behind husbands and wives as they set up their individual households. Georgian families valorized households – not necessarily marriages – as the markers of social and economic adulthood.[31] As Margot Finn has noted, 'while liberal theorists celebrated the economic agency of autonomous individuals, in the market, day-to-day experiences of commerce and the law repeatedly drew attention instead to the embedded nature of the individual's economic activities'.[32] Like others who 'shared economic and social bonds', siblings 'needed to imagine and frame their emotional connections to each other through the household . . . even an imagined one, to make sense of their hierarchies, authorities, and status'.[33] Connected to the individual households run by masters and mistresses were links to sibling households (whether married or not) that established a virtual, or imagined, household shared by families of origin even after the dispersal of the physical household into new marital or nuclear units. Both married and unmarried siblings shared physical households throughout adulthood and old age.[34] Sibling economics encompassed household management via physical care (of children, the ill, and the dying), financial transactions, and the more intangible exchange of social credit (including courtship, education, and occupational assistance). In short, siblings influenced whether life glided on 'smoothly' or whether it was 'ruffled' by 'frequent commotion'.

Households

Georgian brothers and sisters were embedded in the daily routines of one another's households across the social spectrum. It was only the absolutely destitute whose efforts crumbled under the combined weight of dire household conditions and a lack of sibling support; other siblings combined resources and services within and across households.[35] Some siblings pooled their resources (including assistance from the parish poor relief) and shared a household. Charles Cook and his brother combined their money and poor relief to afford an annual rent of £25.[36] Samuel Hill, a shoemaker's apprentice, lived with his brother and sister for a year in London. The pastry maker George Medhurst and his sister Anna Maria lived and worked together.[37] Jane Hide, against the order of the Overseers of Chedworth, Gloucestershire, returned to live with her brother and gave birth to her illegitimate child there.[38] The Jackson siblings exchanged apricot jam, news from cousins, and loans.[39] The Cumberlands exchanged courtship advice and bought and sent clothing for one another.[40] The Travell and Miller siblings paid one another's servants.[41] The Ryder siblings shared the interrogation of one sister's unmarried maid about the maid's pregnancy.[42] Siblings such as the shopkeeper William Gaze, the yeoman William Mason, and the cordwainer Thomas Goscombe all relied on their brothers, who were their principal creditors.[43] Siblings from the labouring and service strata could pass on employment opportunities to each other, as when George Woodward recommended his gardener's sister for a position in his friend's household.[44] In this way households could have multiple sibling networks – those between the householders themselves and those among their servants – both types being mutually supportive. Unfortunately, in Woodward's case the householder was annoyed when his servant's siblings overstayed their welcome and even courted other servants.[45] Throughout the eighteenth century brothers and sisters were cited by courts to execute wills, provide inventories, distribute household items, pay debts, and manage estates after the deaths of their siblings. As a testament to the lifelong importance of sibling economics, an analysis of over 3,000 will abstracts reveals that nearly a third of the testators mentioned their siblings as either beneficiaries or executors.[46] What is remarkable about this sample is the nearly equal distribution between testators and testatrixes. This suggests that, despite the purpose of wills to distribute property to subsequent generations, the recognition of living lateral kin as well as hopes for future family economic prosperity required the continued connection to siblings.[47] Whether from a trade, farming, or gentry family, testators often requested that their siblings provide for their children, arrange apprenticeships, or help their children execute and administer the will. In this way, siblings encouraged the expansion of imagined sibling households to include younger generations.

Brothers and sisters performed a variety of tasks that bound their households together. In a 1747 letter to his brother, Walter, Thomas Edwards thanked him for his advice, updated him on the price of a watch chain he wanted for their cousins, commented on a newsworthy trial, wished for good

Sibling economics 119

relations between Walter and their father, and reported on his contribution to Walter's household. 'I am glad to hear', he wrote, 'the Stockings fitted; I will send you an other pair with the 3 pair of Thread, which he has promis'd me the end of this week, by Monday's Coach.'[48] Thomas and Walter did not share a physical household, but an imagined one. Like the sister of the servant Ralph Trumper, who cut up one of his old shirts to make a night cap for him and then defended him in court about the cap's theft, the Edwards brothers found that their small household expenditures and errands tied them together and became the strings which they could pull for heavier, more intricate, emotional work.[49] Sisters as housekeepers could walk the fine line between servant and co-manager of the household. Many households benefited from sisterly management. Robert Bakewell's 'energetic sister' managed his household, Elin Stout 'freely offered to be housekeeper to her brother, and Elizabeth Sharp's brother William determined that she should join him from Northumberland to help him run his household in London.[50] Thomas Sharp, their father, wrote to Elizabeth about William's designs:

> Now as Billy went to Housekeeping that self same day in the Evening, viz. Monday the 23rd I must tell you how he goes on; because you are intitled to know this, as you are (he says) to be his housekeeper.

Their father continued by describing the details of William's management to impress Elizabeth with her brother's housekeeping skills, indicating that if she joined her brother she would be sharing the household duties, not taking them on alone.

> On Tuesday morning he bought a shoulder of Mutton for dinner. and says his Maid roasted it extreamly well, only Mrs. Reed scolds because he used his new pewter: without scowring it first. Yesterday he had pancakes and what was left of the shoulder the day before . . . And I must not forget his frugality in making the drippings of ye shoulder [or] Mutton on Tuesday serve to fry the batter of ye pancakes on Wednesday.[51]

William Sharp did not seem to regard his sister as a cheap form of domestic labour, but rather, as a newly established householder, he recognized the need for a housekeeper, which was a female occupation. As his brothers James and Granville had also been apprenticed to London tradesmen it must have seemed natural to William to have the next sibling, a sister, join them as well; as there were few skilled trades open to women, housekeeping seemed the gender-appropriate occupation for their sister. It was also a way, after apprenticeship had moved him to London from Northumberland, to reincorporate his sister into his daily life as apprenticeship and employment had done for his brothers.[52] Elizabeth never joined William as a housekeeper, but the following year she and her mother made a special trip to see his house in Mincing Lane, stopping along the way to visit her eldest brother John at Cambridge.[53]

Not all sisters enjoyed felicitous household arrangements with their siblings and siblings-in-law. Tension could enforce unequal status within the household, as when Ann Horn and Mary Clarke lived as servants to their sisters.[54] In the worst situations it could erupt into violence and chaos, as it did when sisters Mary and Sarah Punter verbally and physically abused their brother's wife, Dorothy, and 'did take [th]e government of his house upon them and would not suffer the said. Dorothea his wife to intermeddle w[i]th the household affaires w[hi]ch belonged unto her as his wife'.[55] The presence of unmarried sisters in the households of their siblings, particularly brothers, is often cited as an example of female dependence and subjugation.[56] That is part of the story, but it was precisely because sisters did not consider themselves inferior to their brothers that they could bitterly resent being subject to their household governance. Household management and housekeeping were not the problem – for some families they could be an opportunity to continue shared living – it was the power to control that work that caused troubles for siblings. For sisters accustomed to thinking of a brother as their peer, attempts by him or his wife to render them subservient were bound to be uncomfortable. Unmarried men such as Granville Sharp may have had fewer conflicts when they lived with married siblings because other avenues for contributing to the household were open to them.

For many families good relations mixed with occasional resentment at the heavy burden that sibling household sharing could cause. In a brief diary entry from a summer day in 1794 Agnes Travell Witts remarked on the 'very fine' weather and then explained that she was denied the opportunity to enjoy it, 'being much taken up by the arrival of Mr. Broome Witts'. Broome, her husband's brother, had arrived not only with his luggage, but also with a fever and a sore throat. His arrival necessitated arranging the household to accommodate him and then the added duty of hunting for a doctor (their regular doctor being out of town) and caring for him during his illness. Previously, while living in Edinburgh, Agnes and Edward welcomed visitors, especially visitors like Edward's siblings, with whom they enjoyed friendly relations. Broome's need for medical help and nursing was not unreasonable or unusual; caring for the ill was a regular component of household life. Yet Agnes could still mourn at having 'very little power of being out or engaging' in the fine weather because of Broome's arrival.[57] Compared with the malevolence revealed in probate disputes and described in prescriptive literature this type of expression is subtle enough to almost escape notice, but it was such small, even fleeting, tensions and resentments that sprinkled even the most healthy and loving of sibling relations and affected how services and support flowed between households.[58] Awareness of these tensions and the efforts to ameliorate them took constant, daily labour from siblings.

Even if they did not share a physical household, siblings moved objects between their homes, linking them with physical reminders of sibling connections. Gifts, like the silver toothpick that Tom Rumney gave his sister before her death, might circulate into the households of other siblings, thereby reminding them of their links to one another and memorializing those who had died.[59] An orphaned dressmaker's apprentice in Cheshire left her rings to her younger brother and sister.[60] Anne and Catherine Travell 'walked to Slaughter betwixt Breakfast & Supper to fetch my Brother['s] Shaving Pot'.[61] George and Richard Cumberland exchanged letters, books, food, and even a pet dog.[62] In all these ways siblings lived in, visited, and placed material objects in one another's households. By managing those objects and visits they also built the imagined space they shared with their brothers and sisters.

Physical care

At 3.00 a.m. on 25 February 1783 Agnes Travell Witts 'took ill', and through the night she was 'most miserable'. By the morning of the twenty-sixth she was in the 'highest spirits' when at 4.45 she gave birth to her first son, Francis Edward.[63] Having had 'several miscarriages', she went to Cheltenham 'to lie in, to avail herself of the skill of a celebrated accoucheur of the place'.[64] The next few days were filled with learning the details of mothering, particularly the struggle to breastfeed and the announcement of the birth via correspondence: between thirty and forty letters were written on 25–6 February. On 12 March Francis Edward was 'half-baptized', perhaps to assuage Agnes's worries, as she had been unable to have a living child in her previous six years of marriage, and that afternoon all the family gathered to have tea with Agnes. This rather intimate, and detailed, peep at the early days of Francis Edward's life comes not from his doting mother or from the accoucheur, but from his aunt Anne. It was Anne who carefully noted the beginning of Agnes's labour and the arrival of her 'd[ea]r nephew'; it was Anne who monitored the efforts to help Agnes breastfeed; it was Anne who wrote those letters to family and friends; and it was Anne who gathered the household, which consisted of herself, Catherine, and Ferdinando with his two teenaged daughters, to drink tea with the new mother.[65]

While Anne's account gives unusual details about non-parental child care, it was not unusual for eighteenth-century women and men to care for their younger siblings and for nieces and nephews, even across great distances.[66] This care could involve providing financially, socially, and physically for younger siblings or for nieces and nephews. Whatever the later relationship between nieces and nephews and their uncles or aunts, the origins and foundations of that relationship were with the child's parents and their relationship with their siblings. When sisters took in infant nieces or nephews for weeks at a time, they were fulfilling familial obligations and expectations shared with their sibling, not with the infant. Caring for a niece or nephew performed a service for both the parent and the child, but in the case of young children it was the parents that recognized the service. Other than off-hand references to apprenticeships with uncles and basic schooling at the hands of a single aunt or fictive aunts, prescriptive literature had little to say about siblings as child-raisers and care-givers.[67] Despite assumptions that children were under the control only of their parents and masters, families of various social backgrounds relied on child care rendered by older siblings, aunts, and uncles.[68]

Both sisters and brothers were important care-givers for children. Many sisters assisted at the births of their nieces and nephews much like Anne did, though few made the journey that Frances Sharp did when she travelled 300 miles to Northumberland to assist at the birth of her niece in 1762.[69] Along with Mary Sharp's parents, her aunts and uncles rejoiced when after eighteen or twenty miscarriages her mother successfully gave birth to her – a 'great Blessing... felt most thankfully by us all', her aunt recounted.[70] Gendered practices of childbirth usually excluded brothers from participating in this form of child care, but after the birth both brothers and sisters shared in the care, upbringing, education, and training of their younger siblings and nieces and nephews.[71] Walter Pringle cared for his nine nieces and nephews after the deaths of both his brother and his sister.[72] The niece to whom Frances Sharp travelled was the same niece who fifteen years later had her uncle, Granville Sharp, scouring London for a suitable ear trumpet for her.[73] As a young man, newly apprenticed to a London draper and hundreds of miles from his parents, Granville himself had benefited from sibling child care when his two older brothers bought him a work apron, helped procure his furniture, and generally assured their father that they would regularly check on 'Greeny'.[74] Richard Rose Haines, after several years' employment, was 'then apprenticed to his brother William Haines of Broad Campden, shoemaker for 7 years and served 2 then returned to Blockley where he worked for himself paying his brother 6d a week in lieu of working for him'.[75] Leonard Williams went to live with his uncle when he was five or six years old, was subsequently trained by his uncle, and did not leave the household until he married.[76] When Anne Travell corresponded with her sister's brother-in-law, Broome Witts, in 1800 about how they might keep their common nephew 'afloat', she participated in a practice that most families would have recognized.[77]

Child care also could allow childless siblings the opportunity to engage in parent-like behaviour and reap some of the benefits of parenting.[78] As cultural assumptions about femininity increasingly emphasized motherhood, as opposed to wifehood, in the latter part of the eighteenth century and the beginning of the nineteenth century unmarried sisters could participate in surrogate motherhood.[79] In *Persuasion* Anne Elliot finds that 'in the children, who loved her nearly as well, and respected her a great deal more than their mother, she had an object of interest, amusement, and wholesome exertion'.[80] Marriage drastically decreased the amount of child care that siblings could provide for their nieces and nephews, but widowhood, as it did for Elizabeth Sharp Prowse and others, could return them to the pool of potential caregivers.[81] The employment of siblings as surrogate parents began very early in life in some families. For example, the young Ann Jemima Sharp travelled with her aunt Judith, or, as one sister put it, 'under Sister Juds care', throughout her childhood. And her cousin Jack travelled alone with his aunt Frances when he was three.[82] This type of parenting practice can be difficult to fathom in a culture that idolizes the bond between infants and their biological parents, especially mothers, but in eighteenth-century England it was not uncommon. Aunts and uncles watched over infant nieces and nephews, took them to physicians to be inoculated against smallpox (and kept careful track of the progression of any symptoms), funded or provided training, monitored their development often just as studiously as their parents, and left them bequests in wills. Often, especially in lower economic classes, elder children acted as nurses and schoolteachers, and the employment of one's younger siblings was not unusual.[83] In 151 will abstracts for Cornwall covering the years 1608–1847, the giving of goods, money, and land to nieces and nephews, and making siblings guardians for nieces and nephews, were common to gentlemen, shoemakers, yeomen, and even one 'holemaker'.[84] What is remarkable about the sample is that over a third of the testators also had children.[85]

Poor Law records also contain references to brothers and sisters providing – grudgingly or willingly – financial support for their siblings' children. The recently widowed soldier Roger Taylor, for example, left his young daughter at the house of his deceased wife's brother in 1768.[86] Brothers could also be bound to care for their siblings' illegitimate children, as the yeoman John Wilkes was for his sister's child, the cordwainer Edward Dummer was for his brother's daughter, and the gardener William Tomlins was for his brother's child.[87] When Amy Wilkes gave birth to an illegitimate son in 1731 the parish turned to a variety of male relatives for agreements to support the child should he ever sink into poverty. This group of bound supporters included her father and brother as well as John Mayo, the man whom Amy Wilkes had married since her child's birth, and Mayo's son from a previous marriage.[88] The brother of the birth father could also be bound to help maintain his illegitimate niece or nephew, as the shoemaker Ephraim Wells was in 1737 when he agreed to be bound to care for the illegitimate child of his brother William.[89]

For those with fewer social and financial resources the competing pressures of sibling economics and parish economics could be very uncomfortable. Between October 1776 and October 1778, the prostitute Elizabeth Faddock wrangled with parish and gaol officials as she repeatedly returned to ply her trade in Cambridge. Eventually she was released, 'her brother appearing and agreeing to take her to London with him where he lives'. How much of this was due to inclination (Elizabeth's brother later named a child after her) and how much was from desperation (why did he not come to help her two years previously?) is not clear.[90] In the early months of 1772 Jane Hide, mentioned previously, a widow pregnant with an illegitimate child, moved into the rented cottage of her brother, Samuel Jones, in Wheatenhurst, Gloucestershire. Samuel was a labourer (and later described as a yeoman) and had already roused parish officials' suspicions by 'receiving inmates at great detriment and nuisance' into his cottage. Parish overseers, not enthused at the prospect of Jane and her child staying, had removed her to Standish on 3 March 1772, but she had 'returned the same day to her brother and she there gave birth to a bastard child'. Later evidence stated that Samuel was guilty of having 'unlawfully lodged Jane Hide widow who remained there from 30 Mar until 20 Apr 1772'.[91]

Caring for their younger siblings and nieces and nephews overlapped with siblings' care of the ill and dying. In April 1764 Elizabeth Leigh and her sister gathered at their brother William's bedside. He had been recovering from smallpox, but had suddenly taken a turn for the worse and lay dying. During his last moments, with his sisters 'weeping by his bedside . . . he talk'd most pathetically to each'. According to Elizabeth his final words were encouraging and affectionate; he promised that he would never forget them and that he hoped that they might 'meet again in a more perfect state'.[92] The scene was so affecting that Elizabeth remembered it throughout her life and remarked on it on the twenty-sixth anniversary of her brother's death. Siblings often gathered during illnesses (where circumstances permitted), and it was not unusual for widowed brothers or sisters to spend their final days with their siblings instead of their children. This type of care required that those involved had the means to provide it. For those at the very bottom of the socio-economic scale it was often impossible. For anyone of even slightly secure financial standing the expectation was that they would care for their own, as the 'poor laboring man' Richard Harrison did for his sister, Mary Vezey, for the fortnight after she fled her abusive husband, two weeks being all he could afford. Richard offered to 'take her home, if he [her husband] would allow me for her Maintenance . . . but he would not take my single Bond, and I could get no Body to be bound with me.'[93] Recourse to parents, aunts, and uncles was of course possible, but as members of this generation died or became infirm, siblings and siblings-in-law turned to one another. Joseph Weyman stayed with his sister, Mary Everett, during his final illness, despite their religious differences and despite his having children who could have housed him. Mary and her yeoman husband, both Presbyterians, may not have agreed with Joseph's legacy to a Church of England parish, but it did not prevent them from housing and caring for Joseph.[94]

On Wednesday 16 December 1767, Anne Travell noted that she and Catherine had travelled to Glympton, Oxfordshire, to stay with Miss Wheates and to join Frances Mary (Fanny), who was already staying there. The following Monday 'Poor Fanny [was] taken ill with a fever'. Dr Parker had been visiting the household regularly, but began to visit, dine, and even spend the night more frequently. That Friday Anne paid Mr Coles, 'my Sisr. Fannys apothocarry', five shillings. Dr Parker 'went away' on 28 December, but Ferdinando and Martha spent the twenty-ninth in Glympton and Ferdinando returned with his friend Mr Whalley on the thirty-first. The family seemed to be gathering for what might be Fanny's last illness. Though Anne's daybook for 1768 does survive, the pages for the first six months are blank. She continued to note the amounts she paid to the apothecary and others for 'Dear Fanny' or 'poor Fanny in her illness' at the back of the 1767 daybook and the opening pages of that for 1768. Though she did not record the date of Fanny's death, she noted in the 1768 daybook finding a mantua maker who charged only 14s for 'Body lining' made up with 'little Silk', presumably for Fanny's burial, and an additional sum of 4s 6d that she spent on a pair of 'Shoes for poor F'.[95] In this mundane way Anne continued the housekeeping details and the physical care of her older sister even as Frances Mary passed from their shared household.

Sibling obligations and material connection did not terminate with death, however. Brothers' and sisters' efforts for their ill and dying siblings often extended to financial and probate obligations lasting months and possibly years beyond the death. Many sisters and brothers witnessed and executed wills, or distributed property of siblings who died intestate, and many siblings temporarily managed business and household affairs for deceased siblings until more permanent arrangements could be made, or else permanently assumed the duties themselves. The Sharp siblings, in addition to their care of their dying brother, James, managed his business affairs during his illness, and after his death they worked with his widow to ensure her continued solvency. As youngest brother Granville wrote to the eldest brother, John, two days before James's death, 'With respect to his affairs in business, however, I can with satisfaction acquaint you that Mr. Barwick [William's father-in-law] & myself spent most part of 3 days last Week in examining the States of his annual accompts for several years back and find that there will be a very handsome balance in favour of my sister & her Daughter.'[96] This administration of business, property, and inheritance done by siblings was at once the performance of a duty to a deceased brother or sister and an extension of the practice of shared household management. Immediately after James's death, Granville wrote to John about their efforts to find James's will because 'most part of my Brother William's Fortune & all the Fortunes of my Sisters & my self are invested in it; so that we have much at stake'.[97] Similarly, with her will Frances Mary Travell contributed to her sisters' continued household and financial stability. In the will she acknowledged that her parents' and grandparents' wills had provided for her brothers, and that her responsibility was to temper that inequality by granting greater portions to Anne (who received £300 compared with her brothers' £100). Simultaneously, she honoured the position of elder siblings as leaders and managers, granting Anne the £300, but not mentioning her two youngest sisters, whose youth, she may have considered, put them under the protection and provision of Anne and the brothers. She also recognized the impact that being single and female could have on financial prosperity when she gave £10 to each of her unmarried aunts and her young niece.[98]

From the cradle to the grave siblings provided physical care, especially for children, the ill, and the dying. Though legal tradition privileged spouses and children, real families needed the work of siblings, married and single.[99] Sisters and brothers 'rushed [to] ... offer comfort and support' at the death of siblings and siblings-in-law.[100] They acted as executors and administrators of their deceased siblings' estates. And they, like John Little, did 'Desier for my to Brothers to com to my buriell'.[101] Their work in determining money owed to the estate, debts owed to creditors, and the whereabouts of items and money given to beneficiaries was often recognized with a gift of household items or money. Any household items would then be incorporated into the surviving siblings' homes as visual reminders of the deceased: reminders that required maintenance and management in the new household.

Social and financial credit

In addition to involving physical care, sibling economics were based on a world of reciprocal social and financial labour. This labour could manifest itself as educational and occupational help, marriage and courtship advice, and financial support and counsel. Single sisters might care for their nieces and nephews in exchange for free room and board from their married siblings. Siblings, even groups made up only of sisters, might invest together in expanding capitalist markets.[102] Brothers with fewer monetary resources might receive allowances from more prosperous siblings in exchange for help in their trade, or in performing errands or balancing the books. Brothers like Tom Rumney might engage for months or years in writing to relatives, counselling about careers, and lending money to brothers (or sisters) whose financial acumen was less astute than theirs. In exchange they might, like him, ask a sibling to mediate in difficult relations with a parent.[103] While the tasks could vary depending on the sibling's gender, marital status, and position in the family, the real value of sibling economics rested in the built-in expectation of exchange and reciprocity, not in the task itself. 'Work of various kinds flourished here very much', Anne once wrote to a friend, and siblings' performance of those various labours was the backbone of sibling relationships and the sinews of family survival.[104] The connection to financial interests and the frequency with which siblings provided for one another physically and financially would make this of obvious interest to brothers and sisters.

Though this is only occasionally referenced in advice and prescriptive literature, in their daily interaction and correspondence siblings of various backgrounds took an intense interest in one another's training and present and future occupational security.[105] Numerous siblings participated in joint literary and scientific endeavours. Siblings supported one another's efforts in poetry, science, medicine, religion, and history. In these and other areas they found themselves writing biographies and editing works on subjects far from their own interests.[106] Siblings also worked together in a variety of occupations, some even committing crimes together.[107] One brother and sister referred to their literary collaboration as their mutual 'offspring'.[108] The eighteenth and nineteenth centuries produced a bevy of famous literary siblings: the Fieldings, the Sheridans, the Lambs, the Wordsworths, and later the

Brontës. While it is possible that there were some financial motivations for these efforts, it is more likely that supporting a sibling in his or her occupation was a way of performing a duty to defend one's siblings, a method of expressing love and affection, a contribution to the family's honour, and a confirmation of one's own status as an intimate of such a successful or insightful person – a way of building a sense of self by sharing.

Previous histories have described the difference between men's and women's educational prospects as a 'wedge' between them.[109] Siblings' involvement in one another's occupational and educational successes meant that the 'wedge' between their experiences did not automatically create a distant or discordant relationship. Assuredly, jealousy and rivalry over differing educational and occupational possibilities existed, and the occupational advice given to brothers and sisters often did differ. However, for most people their own financial stability was often so inextricably linked to that of their siblings that the jealousy had to be subsumed in order to ensure the survival of the family. Brothers were counselled in their efforts at formal education and in the professions. Brothers conducted joint teaching duties or worked at the same school, and brothers and sisters organized and ran schools together.[110] Sisters encouraged each other's learning (though usually in a less formal setting) and in 'housewifery arts' that would prepare them for the occupations or duties of wife, mother, and housekeeper.[111] Brothers, in addition to encouraging one another's educational pursuits, often used their influence with others to provide apprenticeships, or to obtain posts and promotions for their siblings, as Richard Rose Haines's shoemaker brother did in 1757.[112] After their father's death, Thomas Oliver's elder brother paid for his apprenticeship to a shoemaker in his native Berkshire, even if he was of 'such a roving Temper that he could not follow it for himself'.[113] Twenty-year-old Matthew Lee from Lincolnshire learned to read and write at school, was apprenticed at eleven to a shoemaker, and, when his time was completed, went to London 'upon the Invitations of a Brother'. Discovering upon his arrival that he did not have appropriate skills for urban shoemaking, he 'had Recourse to his Brother and other Friends, and laid before them his unhappy Situation'.[114]

Siblings' involvement with one another's education and training overlapped with their occupational support. This could be as simple as providing the training of a sibling, as it did for John Perrott who was apprenticed to his half-brother in Hempsted, Hertfordshire.[115] It could also encompass more indirect support. Sisters could be called upon to help in shopkeeping and trade families, or they could dispense 'shrewd advice', as Edward Barlow's servant sister did when he encountered employment difficulties in London.[116] Sisters may not have had professional connections, but they did have social connections that they could employ to improve the position of a brother. Joseph Jackson wrote his brother Nicholas in 1742, 'I am sorry no measures are thought of for promoting my Bro[ther] Will. I was thinking to write to my Sist[e]r Molly', thus incorporating both a brother and a sister in efforts to promote another brother's occupational outlook.[117] The Leigh siblings engaged in a long letter-writing campaign on behalf of their brother, William, to have his appointment to a living renewed. Years previously, William had suffered from a fever that nearly killed him and damaged his health and mental abilities, and when he recovered his brother James went to work to have him reinstated in his previous post.

The Sharp siblings were especially good at occupational support. They exchanged news of James's latest inventions (often related to wagons and carriage wheels) and Granville's speeches, and they approved of how their sisters and sisters-in-law managed households. They seemed especially fond of exchanging news of Granville's work and successes. Because he was the youngest brother, his elder brothers had been intimately connected with his education and occupation from the beginning. As the only bachelor brother, and as one engaged in noble, but unpaid, philanthrophic work, he depended upon his siblings for room and board. His siblings were therefore able to witness his efforts and his ambitions, including his anti-slavery work.[118] He informed his siblings of his publications, and they in return bought copies, offered editorial comments, and generally tracked his career. In turn, Granville kept his brothers' London accounts, and after the death of his brother James in 1783, he helped his widowed sister-in-law manage James's business. Though Granville received the most attention, the success of other brothers was not ignored. Elizabeth made careful mention in her diary of James's inventions and of Thomas's and John's success in the church. William's career as a surgeon to the King received fewer remarks in Elizabeth's record, but someone in the family took the time to preserve a sketch that William made of a kidney stone he had removed, as a memento of his professional life.[119]

Though such educational and occupational assistance went unmentioned in popular literature, this literature overflowed with stories of siblings' involvement in romance and marriage. While 'neither the number of siblings of the same sex within a family, nor the rank of individuals within the sibling set appears to have had a significant influence upon the timing of marriage', they could definitely influence the choice of marriage partner.[120] Siblings were among the 'host of intermediaries' between couples, kin, and neighbours who negotiated marriage in early modern England.[121] While their presence has been noted, the impact they had on courtship and child–parent relations is rarely considered.[122] The tension between romantic expectations and practical realities was played out repeatedly in print, on stage, and in families. In novels and plays the bulk of sibling plots revolved around either inheritance issues or marriage.[123] Few siblings could match the drama found in fictional accounts of sibling involvement in marriage and courtship. In *The Brother* of 1771, for example, a battle between the siblings Cecilia and Richard Wentworth over one another's marriage interests leads to insanity, suicide, death, and crushing regret.[124] While real siblings' lives consisted of a much more mundane mix of daily activities and decisions, they also often and consistently discussed one another's marriage prospects. References to one's siblings-in-law by the titles 'brother' and 'sister' were not just pleasantries. Marriage was difficult, if not nearly impossible, to dissolve, thus not only providing an individual with a lifelong spouse, but also giving siblings a lifelong addition. Deciding who was to be allowed into the ranks was no light matter. The potential sibling-in-law needed to match the economic and social status of the family, but of equal importance was her or his ability to blend with the existing family dynamic.

Marriage and courtship also cemented financial and emotional ties between sibling sets. Because 'early death robbed many parents of the opportunity to arrange their children's future', siblings were the closest kin and the logical choice for building 'multilateral consent'.[125] The marriage of Edward Witts and Agnes Travell in 1775 solidified the connections between their families. The families had been associated since youth, and in 1773 Alicia Witts had moved to Cheltenham, near the house shared by the Travell sisters. Just as Apphia's marriage to Lord Lyttelton was disintegrating, Anne Travell included her in the business of ensuring that Edward's suit of Agnes was smooth. In a 1773 letter to Apphia, Anne wrote that she and her sisters 'were in hopes that we should have had the pleasure of seeing [Edward] here, before his departure, he being a great favorite with us all'.[126] That same autumn Edward was happy to report to Apphia that 'I find by the death of Baron Tracy, the 3 sisters get £2000 from the Stanway Estate ... which is a lucky increase to their small fortunes'.[127] Agnes's improving financial standing as well as the encouragement of both Travell and Witts siblings eased the couple's courtship.

Similarly, the Wintle and Boughton families were connected by social ties between their parents and by marriage negotiations between the siblings. In June 1783 John Wintle, of a Severn riverman's family, wrote to his sister (who remained unnamed in her diary account of this letter) and requested her help in his courtship of Jane Boughton.[128] He granted his sister 'powers to settle an affair of the greatest moment between him & Miss Boughton'. She willingly exercised her power in this matter: 'I hope all things may turn out to their mutual happiness', she wrote.¹²⁹ The Boughton sisters were regular visitors at the Wintle home, and the Wintle sisters often returned the visits. The day after receiving this letter from her brother, the diarist made a visit to the Boughtons (her sister Ann was already there to spend the night with Betsy Boughton): The diarist wrote, 'I went there in the evening and opened the matter to Mr. J[oh]n Boughton relating to my brother J[oh]n & Miss Jane.' She continued by relating how the negotiations went: 'he seemed very agreeable to it'.¹³⁰ The writer's parents figured prominently in her description of everyday social and family affairs, but she offered no explanation of why she, rather than their parents, negotiated marriage for her brother. In fact, in that same diary entry she mentioned that her parents had gone to tea elsewhere that evening. She was the first emissary to explore the receptiveness of Jane and her family. Once it was discovered that John's proposal would be well received their parents were called in, and the next day the Wintle parents went to discuss the matter with Jane Boughton's mother. Unfortunately the diary ends before any mention is made of the wedding, but asking for his sister's intervention was an effective courtship ploy by John Wintle; he married Jane Boughton on 6 February 1787 in Westbury-on-Severn, and among the witnesses was his sister Ann.¹²¹

Mary Abbott has remarked that 'men whose fathers were dead and who, therefore, negotiated as free agents on their own account – and there were many of them – generally submitted to the customary constraints'.¹³² Those customary restraints, for both men and women, were often in the control of their siblings. When John Sharp married Mary Dering in 1752 both sets of siblings were involved in the complex management of inheritance and financial stipulations in the marriage settlement.¹³³ When Thomas Sharp married Catherine Pawson in 1770 his elder brother John took the place of their deceased father as a principal party of the marriage settlement.¹³⁴ It was not only in large matters of inheritance and marriage settlements that siblings figured prominently in the planning of marriages. When Elizabeth Sharp married in 1762 her brother William gave her away. Her eldest brother, John (who would become Archdeacon of Northumberland), performed the ceremony, and all her siblings were in attendance. The Sharps' sharing of support in courtship and marriage is echoed in Ellen Weeton's seeking her brother's opinion of the man she proposed to marry, in George Cumberland's constant reporting of his love interests to his brother Richard, and in Thomas Rumney, who counselled his brother about courtship and used his sisters as a frame of reference for his own love interests.¹³⁵

Siblings could also become the buffer between child–parent conflicts over courtship and marriage, as Tom Weeton was for his sister, as Elizabeth Parker was for her brother, and as Thomas Edwards was for his brother. Other relations thought it was Elizabeth Parker's 'power... to prevail with [her] dear papa' that allowed her brother to marry the woman of his choice.[136] For Walter Edwards, it was his friendly and supportive relationship with his brother Thomas that made him call upon his services. In a letter dated 23 January 1747, Walter referred to their relationship as one of 'harmony', referring to his brother as a 'dearest friend'.[137] That affection allowed Walter to make heavy demands on Thomas. Walter had fallen in love with and determined to marry a girl whom his father, for whatever reason, found unsuitable. Over a period of months in 1747 Walter and Thomas corresponded regularly about Walter's romance and what Thomas could do to smooth relations with their father. Walter the younger asked Thomas to mediate between him and their father in order to soften his attitude. In February 1747 Thomas wrote from Oxford: 'I was very much concern'd to hear by yr last, that yr Affairs continued still in so disagreeable state... It was a great Pleasure to me to find, that my Advice was as kindly taken, as it was meant: But wou'd be a much greater, was it to be of the Service Intended.'[138] Thomas see-sawed between elation that things had resolved themselves (as he assumed at the end of the February) and despair that all was not well in March. He again repeated that there would be no complete reconciliation until Walter was willing to make small concessions. Saddened to discover that far from being resolved, things had become worse, he asked leave to give his real opinion, 'without any view, I do assure you to, my own Affairs'. The disagreement between Walter and his father continued in the summer of 1747, and had Walter not died that June, it undoubtedly would have continued further. Despite generally good relations between the father and the sons, the marriage crisis put Thomas in the difficult situation of trying to negotiate between his father and brother – his 'nearest Relations & best Friends'.[139] Walter expected Thomas's advice and desperately wanted him to solve the problem. Marriage and courtship often demanded sibling attention, and when they involved negotiation with parents they required even more intense sibling labour.

From the smallest amount spent on ribbons to commissions to buy a piano and provision for inheritance of property, siblings fulfilled a variety of financial and material functions.[140] These were constituted of small, incremental assistance throughout life and large bequests, legacies, and gifts usually stipulated in a will. For siblings who lacked the means to support themselves because of their age, illness, or lack of education or training, and whose parents were deceased or unable to help, siblings were the first, and potentially longest-lasting, source of financial assistance. One's sibling's lack of income could spell disaster for oneself. The Wittses' bankruptcy, for example, affected relations in the Travell family. The bankruptcy put Agnes and Edward Witts at Ferdinando's mercy; they were dependent on him not only for the restoration of their financial health, but also for their social standing. The smallest indication that Ferdinando was disappointed greatly troubled Agnes, not because of money alone, but because her character and, more importantly in this context, the character of her husband were also at stake. While financial transactions were negotiated with Ferdinando, it was Anne who mediated the familial capital with Agnes and between Agnes and Ferdinando. Francis was excluded from the nuts and bolts of these transactions because he lacked both the financial, familial, and social capital to be of any use. And Catherine, whatever her role, was subsumed into Anne's sphere. Anne's and Ferdinando's positions of influence in this situation were reinforced by the domestic capital they both possessed: at the time they were the only two siblings who were managing their own households well enough to have the capacity to aid others. Simultaneously they employed their familial and social capital to buttress Francis's flagging standing, to support the Wittses in financial crisis, and to build for the future generation embodied in Ferdinando's daughters and Agnes's sons.

Financial support, like every other aspect of sibling relationships, was based on a give-and-take cycle. This was clear to at least one executor. John Tracy (the Travell siblings' uncle) had carefully administered his brother Thomas's will and estate after his death. John wanted his brother's wealthy widow to express her gratitude financially for his services on her behalf: 'There is certainly nothing more obvious than Brothers owing to each other reciprocal services according to their particular circumstances – one Brother has formed an advantageous Connection by Marriage and is in affluence whilst the other has a Possession only for his support.'[141] Like John Tracy and the brothers of Morse Hobbs (discussed previously), Georgian brothers and sisters determined that one sibling's wealth should be shared among them all, particularly after the wealthy sibling died. Morse Hobbs's case demonstrates a complete breakdown of sibling economics and reveals the severe consequences that this had in the lives of the Hobbses and connected families. The reasoning behind much of the testimony in the case shows the elements of sibling economics discussed above and demonstrates the necessity of sibling contributions to the economic, emotional, and social functioning of the family. According to the logic of sibling economics shared by the various advocates, ecclesiastical authorities, servants, neighbours, and friends, Morse's siblings should have cared for him in his illness, they should have had a pattern of lifelong support to fall back on, and he should have reciprocated this by recognizing their strained financial standing and providing for them.[142]

Conclusion

Anne Travell's single status highlights her importance to Travell sibling economics, but her writings also demonstrate the interconnectedness of married and single siblings of both sexes. 'Tranquility', that 'daughter of regularity', drove and sustained Anne as she wrote her daybook and managed the household.[143] Anne clearly had a 'comprehensive outline of order' that, if Hannah More is correct, gave her 'the best regulated mind' and therefore 'the best regulated family'.[144] Sibling economics, the emotional and physical labour exchanged between brothers and sisters, flowed in, through, and from households – both real and fictive – and took a variety of forms. Siblings, like early modern kinship more broadly, 'involved a range of possibilities ... acknowledgement, advice and support, stretched to financial help and career encouragement, and also included emotional comfort and political solidarity'.[145] As David Cressy has noted, '[w]hat mattered was not how far apart you lived or how often you saw each other, but what the relationship was worth when it came to the crunch.'[146] In the end, sibling relationships were worth a great deal. Georgian sibling economics were positioned in a distinctive moment – one that rhetorically privileged the equality and friendship of siblings and yet persisted in ranking them by gender and age, and simultaneously placed heavy physical and emotional demands upon them.

Sibling economics also highlight the unpaid yet necessary tasks performed by brothers and sisters: child care, nursing, account keeping, and marital advice. These were not regarded as exchanges of special gifts; they were manifestations of the easy, natural affection expected of sisters and brothers. Sibling economics show the outward manifestations of friendship and/or rivalry between siblings. Willing compliance with expectations could be an expression of love and would further cement good relations. The refusal to perform family duties, or performing them poorly, could erode sibling ties and even make them dangerously explosive. Whether sharing physical, financial, social, or emotional care, siblings were embedded in other's lives. Yet the injunction to 'share and share alike' one another's lives was only half the story. In the process of negotiating sibling economics sisters and brothers had to navigate a complicated system of sibling politics.

Notes

1 Johnson, *A Journey to the Western Islands of Scotland*; Anne Travell, commonplace and recipe book, c.1780s, GA, D4582/4/18.

2 Anne Travell, daybook, week of 13–19 February 1764, GA, D4582/4/17/1.
3 Anne Travell, daybook, 25 January 1764, GA, D4582/4/17/1.
4 Anne Travell, daybook, 1767, opening quotations from literature, GA, D4582/4/17/3.
5 Anne Travell, daybook, 16 November 1767, GA, D4582/4/17/3.
6 Vickery, *Behind Closed Doors*, p. 188.
7 Anne Travell, daybook, 16 July 1764, GA, D4582/4/17/1.
8 Anne Travell, daybook, 27 July 1764, GA, D4582/4/17/1.
9 Anne Travell, daybook, 9 August 1764, GA, D4582/4/17/1 map of Cheltenham, eighteenth century, GA, map collection.
10 Gwen Hart, *A History of Cheltenham* (Leicester, 1965), p. 127.
11 Vickery, *Behind Closed Doors*, p. 22.
12 Anne Travell, daybook, 1767, GA, D4582/4/17/3.
13 Anne Travell, daybook, 28–9 October 1764, GA, D4582/4/17/1.
14 Gillis, *For Better, for Worse*, p. 75.
15 Ibid., p. 81; Vickery, *Behind Closed Doors*, pp. 6–7, 24, 88.
16 Laslett, *Family Life and Illicit Love*, p. 96; Tadmor, *Family and Friends*, pp. 18–166.
17 These patterns are visible in other homes headed by unmarried sisters. Thomas Hughes, diary, 1763, 1769, GA, D245/IV/20/1–2; Vickery, *The Gentleman's Daughter*, pp. 127–60; Vickery, *Behind Closed Doors*, pp. 22–3, 190–213; Ingrid Tague, *Women of Quality: Accepting and Contesting Ideals of Femininity in England, 1690–1760* (Woodbridge, Suffolk, and Rochester, NY, 2002).
18 Co-resident siblings constituted an important type of household in early modern and nineteenth-century England. Tosh, *A Man's Place*, p. 21; Crawford, *Blood, Bodies and Families in Early Modern England*, pp. 219–20; Laslett, *Family Life and Illicit Love*, p. 96; Richard Wall et al., eds., *Family Forms in Historic Europe* (Cambridge, 1983), p. 500.
19 OBP, 10 May 1722, trial of John Hawkins and George Simpson (t17220510-3).
20 OBP, 16 January 1730, trial of Katherine Pember (t17300116-8).
21 Craig Muldrew, *The Economy of Obligation: The Culture of Credit and Social Relations in Early Modern England* (New York, 1998), p. 158; Tadmor, *Family and Friends*, p. 278.
22 Court baron of 24 December 1774, in James Hodsdon, ed., *The Court Books of the Manor of Cheltenham, 1692–1803* (Bristol, 2010), p. 2795; Anne Travell, tax assessment, Cheltenham, 1818, GA, D4582/4/19; Frances Mary Travell, will, written 31 August 1764 proved 26 January 1768, Prerogative Court of Canterbury, GA, D495/F6; Jane Travell, will, written 5 November 1767, proved 1 December 1767, Prerogative Court of Canterbury, TNA, PROB 11/934; William Travell, will, written 24 November 1770, proved 6 February 1775, Prerogative Court of Canterbury, GA, D495/F6; Edward Witts, Chipping Norton, Oxfordshire, to Apphia, Lady Lyttelton, Buxton Hall, Derbyshire, 17 September 1773, WFP, F255.

23 Anne Travell, daybook, 1769, GA, D4582/4/17/5.
24 Anne Travell, daybook, 1788, GA, D4582/4/17/12.
25 Anne Travell, daybook, 1801, GA, D4582/4/17/15.
26 Muldrew, *The Economy of Obligation*, pp. 148–57; Vickery, *The Gentleman's Daughter*, pp. 127–60.
27 Most likely extracted from Stéphanie Félicité Comtesse de Genlis, *Tales of the Castle: or, Stories of Instruction and Delight* (London, 1785), p. 138, BL, 12623. df.1; Anne Travell, commonplace and recipe book, c.1780s, GA, D4582/4/18.
28 Though the participation of siblings is not specifically analysed, recent scholarship has done much to reveal daily economic encounters in early modern and Georgian England. David Cheal, *The Gift Economy* (London and New York, 1988); Muldrew, *The Economy of Obligation*; Margot Finn, *The Character of Credit: Personal Debt in English Culture, 1740–1914* (Cambridge, 2003); Ilana Krausman Ben-Amos, *The Culture of Giving: Informal Support and Gift-Exchange in Early Modern England* (Cambridge, 2008).
29 R. Schwartz and V. Finucci, 'Worlds Within and Without', in V. Finucci and R. Schwartz, eds., *Desire in the Renaissance: Psychoanalysis and Literature* (Princeton, 1994), p. 5, quoted in Susan Broomhall, 'Emotions in the Household', in Susan Broomhall, ed., *Emotions in the Household* (Basingstoke: Palgrave Macmillan, 2008) p. 1.
30 Keith Wrightson, *Earthly Necessities: Economic Lives in Early Modern Britain* (New Haven, 2000), p. 296.
31 Gillis, *For Better, for Worse*, p. 74; Vickery, *Behind Closed Doors*, pp. 22–3.
32 Finn, *The Character of Credit*, p. 2. Women's contribution to eighteenth-century economics was particularly ignored by their contemporaries; see Beverly Lemire, *The Business of Everyday Life: Gender, Practice and Social Politics in England, c.1600–1900* (Manchester and New York, 2005), p. 206; Vickery, *The Gentleman's Daughter*, pp. 127–60. The connection between the social and financial credit of households had medieval roots and persisted into the nineteenth century; see Richard Britnell, 'Markets, Shops, Inns, Taverns and Private Houses in Medieval English Trade', in Bruno Blondé et al., eds., *Buyers and Sellers: Retail Circuits and Practices in Medieval and Early Modern Europe*, Studies in European Urban History 9 (Turnhout, Belgium, 2006), pp. 109–23; Rebecca Stern, *Home Economics: Domestic Fraud in Victorian England* (Columbus, 2008).
33 Broomhall, 'Emotions in the Household', p. 17.
34 Froide, *Never Married*, pp. 44–86; Ottoway, *The Decline of Life*, pp. 141–72.
35 Hindle, *On the Parish?*; Crawford, *Parents of Poor Children*.
36 Charles Cook, settlement examination no. 3, Duntisbourne Abbots, Gloucestershire, GA, P122 OV 3/4.
37 OBP, *Ordinary of Newgate's Account*, 23 March 1752 (OA17520323); 6 December 1797, trial of William Murrell (t17971206-51).
38 Thomas King v. Samuel Jones, settlement brief, Whitminster, Gloucestershire, 3 March 1772, GA, P362 OV 3(v).

39 Robert Jackson to his siblings at Sneyd Park, Gloucestershire, 1743–63; Nicholas Jackson the younger to his siblings at Sneyd Park, Gloucestershire, 1752–61, GA, D153.
40 Black, ed., *The Cumberland Letters*, 28, 94.
41 Anne Travell, daybook, 1764, GA D4582/4/17/1; William Hawkes, ed., *The Diaries of Sanderson Miller of Radway Together with his Memoir of James Menteath* ([Stratford-upon-Avon], 2005), pp. 186–7.
42 Bridget Hill, *Servants: English Domestics in the Eighteenth Century* (Oxford, 1996), p. 48.
43 William Gaze, testamentary cause, October–November 1785, GA, GDR B4/2/G25; William Mason, administration, 7 August 1733, GA, GDR Wills 1733/168; William Mason, testamentary cause, 1734–35, GA, GDR B4/2/M37; Thomas Goscombe, testamentary cause, December 1757, GA, GDR B4/2/G41. See also Robert Giles, testamentary cause, February 1739, GA, GDR B4/2/G28; William Hope, testamentary cause, April 1734, GA, GDR B4/2/H139.
44 Hill, *Servants*, p. 176.
45 Ibid., pp. 186–7.
46 The abstracts cover principally Derbyshire and Cornwall and range from the middle of the seventeenth century until the shift to civil control in 1858. See http://freepages.genealogy.rootsweb.ancestry.com/~sterth/will_index.htm; http://webs.lanset.com/azazella/willscor_pen.html; www.genuki.org.uk/big/eng/DBY/ProbateRecords/index.html; www.genuki.org.uk/big/eng/CUL/ProbateRecords/index.html; and http://wills4all.netfirms.com/cambridge.htm (accessed January–April 2009). My thanks to Debbie Gurtler, Dan McKendrick, and Cassie Lloyd, who helped gather this information.
47 The sample contained 3,009 will abstracts (of 2,484 testators, 525 testatrixes). Siblings were listed as heirs and/or executors or executrices in 889 of the wills (729 men's wills and 160 women's). These formed 29.35 per cent of the men's will abstracts, 30.47 per cent of the women's, and 29.54 per cent of the total.
48 Thomas Edwards, Oxford, to Walter Edwards, London, 27 February 1747, GA, D2002/13/4.
49 OBP, 4 April 1733, trial of Thomas Baker (t17330404-45). The trial dissolved into a dispute about whether Thomas Baker's mother or Ralph Trumper's sister had the made cap that Trumper accused Baker of stealing.
50 Hill, *Servants*, pp. 116–17, 120, 122–5; Thomas Sharp London, to Elizabeth Sharp, 26 April 1750, GA, D3549/14/1/3.
51 Thomas Sharp, London, to Elizabeth Sharp, 26 April 1750, GA, D3549/14/1/3.
52 Vickery, *The Gentleman's Daughter*, pp. 128, 140–1, 160.
53 Elizabeth Sharp Prowse, diary and commonplace book, GA, D3549/14/1/1 (p. 16), 1751.
54 OBP, 22 June 1796, trial of Joseph Rogers, Frances Wheeler, and Ann Horn (t17970622-51); 15 January 1720, trial of Jane Griffin (t17200115-35).

55 Dorothy Punter v. Robert Punter, matrimonial cause, Gloucester Consistory Court, 1711, GA, GDR B4/1/1263.
56 Hill, *Women Alone*, pp. 67–80; Vickery, *Behind Closed Doors*, pp. 24, 188–212.
57 Agnes Travell Witts, diary, 29 August 1794, WFP, F187.
58 Broomhall, ed., *Emotions in the Household*, pp. 1–37.
59 A.W. Rumney, ed., *Tom Rumney of Mellfell* (Kendal, 1936), p. 89.
60 Sarah Drinkwater, nuncupative will, recorded January 1712, proved 3 November 1713, CALS, WS 1713.
61 Anne Travell, daybook, 12 December 1768, GA, D4582/4/17/4.
62 Black, ed., *The Cumberland Letters*, pp. 28–30, 70–2, 114.
63 Anne Travell, daybook, 24 February–12 March 1783, GA, D4582/4/17/7.
64 Verey, ed., *The Diary of a Cotswold Parson*, p. 45.
65 Anne Travell, daybook, 24 February–12 March 1783, GA, D4582/4/17/7. For another example of sisters' attention to the birth and breastfeeding of nieces and nephews see Stella Tillyard, *Aristocrats: Caroline, Emily, Louisa, and Sarah Lennox, 1740–1832* (New York, 1994), pp. xvii–xviii.
66 Wrightson, *Earthly Necessities*, p. 85; Ben-Amos, *Adolescence and Youth*, pp. 165–70.
67 Perry, *Novel Relations*, pp. 109, 336–71; *A Precious Testimony for Jesus, in the Experience of Two Children*, 5th edn (London, 1793), BL, 4903.ccc.6.
68 Wrightson, *Earthly Necessities*, p. 66; Ben-Amos, *The Culture of Giving*, pp. 15–44. Wrightson and Ben-Amos mention siblings in passing, but do not consider the specific parameters of sibling involvement.
69 Elizabeth Sharp Prowse, diary and memorandum book, 15 November 1762, GA, D3549/14/1/1.
70 Elizabeth Sharp Prowse, diary and memorandum book, 19 April 1778, GA, D3549/14/1/1.
71 Ben-Amos, *Adolescence and Youth*, pp. 61–8, 100, 124–6, 159, 179, 223–4, 284, 285.
72 Ibid., p. 33.
73 Granville Sharp, London, to John Sharp, 18 October 1777, GA, D3549/9/1/4.
74 Thomas Sharp Sr., London, to his daughter Elizabeth Sharp, 26 April 1750, GA, D3549/14/1/3.
75 Richard Rose Haines, settlement examination no. 38, Blockley, Gloucestershire, 1 November 1757, GA, P52 OV 3/4/1.
76 Leonard Williams, settlement examination, Awre, Gloucestershire, 1806, GA, P30 OV 3/4.
77 Broome Witts, Nibley House, to Anne Travell, Cheltenham, 27 July 1800, GA, D4582/4/9.
78 Helen Berry and Elizabeth Foyster, 'Childless Men in Early Modern England', in Helen Berry and Elizabeth Foyster, eds., *The Family in Early Modern England* (Cambridge, 2007), pp. 158–83; Perry, *Novel Relations*, p. 109; Davidoff and Hall, *Family Fortunes*, pp. 339–42, 347.

79 Marilyn Yalom, *A History of the Wife* (New York: Harper Collins, 2001), pp. 172–4; Davidoff and Hall, *Family Fortunes*, pp. 321–56; Vickery, *The Gentleman's Daughter*, pp. 92, 286.
80 Jane Austen, *Persuasion*, chapter 6.
81 Erickson, *Women and Property*, pp. 204–22. Elizabeth Sharp Prowse, diary and memorandum book, 23 December 1777, August 1780, October 1780, 17 October 1793, GA, 3549/14/1/1.
82 Elizabeth Prowse Sharp, diary and memorandum book, 8 February 1765, 15 April 1768, 6 May 1768, GA, D3549/14/1/1.
83 Gillis, *Youth and History*, pp. 13–18; Ben-Amos, *Adolescence and Youth*, pp. 42–3, 124–5, 149, 160.
84 Taken from 2,853 abstracts of wills and administrations for Cornwall (1602–1859) from http://freepages.genealogy.rootsweb.ancestry.com/~sterth/will_index.htm and http://webs.lanset.com/azazella/willscor_pen.html (accessed January–April 2009). See also the examples of John Clarke (1634) and Anne Sparke (1632), who both provided financial support and funded training and education for their nieces and nephews, in Jane Whittle, 'Servants in Rural England c.1450–1650: Hired Work as a Means of Accumulating Wealth and Skills before Marriage', in Maria Ågren and Amy Louise Erickson, eds., *The Marital Economy in Scandinavia and Britain, 1400–1900* (Aldershot, Hampshire, 2005), p. 100.
85 In wills naming nieces and nephews as beneficiaries 38.5 per cent also mentioned children. The absence of mentions of children in the other 61.5 per cent does not necessarily mean that those testators did not have children. See Arkell, Evans, and Goose, eds., *When Death Do Us Part*, p. 196; Ben-Amos, *Culture of Giving*, p. 49; www.genuki.org.uk/big/eng/BRKwills/datix4.html; http://freepages.genealogy.rootsweb.ancestry.com/~sterth/will_index.htm; and http://webs.lanset.com/azazella/willscor_pen.html (accessed January–April 2009).
86 St Mary de Crypt, Gloucester, vestry account book, Overseers of the Poor Records, 1768, GA, P154/11 OV 2/3.
87 Amy Wilkes, bastardy bond, Cheltenham Overseers of the Poor, 15 September 1731, GA, P78 OV 5/2; Anthony Drummer, bastardy bond, Cheltenham Overseers of the Poor, 9 January 1758, GA, P78 OV 5/2; Samuel Tomlins, bastardy bond, Chipping Campden Overseers of the Poor, 27 June 1737, GA, P81 OV5.
88 Amy Wilkes, bastardy bond, Cheltenham Overseers of the Poor, 15 September 1731, GA, P78 OV 5/2. For another example of the mother's brother being bound see Sarah Harrison, bastardy bond, North Nibley Overseers of the Poor, bastardy papers, 1685/86, GA, P230 OV 5/1.
89 Mary Page and William Wells, bastardy bond, Cheltenham Overseers of the Poor, 5 April 1737, GA, P78 OV 5/2. For other examples of the father's brother being bound see Catherine Smith and Anthony Drummer, bastardy bond, Cheltenham Overseers of the Poor, 9 January 1758, GA, P78 OV 5/2; Elizabeth Harbet and Richard Maysey, indemnity bond, South Cerney Overseers of the

Poor, 1740/1, GA, P71 OV 5/5–6; Elizabeth Vizard and Anthony Tuck, bastardy bond, Tetbury Overseers of the Poor, c.1826, GA, P328a OV 5/9; Anny Smyth and William Romin, bastardy bond, Hawkesbury Overseers of the Poor, 3 December 1744, GA, P170 OV 5/1. For a discussion of provisions for illegitimate children in wills see Davidoff and Hall, *Family Fortunes*, p. 321.
90 Michael J. Burchall, 'A Cambridge Woman of the Town in the Late 18th Century: The Career of Elizabeth Faddock', *Genealogists' Magazine*, 29:8 (December 2008), 299–302.
91 Thomas King v. Samuel Jones, settlement brief, Whitminster, Gloucestershire, 3 March 1772, GA, P362 OV 3(v). It is unclear why the parish officials were so concerned about where Jane Hide had her child or whether they knew they might be in violation of the law. Since 1733 parishes had been forbidden to remove pregnant women or women who had recently given birth. Because previous Poor Law statutes had granted illegitimate children settlement in the parish of their birth, parish officials had often tried to remove single pregnant women who they suspected might need poor relief in the future. A 1744 statute, however, granted illegitimate children settlement in their mother's parish, no matter where they were born.
92 Elizabeth Leigh, diary, 2 April 1790, Leigh Family of Adlestrop, Gloucestershire, SBTRO, DR 671/79.
93 OBP, 14 January 1732, trial of Corbet Vezey (t17320114-12).
94 Joseph Weyman or Wyman, testamentary cause, 1730–32, GA, GDR B4/2 E26 and W171.
95 Anne Travell, daybook, 1767, 1768, GA, D4582/17/3–4.
96 Granville Sharp, London, to John Sharp, 3 November 1783, GA, D3549/9/1/4.
97 Granville Sharp, Old Jewry, to John Sharp, 6 November 1783, GA, D3549/9/1/4.
98 Erickson, *Women and Property*, p. 215.
99 'Wills at the Family Records Centre, Part Two: Estate Duty Office (Death Duty) Registers', *Family Tree Magazine*, 17 (October 2001), 19–20.
100 Vickery, *The Gentleman's Daughter*, p. 88.
101 John Little, will, written 1777, proved 2 May 1778, GA, GDR Wills 1778/60; John Little, testamentary cause, GA, GDR B4/2/L49.
102 Anne Laurence, 'Lady Betty Hastings, her Half-Sisters, and the South Sea Bubble: Family Fortunes and Strategies', *Women's History Review*, 15:4 (2006), 533–40.
103 Rumney, ed., *Tom Rumney of Mellfell*, pp. 72, 83–4, 86–90.
104 Anne Travell, Upper Slaughter, Gloucestershire, letter to Apphia Lyttelton, 23 May 1773, WFP, F256.
105 For a seventeenth-century example see Ben-Amos, *Adolescence and Youth*, p. 153.
106 A partial sampling includes: Arthur William Costigan, *Sketches of Society and Manners in Portugal*, 2 vols. (London, [1787]), BL, 1048.k.23; James Gough, *Memoirs of the Life, Religious Experiences, and Labours in the Gospel, of James*

Gough (Dublin, 1781), BL, 1373.b.20; Martha Giffard, ed., *The Works of Sir William Temple* (London, 1750), BL, 91.g.1.

107 I. Wyatt, 'The Cock Road Gang', *Gloucestershire Historical Studies*, 4 (1970), 37. See also *Gloucester Journal*, August 1731, GA, newspaper collection.

108 *United Efforts: A Collection of Poems, the Mutual Offspring of a Brother and Sister* (London and Dover, 1831), BL, 11650.b.64. For a seventeenth-century example see Judith Spicksley, ' "Fly with a duck in thy mouth' : Single Women as Sources of Credit in Seventeenth-Century England', *Social History*, 32:2 (May 2007), 202.

109 Abbott, *Life Cycles in England*, p. 53.

110 Hans, *New Trends in Education*, pp. 70, 75, 96, 122–3, 126, 152, 230.

111 J. Edwards, Berne, to his sister, 23 August 1713, GA, D2002/17/1.

112 Richard Rose Haines, settlement examination no. 38, Blockley, Gloucestershire, 1 November 1757, GA, P52 OV 3/4/1.

113 OBP, *Ordinary of Newgate's Account*, 8 March 1738 (OA17380308).

114 OBP, *Ordinary of Newgate's Account*, 11 October 1752 (OA17521011).

115 OBP, *Ordinary of Newgate's Account*, 11 November 1761 (OA17611111).

116 Ben-Amos, *Adolescence and Youth*, pp. 148–9, 153.

117 Joseph Jackson, Overbury, Worcestershire, to Nicholas Jackson, Sneyd Park, 23 March 1742, GA, D153/59.

118 Elizabeth Sharp Prowse, diary and memorandum book, GA, D3549/14/1/1.

119 William Sharp, drawing of a kidney stone, GA, D3549/10/1/3.

120 Wrigley, Schofield, et al., eds., *English Population History*, p. 169.

121 Diana O'Hara, *Courtship and Constraint: Rethinking the Making of Marriage in Tudor England* (Manchester and New York, 2002), pp. 3, 30–56, 99–121, 190–235.

122 Cressy, *Birth, Marriage, and Death*, pp. 235, 241–8; Vickery, *Behind Closed Doors*, pp. 65, 67, 78; Grassby, *Kinship and Capitalism*, pp. 42, 66–8.

123 Edward Filmer, *The Unnatural Brother* (London, 1697), BL, 544.e.8; Beaumont and Fletcher, *The Bloody Brother*, p. 6; *The Brothers or, Treachery Punish'd*.

124 *The Brother* (London, 1771).

125 Vickery, *The Gentleman's Daughter*, pp. 41, 55. The term 'Multilateral consent' comes from Martin Ingram, *Church Courts, Sex and Marriage in England, 1570–1640* (Cambridge, 1987), p. 136. Siblings' role in courtship and marriage had old roots in English society. See also Gillis, *For Better, for Worse*, pp. 11–54; Catherine Frances, 'Making Marriages in Early Modern England: Rethinking the Role of Family and Friends', in Ågren and Erickson, eds., *The Marital Economy in Scandinavia and Britain*, pp. 40, 42–6; O'Hara, *Courtship and Constraint*, p. 223; Barbara Hanawalt, *The Ties that Bound: Peasant Families in Medieval England* (Oxford and New York, 1986), p. 198.

126 Anne Travell, Upper Slaughter, Gloucestershire, to Apphia, Lady Lyttelton, 23 May 1773, WFP, F256.

127 Edward Witts, Chipping Norton, Oxfordshire, to Apphia, Lady Lyttelton, Buxton Hall, Derbyshire, 17 September 1773, WFP, F255.
128 Though the sex and name of the diarist are unknown, the style and content (in which socializing with sisters and parents takes precedence over any detailed business discussion) suggest a female writer.
129 Wintle (first name unknown), copy diary, 19 June 1783, transcribed by Miss Palser, Palser Family of Wotton-under-Edge Collection, GA, D1559/Z1.
130 Wintle (unknown), diary, 20 June 1783, GA, D1559/Z1.
131 Westbury-on-Severn, Gloucestershire, Parish Register Transcripts, Forest of Dean Family History, www.forest-of-dean.net, citing original parish registers at GA, P 354 IN 1/5 (accessed June 2011).
132 Abbott, *Life Cycles in England*, p. 55.
133 John Sharp and Mary Dering, marriage settlement, 25 November 1752, GA, D3549/9/1/2.
134 Thomas Sharp and Catherine Pawson, marriage settlement, 1770, GA, D3549/9/1/5.
135 Vickery, *The Gentleman's Daughter*, p. 77; Black, ed., *The Cumberland Letters*, pp. 94, 110, 230, 235; Rumney, ed., *Tom Rumney of Mellfell*, pp. 4–7, 12, 83, 88.
136 Anne Pellet, London, to Elizabeth Parker, Alkincoats, 27 December 1753, quoted in Vickery, *The Gentleman's Daughter*, p. 49.
137 Walter Edwards to Thomas Edwards, 23 January 1747, GA, D2002/13/4.
138 Thomas Edwards, Oxford, to Walter Edwards, London, February 1747, GA, D2002/13/4.
139 Thomas Edwards, Oxford, to Walter Edwards, London, letter undated, GA, D2002/13/4.
140 Claire Walsh, 'The Social Relations of Shopping in Early Modern England', in Blondé et al., eds., *Buyers and Sellers*, pp. 335–51.
141 Thomas and Mary Tracy, property documents, 1750s–1760s, Lawrence Family of Sevenhampton Collection, GA, D444/E6.
142 Morse Hobbs, testamentary cause, 1738–40, GA, GDR B4/2 H123.
143 Pope Clement XIV, *Interesting Letters of the Late Pope Clement XIV (Ganganelli)* (Newcastle, 1777), ECCO, extracted by Anne Travell, commonplace book, c.1780s, GA, D4582/4/18.
144 Hannah More, *Strictures on the Modern System of Female Education*, 2nd edn, vol. 2 (London, 1799), p. 6, GA, R.O.L. N3/Mor.
145 David Cressy, 'Kinship and Kin Interaction in Early Modern England', *Past and Present*, 113:1 (1986), 49.
146 Ibid.

5
Sibling politics

> Priority of age demands some respect. If you refuse to pay it to those who are older than yourselves, how can you expect to receive it from those who are younger! ... Nature has joined you by one common tie. Let, then, no mean or sordid Passion, destroy this domestic friendship.
>
> John Burton, *Lectures on Female Education and Manners*, 1793[1]

> After my ... debts are duly paid ... the Residue of my Estate may be left to those of my Family who have not had so plentiful a Provision as the rest of them have had. Therefore ... I give and bequeath unto my beloved Children ... all the distributive part share and proportion of the Personal Estate of my late dear Husband John Tracy ... and also all other my Goods Chattels Personal Estate ... and whatsoever I shall die possessed of to be equally divided between them share and share alike. Except –
>
> Anne Atkyns Tracy, will, 1740[2]

The Travells' maternal grandmother, Anne Atkyns Tracy, recognized that 'share and share alike' did not mean exact symmetry in the bequests she left, nor in the circumstances in which her heirs found themselves. The children she counted as having 'not so plentiful a Provision' were her youngest five children – four daughters and one son – all them unmarried, despite four of them being over twenty-one. Though she did not state it directly, her bequests demonstrate that she knew that the birth order, gender, and marital status of her children had affected and would continue to affect not only their provision, but their relationships with each other. This was so not just because the property she and her husband had bestowed would then flow between them on the basis of those three measures, but because it could confirm long-held beliefs they had about their relative status and impact how they thought about later exchanges. Both Tracy and Travell families practised similar patterns. Anne Tracy Atkyns's eldest unmarried daughter, Catherine, left the bulk of her property, including income due to her upon the death of her eldest, childless brother, Robert, to her unmarried sisters.[3] John Travell's unmarried siblings had passed their considerable resources on to his children, but, like the Tracys, had apportioned it where they saw greatest need according to understandings of birth order, gender, and marital status. Jane Travell, John's younger sister, left to her financially straitened and unmarried nephew, Francis, 'half of whatever bank stock I dye possessed of', to her nieces (none of whom were married) her clothing, and to the 'Eldest of my nieces that has not her Mothers Diamond Earrings my Diamond Earings and my watch to the eldest of my nieces that has never a gold watch of her own'. In his will, William Travell, John's younger brother, left his married niece Agnes only a token of his affection. He left greater amounts to Francis, Anne, and Catherine, who were all unmarried; his married younger nephew Ferdinando received the residue of his personal property.[4]

Despite assertions that 'legitimate relationships in this world were vertical only', the horizontal axis of sibling relationships sometimes paralleled, intersected with, or conflicted with the vertical relationships between spouses or between children and parents.[5] Understanding how birth order, gender, and marital status interacted is necessary in order to understand how Georgian siblings managed their ever-shifting 'alliances', and how Georgian families operated more generally.[6] The stories told about the Travells to this point should indicate the ways in which birth order, gender, and marital status influenced siblings' relative positions within the family. What follows combines their story with probate disputes between siblings to explore further how Georgian families managed these power nexus as they ran households and negotiated emotional and material connections with one another. These various sources reveal power machinations that constituted an alternative power structure within families, with its own unique internal dynamics. Opposing recent assertions that primogeniture granted 'the lion's share of *any* inheritance to the firstborn son' and that sisters had 'no legal leverage to compel ... services' from their brothers, the evidence presented here shows inheritance schemes and sibling power constantly shifting on the basis of gender, birth order, and marital status.[7] The combination of married and single brothers and sisters required careful negotiation by siblings. While the household – both real and imagined – helped siblings to 'make sense of their hierarchies, authorities and status', it did not guarantee that there would be no struggles over those hierarchies.[8] As Keith Wrightson has noted: 'the actualities of domestic decision-making ... could be shaped by a domestic politics of conflicting desires and expectations, reproach and concession, rupture and reconciliation. ... Success or failure in the management of the domestic economy could depend crucially upon the extent to which these claims and counter claims could be satisfactorily resolved.'[9] In eighteenth-century England households were the places where families worked out the distribution of labour and financial support and where siblings made sense of the hierarchies of their gender, birth order, and marital status in making claims for the equality they expected from one another. Novels and sermons seem never to have considered what happened in the cases of elder sisters and middle brothers, or the cases of families comprising several siblings of each sex, or to have considered that sisters and brothers married and were widowed, or that sisters might have a financial security not shared by their brothers. Real brothers and sisters confronted all of these situations and had to work out the cultural and familial expectations placed upon them according to their sex, age, and marital status.

Authors of eighteenth-century prescriptive literature, wilfully ignoring the different property, financial, and educational resources invested in children, counselled parents to raise their children equally and siblings to treat one another equally. These injunctions were complicated by the reality that most families did advance some children above others. Real families' experiences inspired and reflected prescriptive advice. William King, for example, did not want to make a will, because he considered it an 'Injustice in a parent to make an unequal Division of his Property amongst his Children', but he threatened to cut off his daughter 'with a shilling' if she married against his wishes.[10] In short, while he supported the idea of filial equality, King also supported the right of parents to treat siblings unequally on the basis of parental ideals. A father's will might recommend that his wife distribute his estate among their children 'in as equal proportions as may be'; the phrase 'as equal . . . as may be' seems to suggest that the concept was a relative one.[11]

Siblinghood offers a unique opportunity to see gender interlacing not only with birth order, but with marital status.[12] Marital status could influence the limits of friendship and rivalry. Single siblings' lack of spouses and children (other than in cases of illegitimacy) meant that they had no family connection closer than their brothers and sisters, and therefore had the opportunity to have especially close, or especially corrosive, relations with other single siblings. Whether a family saw unmarried sisters 'at best as an unpaid domestic servant, at worst a source of shame' or as 'a significant asset', they, as well as unmarried brothers, influenced how power and services flowed between households.[13] Marital status could drastically alter sibling dynamics. Tom Rumney recognized this when he worried that all of siblings would marry before he did. 'When I have two brothers and two sisters married the number will complete the four corners for the old childish game – of Tom Fool wants a place, but cannot get one, and I shall have to act the part of Tom Fool', he wrote to his uncle.[14] Married brothers and sisters had to make decisions about how they would fulfil their multiple familial duties, and they had to make those decisions repeatedly throughout a lifetime. The decisions were not always clear-cut and perhaps at times were not even conscious choices. Before marriage a decision could be less complex, as all one's family time could be spent with one's natal family without competition from other obligations. After marriage, however, siblings could no longer be equal participants in the sibling network without sacrificing time or effort spent on their spouses and children. Even though the labelling of siblings-in-law equated them with siblings, the acquisition of a spouse meant the supplanting of a sibling by an even more intimate relation.

Property and probate disputes

When discussing sibling relationships, historians of the 1970s and 1980s often emphasized primogeniture and its supposed power 'inevitably' to generate a 'gulf between the eldest son and heir and his younger brothers' and claimed that 'primogeniture sacrificed [younger brothers] for the sake of their elder brothers'.[15] Primogeniture and its connected inheritance schemes – entail and strict settlement (both increasingly popular in the eighteenth century) – explain only the property aspects of sibling relations, and only for the landed classes. Additionally, primogeniture established the position of elder sons, but it signalled paternal power more than fraternal power. Fathers and grandfathers determined inheritance patterns that influenced generations; eldest brothers did not govern this system any more than their younger siblings did – they simply inherited it. Birth order was not merely about elder sons in relation to everyone else. While the eldest son may have been the usual heir of real estate, daughters and younger sons were often more likely to receive monetary remuneration from their parents and other kin. Inheritance practices tried to enforce a type of 'equality' that, while not strictly equal, encouraged brothers and sisters to 'share and share alike'.[16]

Probate disputes between siblings offer an opportunity to see the mixture of gender, birth order, and marital status and their impact upon the financial and social health of households. The ecclesiastical-legal records of English dioceses are particularly suitable for expanding the vision of sibling relations beyond primogeniture's influence. Because dioceses did not have jurisdiction over real estate disputes, their records miss those aspects of family inheritance disputes most influenced by primogeniture and its related manifestations.[17] The families that appeared before the Consistory Court of Gloucester argued about personal property, not about houses and land, and so disagreements over primogeniture cannot explain their conflicts.[18] Instead they offer a view of sibling conflict where the claims between sisters and brothers were much messier. In most cases a final written decision by the court has not survived, but as most petitioners merely asked the court to enforce the rules of probate (proving a will, granting letters of administration, requiring an inventory of the state to be completed), once these tasks were accomplished, the court needed to take no further action.[19]

The sibling probate disputes of the Diocese of Gloucester cover 120 cases between 1715 and 1836, with one additional case in 1700 and another in 1842. The relatively low rate of sibling property disputes demonstrates how rarely sibling conflict descended to this level. The families discussed here are not representative of all siblings, but they are representative of sibling conflict. The 122 cases provide raw data on several hundred siblings from a variety of occupations. Most families were yeomen or farmers, but many skilled trades (particularly textile-based ones) were also represented. Additionally, there were two gentlemen, a labourer, and a miner.[20] The court did not routinely inventory the estates, so their average value is unknown. Of those with an inventory, the value ranged from less than £10 to £500. Fully understanding the structure of sibling relations in these families also required delving into parish registers to discover other siblings not involved in the cases in order to determine sibling set size, birth order, and marital status. Unfortunately, given the limited information on some of the petitions and the limited information in eighteenth-century parish registers and bishops' transcripts, birth order and marital status could not be completely determined for all the families.[21] Therefore the analysis that follows is based on two data sets, showing gender and some marital status data from the 122 families, and birth order and marital status data from 69 of those families identified in the parish registers. Those 69 families contained 407 siblings – giving an average sibling set size of 5.89 (2.72 sisters, 3.17 brothers). If those numbers held true for the remaining 53 families, approximately 700 siblings would have been involved in the total number of cases. In the 122 Diocese of Gloucester cases, there were 152 incidents of conflict between siblings (including siblings-in-law). This number is derived from counting every sibling dynamic at play in each particular case; for example, if a case had involved an older sister and younger brother arguing against a middle brother, it counts as one incident of brother–brother conflict and one incident of sister–brother conflict.

Gender

In general, conflict was more likely between the genders than within them. Mixed-sex disagreements make up 59.2 per cent of the cases (90 incidents), and same-sex conflicts 40.8 per cent (62 incidents) (see Table 1). The single largest category is sister–brother disputes, with 48 incidents. Brothers argued against other brothers (39 incidents) almost as often as they argued against sisters (42 incidents). Sister–sister conflict, however, occurred rarely, making up only 15.1 per cent of the cases (23 incidents). As men were more likely than women to be executors of wills, inheritance traditions set up brothers as the primary targets of disputes. However, with that tendency in mind, it is intriguing that brother-plaintiffs brought cases against their siblings of either gender in roughly equal numbers. When conflict arose, it took a distinctly gendered turn. For women, sibling power struggles most often involved conflict with their brothers; for men, attempts to assert fraternal power could create conflict with either sisters or brothers. Sisters understood that their brothers and brothers-in-law could benefit not only from unequal inheritance practices but also 'from unequal shares of the products of social labour'.[22]

That so many sisters had to resort to legal intervention fits with the notion that women had to use the legal system to enforce the equality that they and prescriptive literature imagined to be possible. As Amanda Vickery has asserted, eighteenth-century women found patriarchy harder to take from brothers than from fathers.[23] These sisters also understood that they could use the legal system to their advantage. They recognized that the law gave them equal share of any personal property of a parent who died intestate (as most parents did) and that judges were inclined to consider 'fairness' in their decisions. In this way, sisters knew how to wield a general patriarchy embodied in the law to conquer a more immediate patriarchy embodied in their brothers.[24]

Contributing to sister–brother conflicts were inheritance practices that supported sisters' demands against their brothers. Early modern fathers and judges, as Amy Erickson has argued, often tried to make inheritance fair between brothers and sisters, whereas mothers and aunts tended to privilege female heirs.[25] Alternatively, Ruth Perry argues, by the late eighteenth century, daughters' portions were declining and brother–sister conflict was on the rise.[26] In general, the Diocese of Gloucester cases show peaks in brother–sister and sister–brother conflict in the 1730s and 1760s, but because of the small number of disputes, it is not clear whether this contradicts or confirms Perry's argument.[27] What is clear is that many cases show brothers pushing against a parent's efforts to equalize or privilege their sisters. William James, for instance, petitioned the court against his sister when their father's will left her with a house, an orchard, and 1.5 acres while he and his brothers received 'one shilling each and no more'.[28]

The case of the Smith family underscores the pull between brothers' and sisters' claims on equality. In her will of 1782, Hannah Smith, a coal miner's widow, gave her 'well-beloved' son Sampson her term in one house and her 'well-beloved' married daughter Sarah her term in another house. Hannah indicated that Sampson and Sarah should contribute equally to the payment of £3 due to another sister. All of her personal property she instructed 'to be Enjoyed by them share and equall share alike'.[29] Hannah made Sampson her sole executor, but he delayed proving the will. His own reluctance to file and comply with their mother's will did not stop him from filing a cause against his sister and brother-in-law in March 1784, demanding that they take out letters of administration on their father's estate. Equally disinclined to comply with her brother and the court, Sarah delayed taking out the letters until 1786. In the mean time, her patience with Sampson's delay wore thin, and in June 1784 she demanded that he bring their mother's will to be proved. Sampson, however, dragged his feet until 1785 before surrendering the executorship to his sister.[30] With no freehold land to inherit, Sampson and Sarah were legally equal, meaning that their conflict had no quick resolution. Sarah, as the elder sister, may not have appreciated her younger brother's efforts to obstruct her inheritance. In turn, Sampson, whose gender would have privileged him in most other interactions, may have resented Sarah's control of their father's goods.

In all of the delay-and-annoy tactics employed by Sampson and Sarah, their sister Hannah and Sarah's husband were virtually invisible. Whatever the nature of the conflict between Widow Smith's 'well-beloved' children, it centred on Sampson and Sarah. The same is true of all the probate cases. Of the forty-eight sister–brother conflicts, forty were between blood siblings, and only eight involved in-laws. When it came to female–male conflicts, blood proved more volatile than water. The Smith case also demonstrates that brothers, despite the privileges of their sex, sometimes had to rely on the court to enforce equitable sibling relations. The male–female cases were the second most common type, but were of two distinct types. Brothers argued against their sisters (nineteen times) nearly as often as they argued against their sisters-in-law (twenty times). This pattern will be discussed later, but it is notable that while sisters fought against consanguineal brothers, brothers fought against both consanguineal and affinal sisters.

What about disagreements between members of the same sex? Generally conflicts between blood relations were more common than disputes between in-laws. Male–male conflict made up thirty-nine incidents, approximately a quarter of all conflicts. The bulk of these were between blood brothers (twenty-nine of the thirty-nine). It was more common for brothers to go against other brothers than against their sisters (twenty-nine versus nineteen incidents), perhaps highlighting men's recognition of other men's predominance in inheritance matters. The smaller amount of sister–sister conflict supports claims that sisters had particularly close relationships; inheritance practices allowed the flourishing of amicability and equality among the 'have-nots'.[31] Further analysis, however, serves as a caution against the perception of conflict-free sisterly ties. Of the twenty-three incidents of female–female conflict, twelve involved sister against sister. Conflicts between a sister of a deceased man and the widow of the deceased were uncommon (eight incidents), as were conflicts started by widows against their husband's sisters, as in the Punter family (two incidents). So sororal conflict between women was much more likely among sisters who had shared a childhood than among sisters-in-law.

The occurrence of mixed-sex conflicts increased in the eighteenth century. In the middle Ages, brother–brother conflict was more common: Barbara Hanwalt's analysis of fourteenth-century interfamilial crime patterns in England has revealed that in manorial land disputes, the biggest proportion of interfamilial conflict was between siblings, particularly brothers (55 per cent of the cases). Sister–sister conflict and brother–sister conflict added up to less than 15 per cent.[32] Some of this may be attributed to inheritance practices that privileged males as owners of land, but it is intriguing that in counties like Norfolk and Essex that practised equal partible inheritance, land disputes were more likely to descend into homicidal rage than in counties like Yorkshire and Northamptonshire, where primogeniture was the practice. And in the seventeenth century families, remarkably, seem to have had less conflict between brothers and sisters.[33] By the eighteenth century, however, social attitudes had changed the nature of sibling conflict. Strict settlement and entail were practised more often, but a language of social equality was more pervasive as old ideas about the natural order started to crumble under the Enlightenment's onslaught. Sibling conflict between the genders increased as women's and men's experiences more often paralleled one another and as debates over women's position grew heated.[34]

Birth order

The Smith siblings' experience hints at the importance of birth order to sibling politics. Adding birth order to the analysis required searching for the squabbling families in parish registers. The sibling sets for sixty-nine cases were identified, representing 56.6 per cent of the total cases. These sixty-nine cases involved 407 siblings (188 sisters, 219 brothers) and eighty-six incidents of sibling conflict. Because siblings not mentioned could not always be identified as living or dead at the time of the case, the sibling set size reflects in each case the total number of children, not just those living, and not just those arguing over the probate. Again, if a dispute involved several siblings, each incident of birth-order-based conflict was counted separately.

Surprisingly, the overall pattern shows a slight prevalence of older siblings arguing against their younger siblings rather than the reverse (see Tables 2 and 3); forty-six of the cases, or 53 per cent, involved older siblings versus younger ones. Even without factoring in gender, this indicates that age alone could not guarantee a sibling any power. Resorting to using the court exposed a sibling's overall lack of power in persuading other brothers and sisters to administer an estate or distribute legacies. Apparently, being the oldest brother could grant one socially and culturally recognized power, but it did not promise any automatically privileged standing with younger siblings of either sex. Despite prescriptive counsel that narrowed sibling birth-order structures to mean only older brothers and their single younger sisters, real families encountered a variety of age and gender combinations that had older siblings seeking extra-familial intervention slightly more often than younger siblings.

Considering the combination of gender and birth order information opens new ways of understanding eighteenth-century sibling interaction. Brothers were almost three times as likely as sisters to be defendants (sixty-two incidents to twenty-four). That is not particularly surprising, but what is surprising is that older brothers were slightly less likely than younger brothers to be defendants (twenty-nine incidents to thirty-three). This tendency highlights the unstable nature of sibling hierarchies based on birth order. Childhood mortality might claim a quarter to a third of a sibling set.[35] Even if siblings survived to adolescence, the vicissitudes of health, injury, and medicine meant that death was a constant possibility.[36] Siblings squabbling in the diocesan court were typically older than thirty, and many of them were older than forty. This meant that whatever their original birth order, mortality had probably reshaped their relative positions and the sibling politics they affected many times. The description above of the Tracy and Travell families' birth order underscores birth order's instability. When John Travell married Anne Tracy in 1725 their marriage settlement stipulated £5,000 for his 'younger children', but just who would constitute that group of younger children could not be known until John's death.[37]

Privileging eldest sons was supposed to guarantee the perpetuation of inheritance and lineage, but it could take years before any individual family knew who would preserve the family lines and property for the future. As discussed previously, Francis Travell became the heir only after reaching adulthood; he assumed the responsibilities of the heir when his parents died within four months of each other during the autumn and winter of 1762–63. After 1763, however, Francis's standing began to decline. In 1763 and 1767 he fathered two illegitimate sons with a woman who was not deemed a suitable marriage partner. These children did not ruin his chances of becoming an appropriately masculine head of a family: he was not yet forty and possessed a comfortable estate, and there was still a chance that he would marry and produce legitimate heirs. He never did. At some point his siblings must have realized that although he occupied their childhood home, he would not be able to pass it on. Settlement stipulations in their grandfather's will had already determined that the estate would go to his younger brother, Ferdinando, if Francis failed to produce legitimate heirs. Once the family realized that Francis would not produce a legitimate heir, their expectations in the 1760s and 1770s must have rested on Ferdinando's ability to inherit and then pass the property to his sons. Ferdinando, trained in the church, well married, and possessed of keen financial skills, seemed ideally suited to assume the role of heir if necessary, or at least to support his brother until his own children could inherit. By 1780, however, this proved impossible, for Ferdinando's wife died, leaving him with their two teenage daughters. Only in his early forties, he could have remarried and perhaps fathered a son, but he never did so. Again, entail would make Ferdinando at best a life-term tenant on the family's land, assuming that he outlived Francis. In the mid-1780s, when the youngest Travell sibling, Agnes, produced three boys in rapid succession, Ferdinando began to direct his considerable talents towards the future of his nephews. First he sustained their father and mother during a bankruptcy, and then he ensured that the lands he had acquired through his own efforts and patronage (most notably a fine manor and living in eastern Gloucestershire) would go to his nephews. Thus even though Francis became heir apparent in 1748, it took until the 1780s to determine completely who would be the ultimate heir of Swerford. In 1749 the Travells assumed that the family heir would be John; in the 1750s and 1760s they assumed that it would be Francis; in the 1770s and 1780s they assumed that it would be Ferdinando. In the end, the property and associated prestige passed not through the eldest son or any of the sons, but through the youngest daughter.[38] Not every family was like the Travells, but many faced similar shifts in family position based on birth – perhaps accounting for elder and younger brothers equally sharing the load as defendants against irate siblings. Additionally, if death could ravage a sibling set by the time they reached adulthood, by the time they reached middle age it could leave a younger brother as the only brother, rendering him simultaneously the younger brother and the oldest male heir.

Printed literature flattened the instability of age-based family positions and emphasized the unfair treatment of younger brothers.[39] The probate disputes, however, demonstrate that brothers brought cases against younger and elder brothers in almost equal numbers (thirteen and fifteen instances respectively). The more common situation involved an older sister bringing a suit against a younger brother (twenty incidents); this represented 23 per cent of the total cases and 43 per cent of all occurrences of older siblings fighting against younger ones. Older sisters brought cases almost exclusively against brothers; the three cases of older sisters against younger sisters pale in comparison. Older sisters, like Sarah (Smith) Fudge, who had the advantage of age, may have chafed when her younger brothers thought they did not need to consider her wishes in administering an estate. Prescriptive literature and scholarship rarely considered this dynamic, where age privileged the female and gender privileged the younger, and the poor fit of this dynamic with prevailing social attitudes may explain its particular explosiveness. It was in such relationships that injunctions about equality and reminders of hierarchy were mixed in volatile ways.

Birth order analysis underscores the fact that sibling conflict was not just caused by resentment of gendered privileges for brothers. As already stated, sisters were more inclined to go after younger brothers (nineteen incidents) than after older brothers (thirteen incidents); younger brothers opposed older sisters on only eight occasions. Fourteen younger sisters who took their older brothers to court knew that they could get the court to enforce a greater equality than their gender and birth order generally determined. Younger brothers were more likely to be defendants than younger sisters (thirty-three cases to thirteen), but of those thirteen younger sisters, ten defended themselves against the claims of older brothers. The idea that the age- and gender-based position was entirely in favour of the brother appears to be just as fragile and contentious as its reverse. While brothers and sisters who brought cases may have been lacking the sibling power to get their way outside of court, they clearly understood the rules of inheritance and knew that with the court's backing they could get their share. In this way they wielded a type of negative power: they were not strong enough to influence their siblings directly, but were determined enough to employ the ecclesiastical-legal system to bend more powerful siblings to their will. Overall, the addition of birth order analysis to the larger pattern of gender conflict among siblings reveals that notions of equality rubbed against real differences of circumstances in sometimes toxic ways. Where sibling relations best replicated accepted attitudes about equality (between sisters, for example), there was relatively little conflict over inheritance. Where lived experience contrasted starkly with ideas of equality, as they did between younger brothers and older sisters, siblings were less able to negotiate their disagreements without legal intervention.

Marital status

Sisters' and brothers' marriages further complicated sibling politics and efforts to maintain equitable relations. Marriage could upset the delicate balance of power among siblings – something which parents, but not prescriptive authors, recognized.[40] Other than Mary Wollstonecraft's remark that single brothers and sisters could get along with a 'tolerable degree of comfort' until a brother's marriage turned the sister into 'an unnecessary burden on the benevolence of the master of the house and his new partner', prescriptive literature rarely detailed what happened to brothers and sisters after a sibling married.[41] Most assumed that elder brothers cared for younger sisters and were in turn refined by their sisters until they both married. After marriage, the role of protector and closest friend shifted to a woman's husband. 'A Woman without a Husband', so the argument went, was 'like a Ship without a Rudder; She may happen to get into Harbour well, but there are great Odds against it.'[42] Yet brothers and sisters could not jettison sibling ties when they married. Many of them spent a considerable length of time as single young adults or as widowed older adults, and they entered matrimony after twenty or thirty years of established sibling relationships and shared memories. Parents, keenly aware of the greater financial instability for single daughters, inadvertently contributed to the uncertain world of sibling politics by allotting more resources to single daughters than to their married sisters.[43]

Determining sisters' marital status in the probate cases is easier than determining brothers' marital status; because marital status did not affect men's legal status, the court records do not mention it. Despite a woman's being legally under her husband's protection, the court documents rarely listed sisters' husbands as co-litigants. Instead, a sister's husband's name and perhaps occupation were listed much as her brother's occupation was. While coverture made a woman's husband the true litigant, it was her standing as a sister (not a wife or daughter) that gave her, and him, legal footing. The Diocese of Gloucester cases contain marital information on sixty-three female plaintiffs and fifty-four female defendants. Married sisters instigated probate cases more often than widowed or single sisters (see Table 4). While some of this discrepancy derives from the higher numbers of married women versus single women, it is still remarkable that widowed and single women combined made up fewer of the plaintiffs than married sisters. A married sister may have determined that a husband's presence would strengthen her standing in a legal battle or may have engaged in the battle at his behest. The high number of married sisters seeking the court's intervention reflects their diminished power among their siblings. Marriage may have bolstered a man's position with his siblings because he was then able to benefit from his wife's emotional and familial labour. Sisters, however, found their labour, always attached as it always was to domestic and familial concerns, diffused over their three families: natal, conjugal, and affinal.

Married sisters, such as Frances (Jason) Perrott, could find themselves doubly disadvantaged. In 1731 Frances charged that her single sister, Ann, administratrix of their brother's estate, had not distributed Frances's portion. When Ann died later that year, she gave money to aunts, friends and servants, a shilling to her brother Robert, and the rest of her property and money to 'my two loving Sisters Catherine Jason and Celia Jason'.[44] Frances was not mentioned. The Jason family conflict, however, does not appear to have stemmed from long-standing resentment between the sisters but rather appears to have been a manifestation of marriage's impact on a sister's standing within her natal family. Before the 1731 case, Frances and her siblings, excluding their eldest brother Warren, had received equal inheritances of either £1,000 or a comparable combination of money and land when they turned twenty-one or married.[45] When their father inherited an additional £800 from his sister, each child received an additional £100, except for Robert who received £200. Warren was under thirty when he died, and he left no widow or children. He also left no will, and the title and any land associated with it therefore devolved to fourteen-year-old Robert. Without a will, Warren's five surviving siblings were entitled to equal portions of his personal property. It was this one-fifth that Frances wanted the court to force Ann to distribute. Ann's will is telling in its lack of information about Frances. Because Robert had inherited the title and land from Warren, Robert's one shilling from Ann was not a one-shilling cut-off but a place marker indicating her remembrance of him.[46] Celia and Catherine, who were twenty-three and twenty-one years old respectively when Ann died, could still hope to marry and needed provision in the mean time. Frances, on the other hand, was married and established and presumably in no need of assistance from Ann. As the eldest sister, Ann decided that her unmarried younger sisters needed her support more, either to maintain economic independence or to attract eligible suitors.[47] All of the Jason siblings received their inheritance when they acquired the mantle of adulthood, either through age or marriage, but marriage shifted the sisters' roles and power within the family. Like Frances (Jason) Perrott, Ann Courtier Hart could not accept her father's injunction that his married daughters 'shall peaceably and quietly quit and surrender their right and power to the . . . unmarried'. She brought a suit against her brother Isaac despite their father's further stipulation that if all his daughters should marry, they should 'have no share, right, or title' to the property 'but shall peaceably and quietly quit the same, after which I give and bequeath the same unto my son Isaac to his own proper use and behoof'. Isaac's marital status did not affect his inheritance.[48]

Though marital status was more influential in women's lives than in men's, it still played a part in brothers' lives and intersected with gender and birth order in the apportioning of sibling tasks. Brothers, especially older ones, were expected to house their single sisters, and for single women, in any class, with few economic avenues open to them, this was an obvious option; brothers, in their role of protector, would be a logical source of physical support.[49] Alternatively, in families like the Travells, a single sister might inherit a small sum that would allow her a level of economic self-sufficiency (and allow her to help her sisters). Marriage could also disrupt sibling relations for brothers. One man's greatest concern in the event that his brother died was that his sister-in-law 'might be unkind to him'.[50]

Despite the lack of information about brothers' marital status, it could affect those whom brothers challenged in court. Brothers did not bring cases against their sisters as often as they did against their brothers' widows (twenty incidents, representing 13.2 per cent of the Diocese of Gloucester cases). In 1799, when Charles Park, brother of the deceased William Park, had the court cite William's 'pretended' widow, he hoped to trump her rights as the widow.[51] William's widow, Ann, argued, correctly, that her rights as the widow superseded his claims as brother. Both parties understood that if she could not prove she had married William, Charles, as William's only surviving sibling, stood to inherit all of his brother's estate. Despite the law's long-standing recognition of widows' rights, eighteenth-century brothers may have considered that their claims could conquer those based on conjugal ties, particularly when the in-law was female (brothers brought suits against their sisters' husbands only four times). Historians have interpreted this attitude as an indication of widows' declining property rights. Alternatively, they have seen the brothers' lack of success as an indication that conjugal rights were increasingly narrowing the scope and rights of other kin.[52] In light of sibling conflicts, however, this pattern reveals deep-seated expectations about the rewards of fraternal ties. If the experience of James Walden's brothers in 1795 and Cowdall brothers in 1740–41 are any indication, perhaps men had reasons to believe that their married brothers would pit fraternal against conjugal responsibilities. James Walden made his wife, Sarah the principal heir of his freehold estate and personal property as long as she did not 'diminish or demolish' any part of it because after her death he intended it for his brother, William, a shopkeeper. Unsurprisingly, given the will's implicit opposition of fraternal and conjugal ties, William based his complaint on Sarah's inventory of her husband's goods. Getting the property valued at just over £141 meant that he could use that as evidence of what he stood to inherit at Sarah's death and to ensure that she did not 'diminish' it.[53] Some brothers tried to attack the validity of their brothers' wills in order to claim a larger portion of the property. The three Cowdall brothers accused their sister-in-law of producing a fraudulent will in 1741. Significantly, despite the fact that the brothers inherited clothes, linen, and wool equally with their sister, their sister did not join in their suit.[54] Brothers like the Parks, Waldens, and Cowdalls seem to have considered their widowed sisters-in-law vulnerable to counterclaims on the deceased's estate. Though the court rarely agreed, many men apparently considered fraternal connections to male inheritance privileges more lasting than conjugal ones.

The case of the Travell siblings demonstrates how gender, birth order, and marital status were negotiated over a lifetime. As discussed previously, Francis's poor financial management and his two illegitimate sons (and his lack of a wife) all contributed to his inability to exert influence to the extent that his well-married, financially well-off brother Ferdinando did. His position as eldest brother and as owner of Swerford House may have allowed him some leniency that a sister or younger brother would not have enjoyed. However, in all practical matters, Ferdinando was the male sibling power-broker among the Travells. Even after he became a widower, Ferdinando always acted as the financial and social bedrock of the family. He helped to bail out Agnes and Edward when they went bankrupt, he made sure his own daughters had enough money to ensure good marriage prospects, he supported Francis in his declining financial situation, and he passed his property and parish on to his nephew, the son of Edward and Agnes.[55] English society and culture granted him greater educational and property rights than his sisters, and in turn he used these advantages to maintain his family financial and social standing as was expected. In most family matters such as executing wills, distributing money, and maintaining social ties, Ferdinando had to work with his unmarried sisters in a relationship that came close to the equality imagined possible for siblings.[56] Similarly, Anne's position as eldest unmarried daughter and the head of household made her Ferdinando's counterpart. Outside the family Anne's gender and marital status would suggest a subordinate role, but within the family the connection made her a powerful figure. The gender- and birth-order-based conflicts in the probate disputes suggest that by working well with her one younger brother, Ferdinando, Anne Travell and her siblings avoided the pitfalls of other relationships between an older sister and a younger brother. Anne and her siblings avoided a potentially explosive power arrangement as the social recognition of his gender rubbed against the familial experience of her age.[57]

Sisters were an integral part of family survival, as Anne Travell's experience suggests. According to the prescriptive literature, brothers were to protect and govern their sisters, but in practice sisters like Anne performed necessary tasks to preserve family unity, financial survival, and emotional support. The shared and imagined Travell households incorporated multiple generations into their horizontal relationships. Francis never married, but his two sons with Elizabeth Hitchman were included and enjoyed regular interaction with their aunts and uncle, both with and without their father. Additionally, Ferdinando and Martha had two daughters in the 1760s, who regularly visited with their aunts and uncle. At a young age the nieces spent long visits with Anne and Catherine, both with and without their parents. Typical were the events of 26 June 1768 when Miss Witts joined the 'two great and 2 little Miss Travells' for tea.[58] Much as they had benefited from their parents' sibling connections, the Travells recognized how gender, birth order, and marital status affected their nieces and nephews. Anne left the bulk of her property to their nieces, and Ferdinando left his living, and attached rectory, to Agnes's son.[59]

For the Travell sisters their combined inheritances made a household separate from their married brothers a possibility, but even those of more modest means made similar arrangements. Women from farming or trading families could hope to stay with a prosperous brother or sister, to enter an occupation or service themselves, or to combine their resources with female cousins or other sisters. For single sisters, living together was one way of ameliorating women's lower educational and wage-earning potential. If, as in the case of Mary and Catherine Heming, their father left them a house, even sisters with small incomes could survive by sharing household expenses. When Mary died in 1778 she left her portion of their shared house to Catherine.[60]

Being unmarried meant that brothers and sisters could assume the roles of husband and wife that their spouses would later assume, as Ferdinando and Anne seem to have done, particularly after Ferdinando wife's death in 1780. The Huntingford family followed a similar pattern. In 1788 thirty-five-year-old Thomas Huntingford became ill and knew he would soon die. He sent for his brother George. When George arrived at his sickbed, Thomas asked him to care for his widow and children, an enormous task considering that there were already six living children and another on the way. George agreed and spent the rest of his life fulfilling that promise, despite the financial strain it proved to be. In the process he became very close to his widowed sister-in-law; he did not just provide for them financially, but also became his sister-in-law's closest friend and companion – a surrogate husband and father. When she fell ill with her final illness in 1814, he was strongly affected. As his nephew Thomas wrote:

> [T]he saddest sight was to see my poor Uncle! His strong mind struggling against grief, but not always able to suppress it! For more than 25 years my mother had been his faithful companion. In breeding up us children, they had known many difficulties; and in uninterrupted peace and harmony had struggled through them. This naturally had endeared them to each other; so that the thought of being parted at last was bitter in the extreme![61]

For weeks after her death, George remained almost inexpressibly saddened at the loss. Through his lifelong assumption of his brother's role he had fulfilled the duties of brother, father, and husband. Undoubtedly, George's remaining unmarried helped him to provide for his brother's family without competing family concerns, as it did for other men such as Granville Sharp, discussed previously. Thomas Cox, a watchmaker, followed a similar pattern; having no children to leave his property to, he left it to the children of his brothers.[62] In their letters to their siblings, brothers demonstrated a familiarity with a variety of topics and duties usually associated with married masculinity.[63] Unmarried sisters also participated in fictive parenthood, as Mary Dyer, a woman of trade and farming background, did. Her will reveals that though she died unmarried and without children, she still participated in the long-term care of her siblings, nieces, and nephews. Her niece, as executrix, was in charge of proving and administering the will, in which Mary provided housing for her brother and left money to his children.[64]

Conclusion

Families, as R. W. Connell has remarked, are unique institutions: 'In no other institution are relationships so extended in time, so intensive in contact, so dense in their interweaving of economics, motion, power and resistance.'[65] The Diocese of Gloucester probate disputes reveal the tensions between normative expectations of gender, birth order, and marital status and the real-life implementation of sibling power. Birth order on its own was not sufficient to determine power. It may have determined who received the second- or third-best set of bedding – as it did for the daughters of the yeoman Samuel Courtier in his 1766 will – but it was their brother's gender that determined that he would receive the best set of bedding as well as the house, livestock, money, and husbandry tools. And it was the sisters' marital status that determined whether they would inherit at all.

In none of the Diocese of Gloucester disputes did siblings resist the maintenance of family property in the hands of one brother, seemingly accepting this niche of inequality as long as other markers of equality were maintained. Primogeniture, strict settlement, and entail affected only a portion of testators, and much about those practices was determined by earlier generations. Beyond that, siblings expected fair and equal treatment in matters of inheritance. They shared the attitude of William King, who in the years before his death resisted his daughter's pressures to make a will, asserting that because he held his children in 'equal esteem regard and affection', they should divide his property equally. William understood the law, as is shown by his statement 'that he had no Houses or Lands to settle, and asked what he should make a Will for'.[66] Siblings realized that if there was land, it would go to the eldest son, and if there was no land, then the sons stood to receive equal portions. Conflict arose when reality did not match their perceptions of that equality. Siblings appealed to the court in order to enforce a system that, while not strictly equal, encouraged brothers and sisters to share and share alike. Much of the tension described here resulted from a confrontation between a long-standing tradition of sibling equality and developing social and political ideals of equality and other practices that privileged some siblings on the basis of age, sex, or marriage. While medieval women 'were never offered anything like equality with men within the family economy', their early modern and Georgian counterparts expected a modicum of equality with their brothers.[67] As John Locke had noted a century before, 'a father may have natural right to some kind of power over his children, is easily granted; but that an elder brother has so over his brethren, remains to be proved'.[68] Eighteenth-century brothers and sisters still considered the need for differential sibling privileges to be unproved and untenable. Elder sisters resisted impositions by their younger brothers, and brothers disputed with both younger and elder sisters. Additionally, despite the positioning of affinal and consanguineal siblings as equals, balancing those relationships proved difficult for some brothers and their sisters-in-law, and for married sisters trying to exert power among their siblings.

Notes

1 Burton, *Lectures on Female Education and Manners*, pp. 255–6.
2 Anne Atkyns Tracy, will, written 12 June 1740, codicil written 4 February 1747, proved 29 May 1762, TNA, PROB 11/874. An earlier version of this chapter appeared as "'That fierce edge': Sibling Conflict and Politics in Georgian England", *Journal of Family History*, 37: 2 (April 2012), pp. 155–74.
3 Catherine Tracy, will, written 4 March 1762, proved 26 January 1764, TNA, PROB 11/895.
4 Jane Travell, will, written 5 November 1767, proved 1 December 1767, TNA, PROB 11/934; William Travell, will, written 24 November 1770, proved 6 February 1775, Prerogative Court of Canterbury, GA, D495/F6.
5 Anthony Fletcher, *Growing Up in England*, p. 47. Fletcher is referring to Davidoff, *Worlds Between*, pp. 50–3.
6 Linda Pollock, 'Rethinking Patriarchy and the Family in seventeenth-Century England', *Journal of Family History*, 23:1 (January 1998), 4.
7 Perry, *Novel Relations*, p. 154.
8 Broomhall, ed., *Emotions in the Household*, p. 17.
9 Wrightson, *Earthly Necessities*, p. 67.
10 William King, testamentary cause, 1805–14, GA, GDR B4/2/K5; Consistory Court of Gloucester, Court Minutes, 1805–14, GA, GDR B3/35-44.
11 John Clark, will, written 13 November 1793, proved 8 February 1802, GA, GDR Wills 1802/19; John Clark, testamentary cause 1801–02, GA, GDR B4/2/C68. See also William Staite, will written 4 August 1764, codicil written 14 July 1769, proved 4 May 1775, GA, GDR Wills 1775/55; William Staite, testamentary cause, GA, GDR B4/2/S104; Elizabeth Wyatt, will, written 16 July 1762, proved 19 October 1764, GA, GDR Wills 1764/207; Elizabeth Wyatt, testamentary cause, September–November 1764, GA, GDR B4/2/W170.
12 Judith M. Bennett and Amy M. Froide, eds., *Singlewomen in the European Past, 1250–1800* (Philadelphia 1999); Hill, *Women Alone*; Wulf, *Not All Wives*; Lee Chambers-Schiller, *Liberty, a Better Husband: Single Women in America: The Generations of 1780–1840* (New Haven and London, 1984).
13 Froide, *Never Married*, p. 79; Hill, *Women Alone*, p. 3. See also Bennett, *Ale, Beer, and Brewsters in England*, pp. 37–59.
14 Rumney, ed., *Tom Rumney of Mellfell*, p. 7.
15 Stone, *The Family, Sex and Marriage in England*, p. 115, also pp. 43–4, 88, 116, 156, 652. Crawford, *Blood, Bodies and Families*, pp. 214–17; Thirsk, 'Younger Sons in the Seventeenth Century', p. 359; Spring, 'The Strict Settlement'; Donna Birdwell-Pheasant, 'Family Systems and the Foundations of Class in Ireland and England', *History of the Family*, 3 (1998), 17–34.
16 Erickson, *Women and Property*, pp. 62–3, 72, 204–22.
17 Arkell, Evans and Goose, eds., *When Death Do Us Part*, pp. 7–11.

18 Though some of the disputed wills reference land, houses, and mills, none of the disputes arose over inheritance of such property – a matter that would have to be settled in Chancery, not the local ecclesiastical courts. See Anne Tarver, *Church Court Records: An Introduction for Family and Local Historians* (Chichester, 1995), p. 57.
19 Arkell, Evans, and Goose, eds., *When Death Do Us Part*, pp. 3–37.
20 The sample included twenty farmers/yeomen, eleven widows, seven people of unknown occupations, five weavers/tailors/shoemakers, four butchers/victuallers, three millers/engineers/blacksmiths, three masons/carpenters/glaziers, two gentlemen, and two miners/labourers. Consistory Court of Gloucester, testamentary causes, GA, GDR B4/2.
21 Because marital status for men usually goes unmentioned in the records, it is not always possible to determine it at the time of the dispute. Occupational mobility, multiple marriages, deaths far from home, and gaps in the parish records mean that it was not possible to trace all siblings over their life course.
22 Connell, *Gender and Power*, p. 75.
23 Vickery, *The Gentleman's Daughter*, p. 8.
24 Pollock, 'Rethinking Patriarchy'; Davidoff, 'Kinship as a Categorical Concept'.
25 Erickson, *Women and Property*, pp. 62–3, 72, 204–22.
26 Perry, *Novel Relations*, pp. 24, 38–76, 107–42, 154–70.
27 Erickson, *Women and Property*, pp. 76, 230; Perry, *Novel Relations*, p. 408.
28 William James, will, written 26 February 1777, proved 12 December 1793, GA, GDR Wills 1793/167; William James, testamentary cause, November–December 1793, GA, GDR B4/2/J41; Church of England, Newent, Gloucestershire, Parish Registers, FHL, British film 91535.
29 Hannah Smith, will, written 17 July 1782, proved 9 August 1785, GA, GDR Wills 1785/111; Hannah Smith, testamentary cause, June–July 1784, GA, GDR B4/2/S68.
30 Samuel Smith, letters of administration, GA, GDR Wills 1786/21; Samuel Smith, testamentary cause, March 1784, GA, GDR B4/2/S84.
31 Froide, *Never Married*, pp. 60–1; Davidoff and Hall, *Family Fortunes*.
32 Barbara Hanawalt, *Crime and Conflict in English Communities, 1300–1348* (Cambridge, MA, 1979), pp. 160–3, 151–83. While Hanawalt recognizes other forms of sibling conflict and rivalry, her analysis tends to reduce it to brother-brother conflict.
33 Perry, *Novel Relations*, pp. 158–67; Erickson, *Women and Property*, p. 230.
34 Mary Hartman, *The Household and the Making of History*; Brewer, *By Birth or Consent*, p. 360. Sibling contention over partible inheritance is also evident in Revolutionary France and nineteenth- and twentieth-century Brittany. See Suzanne Desan, *The Family on Trial in Revolutionary France* (Berkeley, Los Angeles, and London, 2004), pp. 141–77; Martine Segalen, ' "Avoir sa part": Sibling Relations in Partible Inheritance Brittany', in Hans Medick and David

Warren Sabean, eds., *Interest and Emotion: Essays on the Study of Family and Kinship*. (New York, 1984), pp. 129–44.
35 Laslett, *The World we have Lost*, pp. 112–13.
36 Jamoussi, *Primogeniture and Entail*, pp. 14–15, 53. Jamoussi, like others, discusses elder sons as if they were permanent fixtures in the familial and inheritance landscape.
37 John Travell, copy will, 1762, ORO, Flick I/i/4.
38 Travell Family Papers, GA, D4582 and D495, ORO, Flick I/i; Witts Family Papers, private possession of F.E.B. Witts, WFP, F6–F9, F32–F34, F63, F147–F150, F161, F164–F165, F173–F235.
39 Jamoussi, *Primogeniture and Entail*, pp. 77–102; Ray, *A Compleat Collection of English Proverbs*, p. 66, ECCO.
40 Froide, *Never Married*, p. 44; Perry, *Novel Relations*, pp. 51, 119–24, 127, 132–42. This continued a medieval practice of single women having more contact with their siblings than their married sisters did. Judith Bennett, *Women in the Medieval English Countryside: Gender and Household in Brigstock before the Plague* (New York and Oxford, 1987), pp. 138–9.
41 Mary Wollstonecraft, *A Vindication of the Rights of Woman* (1792), ed. Miriam Kramnick (1978), pp. 157–8, quoted in Bridget Hill, *Women, Work, and Sexual Politics in Eighteenth-Century England* (Oxford, 1989), pp. 228–9.
42 *The Younger Brother*, 4.1, pp. 47–8.
43 Erickson, *Women and Property*, pp. 224–5.
44 Ann Jason, will, written 3 May 1731, proved 25 September 1731, GA, GDR Wills 1731/252; Warren Jason, testamentary cause, January 1730, GA, GDR B4/2/J14; John Burke, *A Genealogical and Heraldic History of the Extinct and Dormant Baronetcies of England, Ireland, and Scotland*, 2nd edn (London, 1841), reprinted by Genealogical Publishing Company, Baltimore, 1985, Church of England, Hinton on the Green, Gloucestershire, Parish Register Transcripts, FHL, British film 504474.
45 Robert Jason, will, written 28 February 1721, codicil 22 February 1723, proved 18 April 1723, Prerogative Court of Canterbury, TNA, PROB 11/590.
46 William Blackstone, *Commentaries on the Laws of England in Four Books* (Philadelphia, 1922), book II, p. 958.
47 Robert Jason, will. Frances may have had the last word on the matter, however. Because Frances was the only Jason sibling to have children, her son, John Stanford Perrott, became residual legatee to all of his aunts' and uncles' property and money in 1798. 'Jason of Broad Somerford, England', *Wiltshire Notes and Queries*, 7:10 (1913), pp. 182–4, 241–5, 291–8, 361–5, 396–403.
48 Samuel Courtier, will, written 16 June 1766, proved 19 May 1774, GA, GDR Wills 1774/85; Samuel Courtier, testamentary cause, May 1774, GA, GDR B4/2/ C114; Church of England, Hawkesbury, Gloucestershire, Parish Registers, FHL, British film 856929. For another example see Jonah Whitfield, will, written 3 February 1780, proved 4 November 1786, GA, GDR Wills 1786/263; Jonah

Whitfield, testamentary cause, August 1792–October 1794, GA, GDR B4/2/W119; Church of England, Stone, Gloucestershire, Parish Registers, FHL, British film 427780; Gillis, *For Better, for Worse*, pp. 75–6.
49 A pattern also visible in colonial America and in Victorian England. See Karin Wulf, *Not All Wives: Women of Colonial Philadelphia* (Ithaca and London, 2000), pp. 85–114 and Tosh, *A Man's Place*, p. 21.
50 OBP, 14 May 1719, trial of Mary Dyer (t17190514-15).
51 William Park, testamentary cause, 1799–1803, GA, GDR B4/2/P40.
52 Spring, *Law, Land and Family*.
53 James Walden, will, written 23 April 1795, proved 25 November 1795, GA, GDR Wills 1795/160; James Walden, testamentary cause, November–December 1797, GA, GDR B4/2/W86.
54 Charles Cowdall, will, written 30 October 1740, proved 14 December 1741, GA, GDR Wills 1741/255; Charles Cowdall, testamentary cause, April–December 1741, GA, GDR B4/2/C117.
55 Travell Family Papers, 1781–93, GA, D4582; Francis Travell, will, written 22 July1792, proved 14 July 1801, Prerogative Court of Canterbury, ORO, Flick I/i/5.
56 Crawford, *Blood, Bodies and Families*, pp. 217–23.
57 For example of the conflicts between single sisters and their brothers see Froide, *Never Married*, pp. 60–4.
58 Anne Travell, daybook, 26 June 1768, GA, D4582/4/17/4.
59 Ferdinando Tracy Travell, will, written 1804, codicils 1805, 1808, proved 17 October 1808 in the Prerogative Court of Canterbury, ORO, Flick I/xvi/1; Anne Travell, will, written 21 January 1825, proved 26 April 1826, TNA, PROB 11/1711.
60 Mary Heming, will, written 24 March1778, proved 30 July 1779, GA GDR Wills 1779/122; Mary Heming, testamentary cause, October–November 1778, GA GDR B4/2/H102. See also Froide, *Never Married*, pp. 54–6.
61 Thomas Huntingford, autobiography, GA, PE 98.
62 Thomas Cox, will, written 27 January 1738, proved, 5 January 1740, GA, GDR Wills 1740/02; Thomas Cox, testamentary cause, January 1740, GA, GDR B4/2/C121.
63 Fletcher, *Gender, Sex and Subordination*; Tosh, *A Man's Place*; Alexandra Shepard, 'Manhood, Credit and Patriarchy in Early Modern England c1580–1640', *Past and Present*, 167:1 (2000), 75–106.
64 Mary Dyer, will, written 2 June 1759, proved 11 October 1777, GA, GDR Wills 1777/183; Mary Dyer, testamentary cause, August 1777–July 1778, GA, GDR B4/2/D79.
65 Connell, *Gender and Power*, p. 121.
66 William King, testamentary cause, 1805–14, GA, GDR B4/2/K5; Consistory Court of Gloucester, Court Minutes, 1805–14, GA, GDR B3/35-44.

67 Judith M. Bennett, 'Medieval Women, Modern Women: Across the Great Divide', in David Aers, ed., *Culture and History, 1350–1600: Essays on English Communities, Identities, and Writing* (London, 1992), pp. 147–76, quoted in Hannah Barker and Elaine Chalus, eds., *Gender in Eighteenth-Century England: Roles, Representations and Responsibilities* (London: 1997), p. 14; Bennett, *Ale, Beer, and Brewsters in England*, pp. 6–8, 156–7.
68 John Locke, *First Treatise on Government*, in Ian Shapiro, ed., *Two Treatises of Government and a Letter Concerning Toleration* (New Haven, CT, 2003), p. 69.

Conclusion

> The brother–sister relationship is simultaneously the longest and the most stable, yet also the most unpredictable that many of us experience.
> Valerie Sanders, 2002[1]

As the nineteenth century dawned and the Travell siblings entered their sixties and seventies, their health and households began to lose their vitality, but their connections to one another remained entrenched. Francis was the first to decline both in financial and physical health. Though he had received an adequate inheritance, his lack of financial acuity and the socially irresponsible relationship he had had with his sons' mother had already taken their toll by the time he wrote his will in 1792. While strict settlement meant that his house in Swerford would go to his brother Ferdinando, Francis's will perpetuated the internal hierarchy of sibling politics. To Ferdinando, 'in consideration of his kind pecuniary assistance to the reduced state of my income and as a testimonial however small of the service I bear', he gave a portrait of their great-grandfather, recognizing the flow of goods and services that had been a constant among the Travell siblings for four decades. He also acknowledged the importance of birth order and gender by bequeathing the portrait first to Ferdinando and then to his 'eldest sister and so on in succession according to priority of age to the last survivor'. Besides the eventual inheritance of the great grandfather's portrait he left Anne and Catherine the residue and execution of his will, 'in consideration of their ever kind and friendly conduct towards me and mine particularly my ever valuable and to be regretted deceased son' and 'from the extraordinary kind exertions in some resent transactions'. Anne's and Catherine's incorporation of their two illegitimate nephews into their household and the maintenance of relationships with a brother who had failed to live up to his socially inscribed roles had softened the sibling hierarchy that had originally benefited him. In other words, the three of them seem to have developed the equality so praised in sibling relationships. For Agnes and Francis things were not so easy, though he gave her £50 as a 'testimonial ... of the Regard I bear every part of my Family'. The twenty-year difference in their ages, separation & untoward circumstances lessened the afflict' of Francis's death for Agnes. Though Agnes acknowledged that 'natural affection made me feel the shock' of her brother's death, it paled in comparison to 'the natural affection and confidence' that existed between Francis, Anne, and Catherine.[2] Francis made one last request to rejoin the family household he had left as a young man when he asked to be buried in Swerford beside his parents and his 'ever blessed elder brother', John, whom he had replaced as eldest son nearly fifty years previously.

Francis was followed by Catherine, who, 'quite worn out with her long & constant state of suffering', died in October 1804, leaving Anne, at sixty-seven years old, alone for the first time in her life.[3] Immediately after Catherine's decease, Ferdinando and his grown daughters travelled to Cheltenham, gathered up Anne, and bundled her back to Ferdinando's house in Upper Slaughter. Anne wrote very little in the week Catherine died, leaving raw-looking spaces in her daybook. There was a sense of relief in Anne's entry for 29 October when she recorded her journey to Upper Slaughter and noted that now she, her nieces, and her brother were 'all at home'.[4] Ferdinando, who had been a widower for over twenty years, was the perfect solace for someone now bereft of her companion. Four years later Ferdinando died in his home, in the company of Anne. Agnes 'rec'd the Melancholy news of the Death of my poor Brother at 4 that afternoon in a letter from my Sister'.[5] In a continuation of his support of Agnes's household, Ferdinando passed his house and the living along to her son, providing financial and occupational backing to his nephew much as he had done previously for his brother-in-law.

While the physical households that Ferdinando had controlled new went to his children, grandchildren, and nephew, the fictive household he had managed with Anne became entirely her responsibility, but that imagined household was quickly dissipating. Agnes became a widow in 1816 when Edward died. Though Agnes had relatives, including her son and sister, with whom she could live, she no longer governed any household. Living with her son made her a guest in the home run by him and his wife; living in a house left by her husband meant that she was merely a trustee for her son's property; and living with Anne made her once again the subordinate younger sister. Her son seems to have recognized the importance of his mother having a place to call her own even as her health declined: in the last weeks of her life he persuaded her to 'quit Stanway House [the home of maternal relatives] for her own home' in Cheltenham near her sister.[6] In so doing she returned to the place from which she had started out as a young bride in 1775. In this way Francis, Catherine, Ferdinando, and Agnes ended their lives right where they had begun – largely in the company of their siblings. By 1825 there was only Anne left – the last vestige of a sibling network founded a century before.

The Travell siblings' lifelong economics – both emotional and material – were, in Leonore Davidoff's words, 'a central element in active kinship'.[7] Families composed of several siblings (some married, some not) and nieces and nephews depended on the households and economic activities of both women and men, not just the husband and father and the wife and mother, but also the sisters and brothers in a series of interconnected households. The comforts that sisters and brothers enjoyed were possible only through the careful balancing of friendship, family, and finances demonstrated in sibling economics. The fortunate ones, like the Travell siblings, successfully negotiated their way from their shared childhood through the practicalities of running connected households and the difficulties of maintaining friendly relations, despite the differences of age, gender, birth order, and marital status. The unfortunate collapsed under, or resisted, the weighty expectations placed upon them, thus dismissing or destroying their sibling relationships.

In February 1826, approaching her ninetieth year, Anne Travell was the last of the Travell siblings to die, retaining 'her faculties to the last'.[8] The 1826 Gloucestershire obituaries listed in the *Gentleman's Magazine* contained this short entry for 2 February: 'at Cheltenham, aged 87 Mrs. Anne Travell.' With these few words Anne slipped into obscurity. Like her aunts before her she left the bulk of her property to her nieces, much to her nephew's annoyance. And in the months following her death those nieces gradually distributed, packed, and sold the items bequeathed to them. By April 1826 the packing and the execution of the will were complete and Martha Travell Whalley, Ferdinando's daughter, took one last moment to appreciate her aunt's home. 'For the last time now am I seated in this beloved house; this cheerful room, where I have spent so many happy days', she wrote. 'I shall never see again – how much of the comforts of my life for many years did I derive from the affection & society of Her who is now no more – when sickness & sorrow seemed nearly to overcome me; her constant attention, unremitting kindness & lively [converse] revived my dro[op]ing spirits.'[9] Martha recognized the emotional labour that her aunt had engaged in, the memory evoked by sitting in Anne's house: the house where each of her three sisters had lived and where she and Catherine had died, the house where her nephew was born, the house where her brothers visited, where the socially well-connected visited, dined, and played whist, the house where she hired, directed, and managed servants, the house where she kept meticulous accounts of finances, journeys, and the health of her siblings, the house where she wrote letters about the emotional and material economics at the foundation of sibling life.

Anne Travell died just as Victorian mourning rituals were coming into play – rituals that accorded lengthy grieving periods to spouses and children, but only six months to siblings. The mourning of a sibling such as Anne's for Catherine or Agnes was already becoming less important in the narrowing public conceptions of grief and family. She had known Catherine and lived with her for longer than all but the longest-living spouses, but because they were not spouses their relationship was presumed to be a lesser connection. In an expanding individualistic, capitalist culture the language of kin support and credit was gone, and rhetorical space for sibling support began to dissolve over the course of the nineteenth century. Georgian siblings, in all of their rivalrous and friendly glory, inhabited a different time. Previous understandings of sibling rivalry and increasing emphasis on sibling friendship, coupled with legal and cultural practices that insisted on equality while simultaneously perpetuating hierarchy, all collided in eighteenth-century families. In a time with limited educational and economic prospects for women and with few financial resources outside family networks, siblings were essential to one another's social, emotional, and material survival. In performing or refusing to perform voluntary and obligatory exchanges of goods, services, and support, eighteenth-century sisters and brothers 'shared and shared alike' the labour of siblinghood. Conjugal family forms have become ascendant in contemporary conceptions of family life, but sibling ties have become the definitive language for much of current social, religious, and political thought. Siblings' lived experience coincided with notions of fictive siblinghood – both to those who valorized the unity and equality it represented and to those who worried that it would destabilize ancient hierarchies. Understanding just what it meant to be a sibling at the time when this language began to gain momentum can only help us to understand better the possibilities and pitfalls of familial and social relations.

In the eighteenth century, siblings, at times more than parents, were essential to one another's social, financial, familial, and emotional well-being, and for sheer longevity nothing outdid the sibling tie. Sibling relationships were intricately complex, and understanding siblings is necessary to understanding early modern family and gender relations, and equally necessary to appreciating the role of family relations in social interaction. If they lived close to one another, siblings' frequent visits to each other deepened their relationships (whether positively or negatively or even ambiguously). Siblings marrying a set of siblings from another family, whether related or not, solidified connections. And of course, letter-writing, that great passion of the eighteenth century, could bind and inform across great expanses of time and distance. Because siblings, no matter what their station, were essential to one another's economic, social, material, and emotional lives it is not surprising that so many made the effort to maintain the connection, even if it was not accompanied by the warmest of feelings. Ideally sibling relationships were based upon love, affection, and friendship, and among functional sibling groups those three attributes were manifested in a variety of social, emotional, material, and physical actions. Conversely, and simultaneously, siblings were also enjoined to avoid the natural pitfall of rivalry and the inappropriate familiarity of incest. When acrimonious relationships developed between siblings all of the avenues available for expressing love and friendship could be denied or used to deepen conflict. In addition to receiving mixed messages about their natural friendship and rivalry, siblings inhabited another contradictory position. Cultural expectations and many family practices told siblings that they were equal, yet legal practices and co-existing social norms imagined them in a hierarchy of equality – a hierarchy based upon gender, birth order, and marital status. This hierarchy of equality affected siblings both within the family circle and beyond it. Ideas of social or political equality embodied in a sibling language hid the built-in hierarchies that were still in play both in families and in larger groups.

As the Georgian period ended there was a decline in siblings' material and economic interdependency and a simultaneous intensification in the literary portrayal of their emotional connections.[10] Sibling economies seem to have developed from 'practical means for mutual aid' into 'symbolic media for managing the emotional aspects of relationships'.[11] Sibling relationships were described as emotionally intense in the nineteenth century, but a recognition of their complexity declined. As 'family' came to mean an increasingly narrow group of people, some sibling work went underground and sibling conflict was reduced to birth-order-based rivalry. Siblings remained and remain important to emotional and social development, but they have lost the recognition of their importance. Sociology and psychology have recently demonstrated the importance of siblings throughout the life course, but the tone of these findings consistently emphasizes their discovery of an underappreciated and under-studied phenomenon.[12] At first glance it would appear that the change in economic patterns, in the parameters of women's lives, and in demographics has permanently altered the structure of sibling life. The emotional expectations of enduring friendship and the fears of combative rivalry seem to have survived intact.[13] How the stability of the immaterial aspects of siblinghood works when the material tools for expressing it have changed so drastically is a question yet to be answered. For some populations the economic and material interdependence of siblings lasted well into the twentieth century, and among many families the material and economic exchanges continue to exist, but its impact is only just beginning to be appreciated.[14]

In the thoughts and imaginations of most people, however, siblinghood has been stripped of its eighteenth-century functionality. In popular media 'brotherhood' conjures up nebulous ideas of solidarity and rugged friendship shared between fire-fighters or soldiers, and sisterhood is relegated to soft-focus, black-and-white photo spreads in coffee-table books.[15] One offering, a collection of short essays, each accompanied by a black and white photo of the sisters under discussion, shows them in close physical contact, often embracing (except for the teenage duo who are shown back to back and still in the midst of adolescent rivalry). The message is one of the universal bond of sisterhood – a bond that provides women with stability, a sense of safety, and support for a lifetime. 'Sisters are girlfriends', Saline writes, 'rivals, listening posts, shopping buddies, confidantes, and so much more.'[16] It was the 'so much more' that was a recognized element of both sisterhood and brotherhood in the eighteenth century. Coffee-table books and pocket gift books extolling the virtues and special characteristics of sisterhood are not currently produced for brothers. Other family relationships, including that between fathers and sons, also receive these kinds of popular memorials, but brothers lie beyond the pale of such discussions (as, apparently, do brother–sister relationships). This literature, while supportive of sisterhood, has narrowed the expansive definition and function of siblings expected for both brothers and sisters in the eighteenth century.

Despite assertions that conjugal family forms were triumphant, sibling ties and their relation to marriage continued to be hotly contested throughout the nineteenth century, as the debate over marriage with a deceased wife's sister demonstrated. The Marriage Act of 1835 prohibited this practice, but the already century-old debate over the issue continued unabated until 1907. In essence, it was not the nineteenth century but the twentieth century that saw conjugal ties completely triumph over the fraternal connections in legal statute. Marriage to a deceased wife's sister or a deceased husband's brother was made legal in 1907 and 1921 respectively – thus subsuming all affinal sibling ties to conjugal ties.[17] These Acts, combined with the criminalization of incest in 1908 constituted the final step in establishing biology as the sole marker of fraternal ties and thus eliminating the tension between the conjugal and the fraternal, as blood-related siblings had always been within the degrees of prohibited marriage. The final marker of the primacy of the conjugal over the fraternal, however, was not visible until 1985. Between 1908 and 1985 the range of relationships classified as incest or for whom marriage was prohibited continually narrowed as step- and god-relations (over the age of eighteen) were allowed and as people once related through marriage were permitted to establish marital or sexual relations after divorce or death. In reviewing the incest law of 1908, the 1985 report from the Criminal Law Revision Committee recommended a radical rethinking of sibling incest, suggesting that 'sexual relations between brothers and sisters should 'cease to be an offence where they have both reached the age of 21'.[18] Though this never became law the mere suggestion that sexual and conjugal relationships could replace and trump sibling relations was the culmination of two centuries of wrangling.

Instead of emphasizing the triumphant conjugal family of the nineteenth century or our current nostalgic renderings of sibling relations, further attention to the practicalities of siblinghood elucidates the nuances of eighteenth-century family life and the ideas of social organization that took their model from families. As the century progressed, social and political theorists employed sibling language to suggest friendly, equal alliances and encouraged the diminishment of its rivalrous connotations.[19] The most radical rethinking of sibling relations, both consanguineal and fictive, occurred when the French National Convention gave illegitimate children the same inheritance rights as their legitimate siblings and equal treatment to sons and daughters. Though this law did not last and nothing like it was passed in Britain (despite political recognition of unequal inheritance practices since at least the Interregnum), it demonstrates the contemporary tension between a sibling-based language of equality and continuing unequal hierarchies between real brothers and sisters.[20] By the end of the Georgian period siblings had not resolved the tension between equality and hierarchy. It could be claimed that once women were no longer barred from the vote, higher education, and certain occupations, they and their brothers no longer struggled with inequality. From a legal perspective it is possible to claim that the 1925 Administration of Estates Act, which ended primogeniture finally made siblings truly equal in property matters. But these must be balanced against the persistent, and even worsening, condition of women's economic and legal status in the nineteenth century, even as the language of equality became more prevalent. Simultaneously, fictive siblinghood strengthened its hold on English society just as real siblinghood lost many of its material elements and as conjugal forms dominated discussions and research.[21] Legal and social reforms of the nineteenth and twentieth centuries repeatedly played up the language of shared siblinghood to conjure notions of 'one for all and all for one' equality and reciprocity. Whether in labour reform, abolition, voluntary associations, religion, or feminism, fictive siblinghood continues as a powerful metaphor of social and political organization.[22] The contemporary metaphor, however, based as it is on a narrower, less practical understanding of siblinghood, misses the real contours of sibling relations, fictive or real. Though built-in privileges for males and older children have largely been dismantled in the last 150 years, the language of equality continues to belie, for better or worse, the very different social, financial, and familial fortunes of siblings.[23] And in that there is a lesson for political and social organization. Unless it analyses how real siblings managed a relationship meant to be equal but fraught with competition, envy, hierarchy, and resentment, contemporary society misses the opportunity to ponder how ideas of social fraternal equality hide other hierarchies. By borrowing the language of siblinghood without understanding its meaning we misinterpret the costs and benefits of sharing and sharing alike.

Notes

1 Sanders, *The Brother–Sister Culture*, p. 31.
2 Francis Travell, will, written 20 July 1792, proved 14 July 1801, Prerogative Court of Canterbury, ORO, Flick, I/i/5; Agnes Travell Witts, diary, 23 June 1801, WFP, F199.
3 Anne Travell, daybook, 22 October 1804, GA, D4582/4/17/18; Agnes Travell Witts, diary, 24 October 1804, WFP, F205.
4 Anne Travell, daybook, 29 October 1804, GA, D4582/4/17/18.
5 Agnes Travell Witts, diary, 27 September 1808, WFP, F212.
6 Verey, ed., *The Diary of a Cotswold Parson*, p. 35.
7 Davidoff, 'Kinship as a Categorical Concept'.
8 Verey (ed.), *The Diary of a Cotswold Parson*, p. 45.
9 Martha Travell Whalley, pious diary, 26 April 1826, GA, D4582/5/9.
10 Mink and Ward, eds., *The Significance of Sibling Relationships in Literature*; Sanders, *The Brother–Sister Culture*.
11 Cheal, *The Gift Economy*, p. 5.
12 DeVita-Raeburn, *The Empty Room*; Victor G. Cicirelli, 'The Role of siblings as Family Caregivers' in W. J. Sauer & R. T. Coward, eds., *Social Support Networks and the Care of the Elderly* (New York, 1985), pp. 93–107; Ann Goetting, 'The Developmental Tasks of Siblingship over the Life Cycle', *Journal of Marriage and the Family*, 48:4 (November 1986), 703–14; I. A. Connidis, 'Siblings as Friends in Later Life', *American Behavioral Scientist*, 33:1 (1989), 81–93; Victor G. Cicirelli, 'Sibling Relationships in Cross-Cultural Perspective', *Journal of Marriage and the Family*, 56:1 (February 1994), 7–20; Eunice G. Pollack, 'The Childhood we have Lost: When Siblings were Caregivers, 1900–1970', *Journal of Social History*, 36:1 (Autumn 2002), 31–61; Berit Ingersoll-Dayton et al., 'Redressing

Inequity in Parent Care among Siblings', *Journal of Marriage and the Family*, 65:1 (February 2003), 201–12; Hilde Bras, 'Kinship and Sibling Networks: A Regional analysis of Sibling Relations in Twentieth-Century Netherlands', *Journal of Family History*, 32:3 (2007), 296–322.

13 Rowe, *My Dearest Enemy, my Dangerous Friend*.

14 Michele Stairs, 'Matthews and Marillas: Bachelors and Spinsters in Prince Edward Island in 1881', in Nancy Christie and Michael Gauvreau, eds., *Mapping the Margins: The Family and Social Discipline in Canada, 1700–1975* (Montreal, 2004), pp. 247–67; Gerald O'Brien, 'Rosemary Kennedy: The Importance of a Historical Footnote', *Journal of Family History*, 29:3 (July 2004), 225–36; Joan Marie Johnson, '"How would I live without Loulie?" Mary and Louisa Poppenheim, Activist Sisters in Turn-of-the-Century South Carolina', *Journal of Family History*, 28:4 (October 2003), 561–77; Desan, *The Family on Trial*, pp. 141–77; Sylvie Perrier, 'Coresidence of Siblings, Half-Siblings, and Step-siblings in *Ancien Régime* France', *The History of the Family: An International Quarterly*, 5:3 (2000), 299–314; Hemphill, *Siblings: Brothers and Sisters in American History*.

15 For example, the brotherhood image used extensively to describe fire-fighters around the world after 11 September 2001 and the popular television series *Band of Brothers*, depicting World War II soldiers.

16 Carol Saline with photographs by Sharon J. Wohlmuth, *Sisters* (Philadelphia and London, 1994), p. 13; *Sisters*, a Helen Exley Giftbook (New York and Watford, 1995).

17 Sybil Wolfram, *In-Laws and Outlaws: Kinship and Marriage in England* (London and Sydney, 1987).

18 Ibid., p. 44.

19 Leonore Davidoff, 'The Sibling Relationship and Sibling Incest in Historical Context', in Prophecy Coles, ed., *Sibling Relationships*, p. 36.

20 Beste, *The Christian Religion Briefly Defendeds*, ECCO.

21 Hylson-Smith, *Evangelicals in the Church of England, 1734–1984*, p. 209; Ronald A. Hill, 'Siblings, Religious Brotherhoods, or Neither: Oliver, Pratt, and Fowler or Foley Families of Whitehaven, England', *National Genealogical Society Quarterly*, 96:4 (December 2008), 283–98.

22 Wrightson, *Earthly Necessities*, pp. 79–82, 327–8; Offen, *European Feminisms*, p. 41; Juliet Flower MacCannell, *The Regime of the Brother: After the Patriarchy* (London and New York, 1991).

23 Conley, *The Pecking Order*.

Appendix 1
Tables

Table 1 Gender composition of sibling probate disputes, Diocese of Gloucester, 1700–1842

Gender conflict	Number	Percentage of total
Female v. female	23	15.1
Male v. male	39	25.7
Female v. male	48	31.6
Male v. female	42	27.6

Table 2 Younger versus older siblings in probate disputes, Diocese of Gloucester, 1700–1842

Silings involved (40 incidents)	Number of incidents	Percentage	Percentage of total cases
Sister v. older sister	4	10.0	4.7
Sister v. older brother	14	35.0	16.3
Brother v. older brother	15	37.5	17.4
Brother v. older sister	7	17.5	8.1

Table 3 Older versus younger siblings in probate disputes, Diocese of Gloucester, 1700–1842

Siblings involved (46 incidents)	Number of incidents	Percentage	Percentage of total cases
Sister v. younger sister	3	6.5	3.5
Sister v. younger brother	20	43.5	23.3
Brother v. younger brother	13	28.3	15.1
Brother v. younger sister	10	21.7	11.6

Table 4 Marital status of female litigants in probate disputes, Diocese of Gloucester, 1700–1842

Marital status	Plaintiffs	Defendants
Married sisters	44	20
Widowed sisters	14	25
Single sisters	5	9

Appendix 2
Family trees

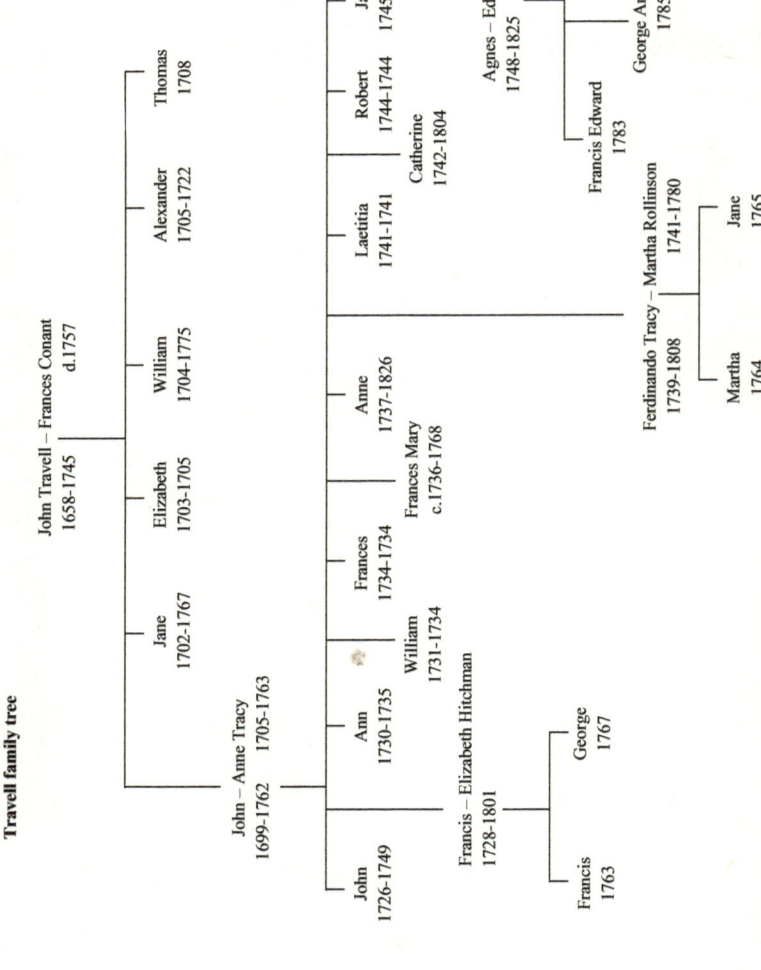

Appendix 2

Tracy, Keck, and Edwards family tree

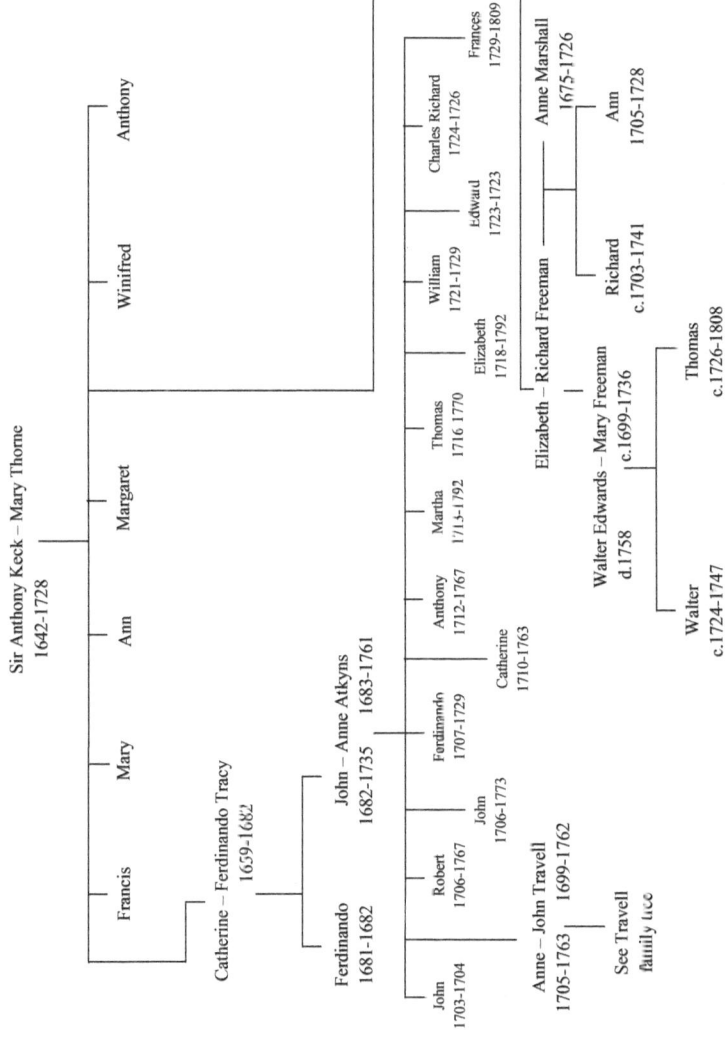

Appendix 2

Sharp family tree

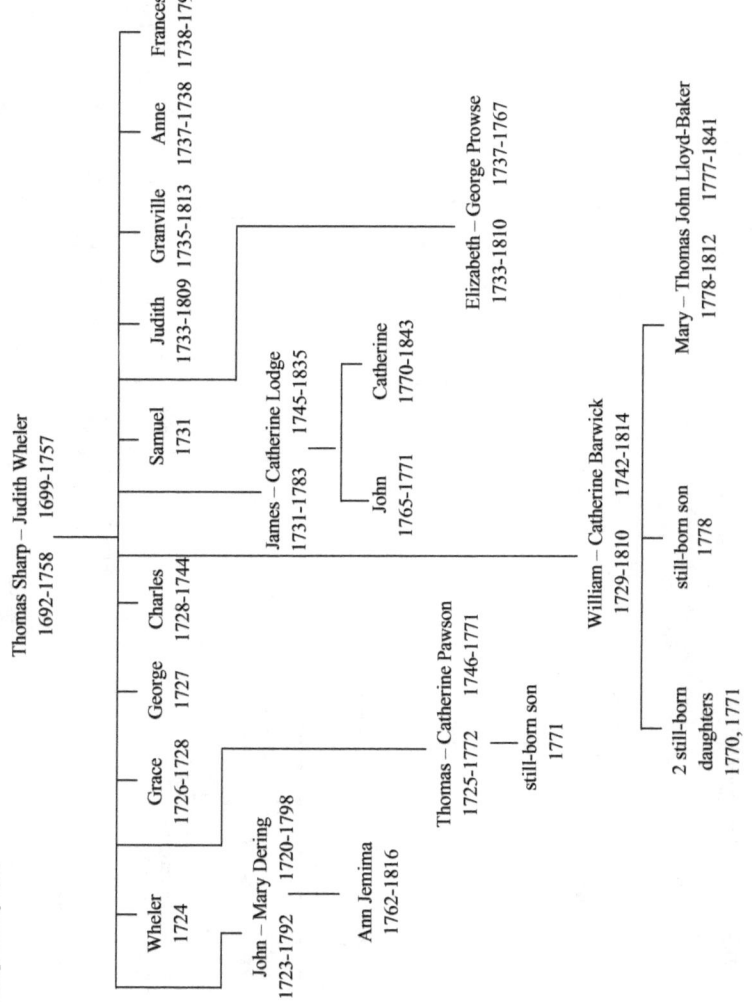

Appendix 2 181

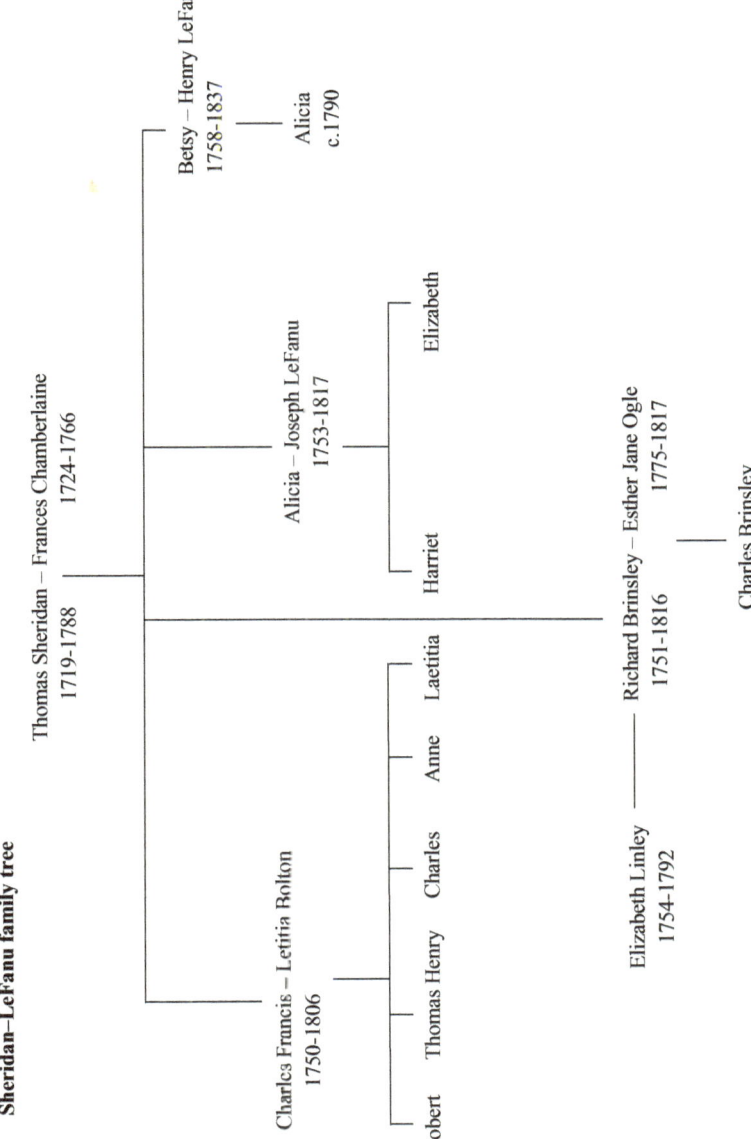

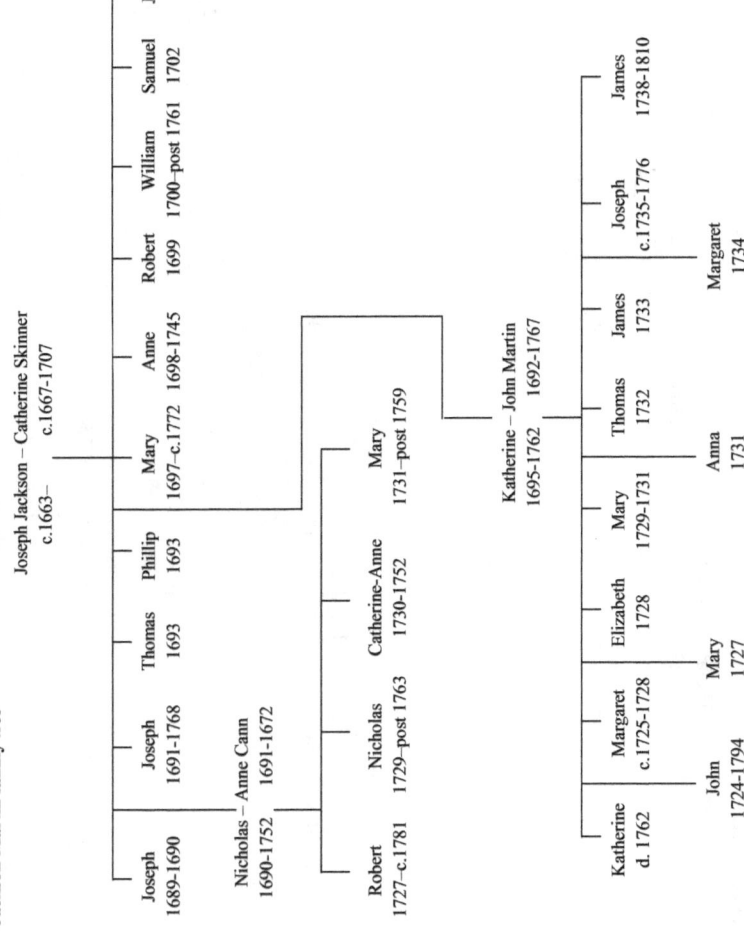

Select bibliography

Secondary sources

Abbott, Mary. *Family Ties: English Families 1540–1920*. London and New York: Routledge, 1993.
——. *Life Cycles in England, 1560–1720*. London and New York: Routledge, 1996.
Anderson, Michael. *Approaches to the History of the Western Family, 1500–1914*. (London and Basingstoke: Macmillan, 1980).
Ariès, Philippe. *Centuries of Childhood: A Social History of Family Life*. New York: Vintage, 1962.
Arizpe, Evelyn, and Morag Styles. ' "Love to learn your book": Children's Experiences of Text in the Eighteenth Century', *History of Education*, 33 (May 2004), 337–52.
Arkell, Tom, Nesta Evans, and Nigel Goose, eds. *When Death Do Us Part: Understanding and Interpreting the Probate Records of Early Modern England*. Oxford: Leopard's Head Press, 2000.
Atkins, Annett. *We Grew Up Together: Brothers and Sisters in Nineteenth-Century America*. Urbana and Chicago: University of Illinois Press, 2001.
Bailey, Joanne. *Parenting in England c.1760–1830: Emotions, Self-Identities and Generations*. Oxford: Oxford University Press, forthcoming.
——. *Unquiet Lives: Marriage and Marriage Breakdown in England, 1660–1800* Cambridge: Cambridge University Press, 2003.
Baine, A. *History of Kingswood Forest Including All the Ancient Manors and Villages in the Neighborhood*. London William F. Mack, Bristol, 1891
Bannet, Eve Tavor. *Empire of Letters: Letter Manuals and Transatlantic Correspondence, 1688–1820*. Cambridge: Cambridge University Press, 2005.
Barry, Jonathan. 'The Making of the Middle Class?', *Past and Present*, 145:1 (November 1994), 194–208.
Bell, Vikki. *Interrogating Incest: Feminism, Foucault and the Law*. London and New York: Routledge, 1993.

Ben-Amos, Ilana Krausman. *Adolescence and Youth in Early Modern England*. New Haven and London: Yale University Press, 1994.
——. *The Culture of Giving: Informal Support and Gift-Exchange in Early Modern England*. Cambridge: Cambridge University Press, 2008.
Bennett, Judith. *Women in the Medieval English Countryside: Gender and Household in Brigstock before the Plague*. New York and Oxford: Oxford University Press, 1987.
——, ed. *Sisters and Workers in the Middle Ages*. Chicago: University of Chicago Press, 1989.
Bennett, Judith, and Amy M. Froide, eds. *Singlewomen in the European Past, 1250–1800*. Philadelphia: University of Philadelphia Press, 1999.
Benzaquén, Adriana. 'Childhood, Identity, and Human Science in the Enlightenment', *History Workshop Journal*, 57:1 (Spring 2004), 35–57.
Berry, Helen, and Elizabeth Foyster, eds. *The Family in Early Modern England*. Cambridge: Cambridge University Press, 2007.
Binion, Rudolph. 'Notes on Romanticism', *The Journal of Psychohistory*, 11:1 (1983), 43–64.
Bloch, Ruth. 'American Feminine Ideals in Transition: The Rise of the Moral Mother, 1785–1815', *Feminist Studies* (1978), 101–27.
Bonca, Teddi Chichester. *Shelley's Mirrors of Love: Narcissism, Sacrifice, and Sorority*. Albany, NY: State University of New York Press, 1999.
Bowdon, Lynne. 'Redefining Kinship: Exploring Boundaries of Relatedness in Late Medieval New Romney', *Journal of Family History*, 29:4 (October 2004), 407–20.
Brant, Clare. *Eighteenth-Century Letters and British Culture*. Basingstoke and New York: Palgrave, 2006.
Bras, Hilde. 'Kinship and Sibling Networks: A Regional Analysis of Sibling Relations in Twentieth-Century Netherlands', *Journal of Family History*, 32:3 (2007), 296–322.
Brewer, Holly. *By Birth or Consent: Children, Law, and the Anglo-American Revolution in Authority*. Chapel Hill: University of North Carolina Press, 2005.
Broomhall, Susan, ed. *Emotions in the Household, 1200–1900*. Basingstoke: Palgrave Macmillan, 2008.
Brown, Sarah Annes. 'The Double Taboo: Lesbian Incest in the Nineteenth Century', *Nineteenth Century Studies*, 18 (2004): 81–98.
Chambers, Lee. *'Rocking the Nation like a Cradle': The Westons Fashion an Antislavery Sisterhood*, unpublished book manuscript, forthcoming.
Chambers-Schiller, Lee. *Liberty an Better Husband: Single Women in America: The Generations of 1780–1840*. New Haven and London: Yale University Press, 1984.
Cheal, David. *The Gift Economy*. London and New York: Routledge, 1988.
Cicirelli, Victor G., 'The Role of Siblings as Family Caregivers', in W. J. Sauer and R. T. Coward, eds., *Social Support Networks and the Care of the Elderly* (New York: Springer, 1985), pp. 93–107.
Cohen, Michael. *Sisters: Relation and Rescue in Nineteenth-Century British Novels and Paintings*. London and Toronto: Associated University Press, 1995.

Cohen, Michèle. ' "Manners" Make the Man: Politeness, Chivalry, and the Construction of Masculinity, 1750–1830', *Journal of British Studies*, 44 (April 2005): 312–29.
Coles, Prophecy, ed. *Sibling Relationships*. London and New York: Karnac, 2006.
Collins, Stephen. 'British Stepfamily Relations, 1500–1800', *Journal of Family History*, 16:4 (1991), 331–44.
Conger, Rand D., et al., eds. *Continuity and Change in Family Relations: Theory, Methods, and Empirical Findings*. Mahwah, NJ, and London: Lawrence Erlbaum, 2004.
Conley, Dalton. *The Pecking Order: Which Siblings Succeed and Why*. New York: Pantheon Books, 2004.
Connell, R.W. *Gender and Power: Society, the Person, and Sexual Politics*. Palo Alto: Stanford University Press, 1987.
Connidis, I. A. 'Siblings as Friends in Later life', *American Behavioral Scientist*, 33:1 (1989), 81–93.
Cooper, Sheila. 'Intergenerational Social Mobility in Late-Seventeenth- and Early-Eighteenth-Century England', *Continuity and Change*, 7:3 (1992), 283–301.
Corbett, Mary Jean. *Family Likeness: Sex, Marriage, and Incest from Jane Austen to Virginia Woolf*. Ithaca and New York: Cornell University Press, 2008.
Coster, Will. *Family and Kinship in England, 1450–1800*. London: Pearson Education, 2001.
Crawford, Patricia. *Blood, Bodies and Families in Early Modern England*. Harlow: Longman, 2004.
——. *Parents of Poor Children in England, 1580–1800*. Oxford: Oxford University Press, 2010.
Cressy, David. *Birth, Marriage and Death: Ritual, Religion and the Life-Cycle in Tudor and Stuart England*. Oxford: Oxford University Press, 1997.
——. 'Kinship and Kin Interaction in Early Modern England', *Past and Present*, 113:1 (1986): 38–69.
Cunningham, Hugh. *The Invention of Childhood*. London: BBC Books, 2006.
Curran, Stuart. 'Dynamics of Female Friendship in the Later Eighteenth Century', *Nineteenth-Century Contexts*, 23:2 (2001), 221–39.
Davidoff, Leonore. 'Kinship as a Categorical Concept: A Case Study of Nineteenth Century English Siblings', *Journal of Social History*, 39:2 (Winter 2005), 411–28.
——. *Thicker than Water: Siblings and their Relations, 1780–1920*. Oxford: Oxford University Press, forthcoming.
——. *Worlds Between: Historical Perspectives on Gender and Class*. Cambridge: Polity Press, 1995.
Davidoff, Leonore, and Catherine Hall. *Family Fortunes: Men and Women of the English Middle Class, 1780–1850*. Chicago: University of Chicago Press, 1987.
Desan, Suzanne. *The Family on Trial in Revolutionary France*. Berkeley, Los Angeles, and London: University of California Press, 2004.
Doebler, Bettie Anne. *'Rooted Sorrow': Dying in Early Modern England*. London and Toronto: Associated University Press, 1994.

Dowd, Michelle, and Julie Eckerle, eds. *Genre and Women's Life Writing in Early Modern England*. Burlington, VT: Ashgate, 2007.

Earle, Rebecca. *Epistolary Selves: Letters and Letter-Writers, 1600–1945*. Aldershot, Hampshire: Ashgate, 1999.

Edwards, Rosalind, et al. *Sibling Identity and Relationships: Sisters and Brothers*. London and New York: Routledge, 2006.

Erickson, Amy Louise. *Women and Property in Early Modern England*. London and New York: Routledge, 1993.

Fara, Patricia. *Pandora's Breeches: Women, Science, and Power in the Enlightenment*. London: Pimlico, 2004.

Fildes, Valerie, ed. *Women as Mothers in Pre-Industrial England: Essays in Memory of Dorothy McLaren*. New York: Routledge, 1990.

Finch, Janet, and Jennifer Mason. *Negotiating Family Responsibilities*. London and New York: Tavistock and Routledge, 1993.

——, et al. *Wills, Inheritance, and Families*. Oxford and New York: Oxford University Press, 1996.

Finn, Margot. *The Character of Credit: Personal Debt in English Culture, 1740–1914*. Cambridge: Cambridge University Press, 2003.

Flandrin, Jean-Louis. *Families in Former Times: Kinship, Household, Sexuality*. Trans. Richard Southern. Cambridge: Cambridge University Press, 1979.

Fletcher, Anthony. *Gender, Sex and Subordination in England, 1500–1800*. New Haven and London: Yale University Press, 1995.

——. *Growing Up in England: The Experience of Childhood, 1600–1914*. New Haven and London: Yale University Press, 2008.

Fliegelman, Jay. *Prodigals and Pilgrims: The American Revolution against Patriarchal Authority, 1750–1800*. Cambridge: Cambridge University Press, 1982.

Flinn, Michael. *The European Demographic System, 1500–1820*. Baltimore: Johns Hopkins University Press, 1981.

Fox, Bonnie, ed. *Family Bonds and Gender Divisions: Readings in the Sociology of the Family*. Toronto: Canadian Scholars' Press, 1988.

Franks, D., and D. McCarthy, eds. *The Sociology of Emotion: Original Essays and Research Papers*. Greenwich, CT: JAI Press, 1989.

Froide, Amy. *Never Married: Singlewomen in Early Modern England*. Oxford: Oxford University Press, 2004.

Frye, Susan, and Karen Robertson, eds. *Maids and Mistresses, Cousins and Queens: Women's Alliances in Early Modern England*. New York and Oxford: Oxford University Press, 1999.

Fussell, G. E. *The English Countrywoman: Her Life in Farmhouse and Field from Tudor Times to the Victorian Age*. London: Orbis, 1981.

Gillis, John. *For Better, for Worse: British Marriages, 1600 to the Present*. New York and Oxford: Oxford University Press, 1985.

——. *A World of their Own Making: Myth, Ritual and the Quest for Family Values*. Cambridge, MA: Harvard University Press, 1997.

Select bibliography

———. *Youth and History: Tradition and Change in European Age Relations, 1770 – Present*, Expanded student edn. Orlando: Academic Press, 1981.
Gittings, Robert, and Jo Manton. *Claire Clairmont and the Shelleys, 1798–1879*. Oxford and New York: Oxford University Press, 1992.
Glenn, Evelyn Nakano, Grace Chang, and Linda Rennie Forcey, eds. *Mothering: Ideology, Experience, and Agency*. New York and London: Routledge, 1994.
Glover, Lorri. *All Our Relations: Ties and Emotional Bonds among the Early South Carolina Gentry*. Baltimore and London: Johns Hopkins University Press, 2000.
Goetting, Ann. 'The Developmental Tasks of Siblingship over the Life Cycle', *Journal of Marriage and the Family*, 48:4 (November 1986), 703–14.
Goldenthal, Peter. *Why Can't We Get Along? Healing Adult Sibling Relationships*. New York: John Wiley and Sons, 2002.
Goody, Jack. *The Development of the Family and Marriage in Europe*. Cambridge: Cambridge University Press, 1983.
Grassby, Richard. *Kinship and Capitalism: Marriage, Family, and Business in the English-Speaking World, 1580–1740*. Cambridge: Cambridge University Press, and Woodrow Wilson Center Press, 2001.
Gruner, Elisabeth Rose. 'Born and Made: Sisters, Brothers, and the Deceased Wife's Sister Bill', *Signs*, 24:2 (Winter 1999), 423–47.
Hanawalt, Barbara. *Growing Up in Medieval London: The Experience of Childhood in History*. New York: Oxford University Press, 1993.
———. *The Ties that Bound: Peasant Families in Medieval England*. Oxford and New York: Oxford University Press, 1986.
———. *The Wealth of Wives: Women, Law, and Economy in Late Medieval London*. Oxford: Oxford University Press, 2007.
Hans, Nicholas. *New Trends in Education in the Eighteenth Century*. London: Routledge, 1951.
Hareven, Tamara. *Families, History, and Social Change: Life-Course and Cross-Cultural Perspectives*. Boulder, CO: Westview Press, 2000.
———, ed. *Transitions: the Family and the Life Course in Historical Perspective*. New York: Academic Press, 1978.
Hareven, Tamara, and Andrejs Plakans. *Family History at the Crossroads: A Journal of Family History Reader*. Princeton: Princeton University Press, 1987.
Harrington, Joel F. *The Unwanted Child: The Fate of Foundlings, Orphans, and Juvenile Criminals in Early Modern Germany*. Chicago and London: University of Chicago Press, 2009.
Harris, Amy. 'This I Beg my Aunt may not Know: Young Letter-Writers in Eighteenth-Century England, Peer correspondence in a Hierarchical World', *Journal of the History of Childhood and Youth*, 2:3 (2009), 333–60.
Hart, Gwen. *A History of Cheltenham*. Oxford: Leicester University Press, 1965
Hartman, Mary S. *The Household and the Making of History: A Subversive View of the Western Past*. Cambridge: Cambridge University Press, 2004.

Heal, Felicity, and Clive Holmes. *The Gentry in England and Wales, 1500–1700*. Stanford: Stanford University Press, 1994.
Hemphill, C. Dallett. 'Sibling Relations in Early American Childhoods: A Cross-Cultural Analysis', in James Marten, ed., *Children in Colonial America*. New York: New York University Press, 2007, pp. 77–89.
———. *Siblings: Brothers and Sisters in American History*. Oxford: Oxford University Press, 2011.
Hendrick, Harry. 'The Child as a Social Actor in Historical Sources: Problems of Identification and Interpretation', in Pia Christensen and Allison James, eds., *Research with Children: Perspectives and Practices*. London and New York: Falmer Press, 1999, pp. 36–61.
Hill, Bridget. *Servants: English Domestics in the Eighteenth Century*. Oxford: Clarendon Press, 1996.
———. *Women Alone: Spinsters in England 1660–1850*. London and New Haven: Yale University Press, 2001.
Hilton, Mary, and Jill Shefrin, eds., *Educating the Child in Enlightenment Britain: Beliefs, Cultures, Practices* (Farnham, Surrey, and Burlington, VT: Ashgate, 2009).
Hilton, Mary, Morag Styles, and Victor Watson, eds. *Opening the Nursery Door: Reading, Writing and Childhood 1600–1900*. London and New York: Routledge, 1997.
Hindle, Steve. *On the Parish? The Micro-Politics of Poor Relief in Rural England, c.1550–1750*. Oxford: Oxford University Press, 2004.
Hochshild, Arile Russell. 'Emotion Work, Feeling Rules and Social Structure', *American Journal of Sociology*, 85 (1979), 551–75.
Hockaday, F.S. 'The Consistory Court of Gloucester', *Transactions of the Bristol and Gloucestershire Archaeological Society*, 46 (1924), 195–288.
Houlbrooke, Ralph. *Death, Religion and the Family in England, 1480–1750*. Oxford University Press, 1998.
———. *The English Family 1450–1700*. London and New York: Longman, 1984.
Hudson, Glenda A. *Sibling Love and Incest in Jane Austen's Fiction*. New York: St Martin's Press, 1992.
Hufton, Olwen. *The Prospect before Her: A History of Women in Western Europe*. New York: Vintage, 1995.
Hunt, Lynn. *The Family Romance of the French Revolution*. Berkeley and Los Angeles: University of California Press, 1992.
Hussey, David and Margaret Ponsonby, eds. *Buying for the Home: Shopping for the Domestic from the seventeenth Century to the Present*. Aldershot, Hampshire: Ashgate, 2008.
Hylson-Smith, Kenneth. *Evangelicals in the Church of England, 1734–1984*, Edinburgh: T. & T. Clark, 1988.
Ingersoll-Dayton, Berit, et al. 'Redressing Inequity in Parent Care Among Siblings', *Journal of Marriage and the Family*, 65:1 (February 2003), 201–12.

James, Allison, Chris Jenks, and Alan Prout. *Theorizing Childhood*. Oxford and Cambridge: Polity Press, 1998.

James, Allison, and Alan Prout, eds. *Constructing and Reconstructing Childhood: Contemporary Issues in the Sociological Study of Childhood*. 2nd edn. London and Washington, DC: Falmer Press, 1997.

Jamoussi, Zouheir. *Primogeniture and Entail in England: A Survey of their History and Representation in Literature*. Tunis: Centre de Publication Universitaire, 1999.

Johnson, Christopher H., and David Warren Sabean, eds. *Sibling Relations and the Transformation of European Kinship, 1300–1900*. New York and Oxford: Berghahn, 2011.

Kuper, Adam. *Incest and Influence: The Private Life of Bourgeois England*. Cambridge and London: Harvard University Press, 2009.

——. 'Incest, Cousin Marriage, and the Origin of the Human Sciences in Nineteenth-Century England', *Past and Present*, 174:1 (2002), 158–83.

Laslett, Peter. *Family Life and Illicit Love in Earlier Generations*. Cambridge: Cambridge University Press, 1977.

——. *Household and Family in Past Time*. Cambridge: Cambridge University Press, 1972.

——. *The World we have Lost: Further Explored*. London: Methuen, 1983.

Lemire, Beverly. *The Business of Everyday Life: Gender, Practice and Social Politics in England, c.1600–1900*. Manchester and New York: Manchester University Press, 2005.

Levin, Amy K. *The Suppressed Sister: A Relationship in Novels by Nineteenth- and Twentieth-Century British Women*. London and Toronto: Associated University Press, 1992.

MacFarlane, Alan. *The Family Life of Ralph Josselin, a Seventeenth-Century Clergyman*. Cambridge: Cambridge University Press, 1970.

——. *Marriage and Love in England: Modes of Reproduction, 1300–1840*. Oxford and New York: Basil Blackwell, 1986.

——. *The Origins of English Individualism: The Family, Property and Social Transition*. Cambridge and New York: Cambridge University Press, 1978.

——. 'Review of *The Family, Sex and Marriage in England 1500–1800*, by Lawrence Stone', *History and Theory*, 18:1 (February 1979), 103–26.

McIntosh, Marjorie. 'Women, Credit, and Family Relationships in England 1300–1620', *Journal of Family History*, 30:2 (April 2005), 143–63.

McNaron, Toni, ed. *The Sister Bond: A Feminist View of a Timeless Connection*. New York: Pergamon Press, 1985.

Maddern, Philippa. 'Between Households: Children in Blended and Transitional Households in Late-Medieval England', *Journal of the History of Childhood and Youth*, 3:1 (Winter 2010), 65–86.

Marcus, Sharon. *Between Women: Friendship, Desire, and Marriage in Victorian England*. Princeton: Princeton University Press, 2007.

Mares, Marie-Louise. 'The Aging Family', in Mary Anne Fitzpatrick and Anita L. Vangelisti, eds., *Explaining Family Interactions*. Thousand Oaks, London, and New Dehli: Sage Publications, 1995, pp. 344–74.

May, Leila Silvana. *Disorderly Sisters: Sibling Relations and Sororal Resistance in Nineteenth-Century British Literature*. London: Associated University Press, 2001.

Maynes, Mary Jo. 'Age as a Category of Historical Analysis: History, Agency, and the Narratives of Childhood', *Journal of the History of Childhood and Youth*, 1:1 (2008), 114–24.

Medick, Hans, and David Warren Sabean, eds. *Interest and Emotion: Essays on the Study of Family and Kinship*. Cambridge and New York: Cambridge University Press, 1984.

Mendelson, Sara, and Patricia Crawford. *Women in Early Modern England 1550–1720*. Oxford: Clarendon Press, 1998.

Miller, Naomi, and Naomi Yavneh. *Sibling Relations and Gender in the Early Modern World: Siblings, Brothers, and others*. Aldershot, Hampshire, and Burlington, VT: Ashgate, 2006.

Mink, JoAnna Stephens, and Janet Doubler Ward, eds. *The Significance of Sibling Relationships in Literature*. Bowling Green, OH: Bowling Green State University Popular Press, 1993.

Mitterauer, Michael. *The European Family: Patriarchy to Partnership from the Middle Ages to the Present*. Oxford: Basil Blackwell, 1982.

Moore, Wendy. 'Love and Marriage in 18th-Century Britain', *Historically Speaking: The Bulletin of the Historical Society*, 10:3 (June 2009), 8–10.

Muldrew, Craig. *The Economy of Obligation: The Culture of Credit and Social Relations in Early Modern England*. New York: St. Martin's Press, 1998.

Nicholls, Mark. 'As Happy a Fortune as I Desire: The Pursuit of Financial Security by the Younger Brothers of Henry Percy, 9th Earl of Northumberland', *Historical Research*, 65:158 (1992), 296–314.

O'Day, Rosemary. *The Family and Family Relationships, 1500–1900: England, France and the United States of America*. New York: St Martin's Press, 1994.

O'Malley, Andrew. *The Making of the Modern Child: Children's Literature and Childhood in Late Eighteenth-Century England*. London and New York: Routledge, 2003.

Ottaway, Susanna. *The Decline of Life: Old Age in Eighteenth-Century England*. Cambridge: Cambridge University Press, 2004.

Pearsall, Sarah. *Atlantic Families: Lives and Letters in the Later Eighteenth Century*. New York and Oxford: Oxford University Press, 2008.

Perrier, Sylvie. 'Coresidence of Siblings, Half-Siblings, and Step-Siblings in *Ancien Régime* France', *The History of the Family: An International Quarterly*, 5:3 (2000), 299–314.

Perry, Ruth. *Novel Relations: The Transformation of Kinship in English Literature and Culture 1748–1818*. Cambridge: Cambridge University Press, 2004.

Persson, Inga, and Christina Jonung, eds. *Economics of the Family and Family Policies*. London and New York: Routledge, 1997.

Pinchbeck, I. and M. Hewitt. *Children in English Society*, 2 vols. London: Routledge, 1969.
Pollack, Eunice G. 'The Childhood we have Lost: When Siblings were Caregivers, 1900–1970', *Journal of Social History*, 36:1 (Autumn 2002), 31–51.
Pollock, Linda. 'Childbearing and Female Bonding in Early Modern England', *Social History*, 22:3 (October 1997), 286–306.
——. *Forgotten Children: Parent–Child Relations from 1500 to 1900*. Cambridge: Cambridge University Press, 1983.
——. *A Lasting Relationship: Parents and Children over Three Centuries*. Hanover and London: University Press of New England, 1987.
——. 'Rethinking Patriarchy and the Family in Seventeenth-Century England', *Journal of Family History*, 23:1 (January 1998), 3–27.
——. 'Younger Sons in Tudor and Stuart England', *History Today*, 39:6 (June 1989), 23–9.
Porter, Roy, ed. *Rewriting the Self: Histories from the Renaissance to the Present*. London and New York: Routledge, 1997.
Price, Richard. *British Society, 1680–1880: Dynamism, Containment, and Change*. Cambridge: Cambridge University Press, 1999.
Purdue, A.W. 'John and Harriet Carr: A Brother and Sister from the North-East on the Grand Tour', *Northern History*, 30 (1994), 122–38.
Razzell, Peter. 'The Growth of Population in Eighteenth-Century England: A Critical Reappraisal', *Journal of Economic History*, 53:4 (December 1993), 743–71.
Retford, Kate. *The Art of Domestic Life: Family Portraiture in Eighteenth-Century England*. New Haven and London: Paul Mellon Centre for Studies in British Art, Yale University Press, 2006.
——. 'Sensibility and Genealogy in the Eighteenth-Century Family Portrait: The Collection at Kedleston Hall', *Historical Journal*, 46:3 (2003), 533–60.
Rosser, Gervase. 'Going to the Fraternity Feast: Commensality and Social Relations in Late Medieval England', *Journal of British Studies*, 33:4 (October 1994), 430–46.
Rowe, Dorothy. *My Dearest Enemy, my Dangerous Friend: Making and Breaking Sibling Bonds*. London and New York: Routledge, 2007.
Saffady, William. 'The Effects of Childhood Bereavement and Parental Remarriage in Sixteenth-Century England: The Case of Thomas More', *History of Childhood Quarterly*, 1:3 (1973), 310–36.
Sanders, Valerie. *The Brother–Sister Culture in Nineteenth-Century Literature*. Houndmills, Hampshire: Palgrave, 2002.
Schneider, Gary. *The Culture of Epistolary: Vernacular Letters and Letter-Writing in Early Modern England, 1500–1700*. Newark: University of Delaware Press, 2005.
Slater, Miriam. *Family Life in the Seventeenth Century: The Verneys of Claydon House*. Boston and London: Routledge and Kegan Paul, 1984.
Soliday, G.L., with Tamara Hareven. *History of the Family and Kinship: A Select International Bibliography*. Milwood, NY: Kraus, 1980.

Sommerville, C. John. *The Rise and Fall of Childhood*. Beverly Hills: Sage Publications, 1982.
Spring, Eileen. *Law, Land and Family: Aristocratic Inheritance in England, 1300 to 1800*. Chapel Hill and London: University of North Carolina Press, 1993.
——. 'The Strict Settlement: Its Role in Family History', *Economic History Review*, 41:3 (August 1988), 454–60.
Stabile, Susan. *Memory's Daughters: The Material Culture of Remembrance in Eighteenth-Century America*. Ithaca and London: Cornell University Press, 2004.
Staves, Susan. *Married Women's Separate Property in England, 1660–1833*. Cambridge, MA, and London: Harvard University Press, 1990.
Stearns, Carol Z. 'Introducing the History of Emotion', *The Psychohistory Review*, 18:3 (1990), 263–91.
Steedman, Carolyn. *Strange Dislocations: Childhood and the Idea of Human Interiority, 1780–1930*. Cambridge: Harvard University Press, 1995.
Stern, Rebecca. *Home Economics: Domestic Fraud in Victorian England*. Columbus: Ohio State University Press, 2008.
Steward, James Christen. *The New Child: British Art and the Origins of Modern Childhood, 1730–1830*. Berkeley: University Art Museum and Pacific Film Archive, University of California, distributed by University of Washington Press, 1995.
Stone, Lawrence. *The Family, Sex and Marriage in England, 1500–1800*. New York: Harper and Row, 1977.
Sulloway, Frank J. *Born to Rebel: Birth Order, Family Dynamics, and Creative Lives*. New York: Vintage Books, 1996.
Sweet, Rosemary and Penelope Lane, *Women and Urban Life in Eighteenth-Century England: 'On the Town'*. Aldershot, Hampshire, and Burlington, VT: Ashgate, 2003.
Tadmor, Naomi. *Family and Friends in Eighteenth-Century England: Household, Kinship, and Patronage*. Cambridge: Cambridge University Press, 2001.
Tague, Ingrid. *Women of Quality: Accepting and Contesting Ideals of Femininity in England, 1690–1760*. Woodbridge, Suffolk, and Rochester, NY: Boydell Press, 2002.
Tannen, Deborah. *You were Always Mom's Favorite! Sisters in Conversation throughout their Lives*. New York: Random House, 2009.
Thirsk, Joan. 'Younger Sons in the Seventeenth Century', *History*, 54:182 (1969), 358–77.
Thorne, Barrie, and Marilyn Yalom, eds. *Rethinking the Family: Some Feminist Questions*, rev. edn. Boston: Northeastern University Press, 1992.
Tillyard, Stella. *Aristocrats: Caroline, Emily, Louisa, and Sarah Lennox, 1740–1832*. New York: Noonday Press, 1994.
——. *A Royal Affair: George III and his Scandalous Siblings*. New York: Random House, 2006.

Tippetts, Nancy Lyn. *Sisterhood, Brotherhood, and Equality of the Sexes in the Restoration Comedies of Manners.* New York: Peter Lang, 1994.
Tosh, John. *A Man's Place: Masculinity and the Middle-Class Home in Victorian England.* New Haven and London: Yale University Press, 1999.
Trumbach, Randolph. *The Rise of the Egalitarian Family: Aristocratic Kinship and Domestic Relations in Eighteenth-Century England.* New York: Academic Press, 1978.
Vaught, Jennifer C. *Masculinity and Emotion in Early Modern English Literature.* Aldershot, Hampshire: Ashgate. 2008.
Vickery, Amanda. *Behind Closed Doors: At Home in Georgian England.* New Haven and London: Yale University Press, 2009.
——. *The Gentleman's Daughter: Women's Lives in Georgian England.* New Haven and London: Yale University Press, 1998.
Vincent, David. *Literacy and Popular Culture: England 1750-1914.* Cambridge: Cambridge University Press, 1989.
Wahrman, Dror. *The Making of the Modern Self: Identity and Culture in Eighteenth-Century England.* New Haven: Yale University Press, 2004.
Wall, Richard, et al., eds. *Family Forms in Historic Europe.* Cambridge: Cambridge University Press, 1983.
Waller, Gary. 'Mother/Son, Father/Daughter, Brother/Sister, Cousins: The Sidney Family Romance', *Modern Philology*, 88:4 (May 1999), 401–14
Watts, Richard J. *Power in Family Discourse.* Berlin and New York: Mouton de Gruyter, 1991.
Weil, Rachel. *Political Passions: Gender, the Family and Political Argument in England, 1680-1714.* Manchester and New York: Manchester University Press, 1999
Wilde, Francesca Suzanne. 'London Letters (1720-1728) Written by Mary (Granville) Pendarves to her Sister, Anne Granville, in Gloucester: A Sequence from the Autobiography and Correspondence of Mary Delany, Formerly Mary Pendarves, née Granville (1700-1788)'. PhD dissertation, University of York, 2003.
Wrightson, Keith. *Earthly Necessities: Economic Lives in Early Modern Britain.* New Haven: Yale University Press, 2000.
Wrigley, E. Anthony. *Population and History.* London: Weidenfeld and Nicholson, 1969.
Wrigley, E. Anthony, and Roger Schofield. *The Population History of England, 1541-1871: A Reconstruction.* Cambridge: Cambridge University Press, 1989.
——, et al., eds. *English Population History from Family Reconstitution, 1580-1837.* Cambridge: Cambridge University Press, 1997.
Wulf, Karin. *Not All Wives: Women of Colonial Philadelphia.* Ithaca and London: Cornell University Press, 2000.
Yalom, Marilyn. *A History of the Wife.* New York: Harper Collins, 2001.
Yerby, George. *People and Parliament: Representative Rights and the English Revolution.* Basingstoke and New York: Palgrave Macmillan, 2008.

Primary sources

Published literature

Addington, Stephen. *Religious and Prudential Maxims Collected from the Sacred Scriptures and Other Writings.* London: James Buckland, 1768. ECCO.
Alcott, William A. *Letters to a Sister; or Woman's Mission. To Accompany the Letters to Young Men.* Buffalo: George Derby, 1850. BL, 8415.e.31.
Allestree, Richard. *The Works of the Learned and Pious Author of the Whole Duty of Man.* London and Oxford: John Baskett, 1726. BAN, FBV 4500.A43 1726.
Anonymous. *Advice to the Fair: An Epistolary Essay in Three Parts: On Dress, Converse, and Marriage: Addressed to a Sister.* London: J. Wilford, 1738. BL, 11660.g.
Anonymous. *The Affecting History of Mr. Anley and his Sister.* London: T. & R. Hughes, [c.1810]. BL, 12452.a.34.(2).
Anonymous. *The Barnard Castle Tragedy.* 1718. BL, Roxburghe Ballads Collection, Rox.111.797 (1718).
Anonymous. 'The blood brother', in a collection of songs and ballads. BL, 11630.f.7 (42).
Anonymous ('A Lady'). *The Brother.* London: T. Lowndes, 1771. BL, CUP 404.b.16.
Anonymous [John Warwick?]. *The Brother in Law.* Littlebourne, Kent: Lee Priory, 1817. BL, 18797.
Anonymous. *The Brother and Sisters; A Dramatic Trifle for Children with a Prologue and Epilogue.* London: J. Harris, 1808. BL, 11778.aa.10.
Anonymous. *The Brothers or, Treachery Punish'd.* London: T. Payne, 1730. BL, 1459.b.30.
Anonymous. 'The children in the wood'. In a collection of songs and ballads. BL, 11630.f.7 (20).
Anonymous. *The Elder Brother.* London: Charles Knight, 1836. BL, 1210.d.10.2.
Anonymous. *Extracts from the Letters and Memorandum of Maria Grundy with a Short Notice of a Beloved Elder Sister.* Printed for private circulation, 1847. BL, 4410.g.30.
Anonymous. *The Fair Adulteress: or, the Treacherous Brother.* London: A. Miller, 1743. BL, 1094.e5.
Anonymous. *The Faithful Friend; Or, Two Conversations on Worldly Intercourse and Family Duties.* London: James Nisbet, 1834. BL, 863.d.39.
Anonymous. *Filial Remembrancer. Selection of the Much-admired Poems, My Father, My Mother, My Brother, My Sister,* 3rd edn. Banbury: J. G. Rusher, [c.1820]. BL, 11644.e.74.
Anonymous. *The Friendly Instructor: or, a Companion for Young Ladies and Young Gentlemen.* London, John Wilson and James Hodges, 1741. ECCO.
Anonymous. *The Genuine Account of the Adventures of Mr. Richard Brown, and his Sister.* London: Bailey, 1750. BL, 012611.h.37.
Anonymous. *A Genuine and Authentic Account of the Trial, Life, Behaviour, and Dying Words of Richard Milhill.* London: W. Robins, [1767]. BL, 1568/9284.

Anonymous. *The Good Boy, or the History of Ned Careful and his Sister Ann*. Cork: West & Coldwells, [c.1820]. BL, Ch.790/102.7.
Anonymous. *Letters of Consolation and Advice from a Father to his Daughter on the Death of her Sister*, 2nd edn. London: F. and C. Rivington and J. Hatchard, 1805. BL, 4401.n.6.
Anonymous. *The Life and Amours of Lady Ann F_l_y [Foley]*. London: G. Lister, [c.1782?]. BL, 1414.c.42.
Anonymous. *Memoirs of a Younger Brother*. London: J. Axtell, 1789. BL, 10826. aaa.30.
Anonymous. *The Monk and his Sister*. London: Knevelt, Arliss, and Baker, 1811. BL, RB23.a.19675.
Anonymous. *A Precious Testimony for Jesus, in the Experience of Two Children*, 5th edn. London: C. Boult, 1793. BL, 4903.ccc.6.
Anonymous. *The Rambles of Mr. Frankly. Published by his Sister* Dublin: Messr. Sleater, Lynch, Williams, Potts, Chamberlaine, Wilson, Husband, Walker, Moncrieffe, and Flin, 1773. BL, 1459.d.15.
Anonymous. *To my Sister at Abbotsford with a Bluebell Gathered at Dyrnstein July 1823*. Leaflet, no publication information. BL, 1875.d.b (169).
Anonymous. *United Efforts: A Collection of Poems, the Mutual Offspring of a Brother and Sister*. London: Sherwood, Gilbert, and Piper, and Dover: W. Batcheller, 1831. BL, 11650.b.64.
Anonymous. *The Younger Brother or the Sham Marquis*. London: J. Brotherton, W. Meadows, J. Roberts, and A. Dodd, 1719. BL, 11775.bbb.15.
Atkyns, Sir Robert. *The Ancient and Present State of Gloucestershire*. London: W. Bowyer, 1712. Reprint with introduction by Brian S. Smith, Wakefield, Yorkshire: EP Publishing, 1974. GA. B627/39417GS.
Bartelot, Rev. Grosvenor. *History of Crewkerne School, 1499–1899*. Crewkerne, Somerset: James Wheatley, 1899.
Beaumont, Francis, and John Fletcher. *The Bloody Brother*. London: J.T., 1718. BL, 11773.g.6.
Behn, Aphra. *Love-Letters between a Nobleman and His Sister with the History of their Adventures*, 8th edn. London: L. Hawes et al., 1745. BL, 12614 cc1.
———. *The Younger Brother: or, The Amorous Jilt*. London: J. Harris, 1696. BL, 644.g.19.
Berquin, M. *The Children's Friend, Being a Selection from the Works of M. Berquin*, London, 1788. ECCO.
Beste, Rev. Henry Digby. *The Christian Religion Briefly Defended Against the Philosophers and Republicans of France*. London: John Stockdale, 1793. ECCO.
Budden, Maria Elizabeth. *Always Happy!!! Or, Anecdotes of Felix and his Sister Serena*. London: J. Harris, 1814. BL, 12804.aaa.18.
Burn, Richard. *Ecclesiastical Law*, 2nd edn. London: A. Millar, 1767. ECCO.
Burton, John. *Lectures on Female Education and Manners*. Rochester: Gilman and Etherington, 1793. ECCO.

Chapman, George. *A Treatise on Education.* Edinburgh: A. Kincaid & W. Creech, 1773. ECCO.

Chapone, Hester. *Letters on the Improvement of the Mind,* 2 vols. London: H. Hughes, 1773. ECCO.

Charleton, Walter. *A Natural History of the Passions.* London: R. Wellington and E. Rumball, 1701. ECCO.

Clarke, Joseph. *A Full Refutation of the Pretended Genuine Narrative of the Trial and Condemnation of Mary Edmundson.* [London]: M. Cooper, 1759. BL, 518.f.50.

Cobbett, William. *Advice to Young Men and (Incidentally) to Young Women,* 1830. Oxford: Oxford University Press, 1980.

Cole, K. *Days Gone By. Written on the Anniversary Birth-Day of a Beloved Brother, who Died on the 31st July, 1827.* Dublin: R. Carrick, [c.1827]. BL, 10826.aa.27.

Costigan, Arthur William. *Sketches of Society and Manners in Portugal.* 2 vols. London: T. Vernor, [1787]. BL, 1048.k.23.

Croft, Sir Herbert. *A Brother's Advice to his Sisters,* 2nd edn. London: J. Ridley and J. Wilkie, 1776. BL, 230.k.52.

Davy, Sir Humphry. *Collected Works.* 9 vols. Ed. John Davy. London: Smith, Elder and Company, 1839. BL, 1207.f.18.

Davy, John. *Memoirs of the Life of Sir Humphrey Davy Bart.* 2 vols. London: Longman, Rees, Orme, Brown, Green, and Longman, 1836. BL, 614.f.6.

Dibdin, Charles. *The Younger Brother.* Dublin: P. Wogan, P. Byrne, J. Moore, J. Jones, and W. Jones, 1793. BL, CUP.407.dd9.

Dodd, William. *The Sisters; or the History of Lucy and Caroline Sanson, Entrusted to a False Friend.* London: T. Waller, 1754. BL, 012611.e.21.

Dudley, Howard. *Juvenile Researches.* Easebourne, 1835. BL, C.44.a.14.

D'Urfrey, Thomas. *A Fond Husband: Or, the Plotting Sisters.* London: James Magnes and Richard Bentley, 1677. BL, 1343.k.25.

Fielding, Sarah. *The Adventures of David Simple* [1744] and *The Adventures of David Simple, Volume the Last* [1753]. Ed. with an introduction and notes by Linda Bree. London: Penguin Books, 2002.

——. *The Governess: The Little Female Academy.* Dublin: A. Bradley and R. James, 1749. Project Gutenberg, Ebook 1905 (accessed 10 October 2008).

Filmer, Edward. *The Unnatural Brother.* London: J. Orme, 1697. BL, 644.e.8.

Finch, Thomas. *Early Wisdom, Designed to Improve Young People in Religion and Virtue, in the Knowledge of Themselves.* London: the Author, 1793. ECCO.

Flower, Joseph. *The Prodigal Son, a Poem.* 2nd edn. Bath: T. Mills, [1750?]. BL, 11633.c.21.

Fordyce, James. *Sermons for Young Women.* London: A. Millar et al., 1766. ECCO.

——. *The Character and Conduct of the Female Sex.* London: T. Cadell, 1776. BAN, BV 4282 F6 1776.

——. *Sermons for Young Women* (London: A. Millar et al., 1766). ECCO.

Genlis, Stéphanie Félicité, Comtesse de, *Tales of the Castle: or, Stories of Instruction and Delight.* London: G. Robinson, 1785. BL, C.175.I.6.

Giffard, Martha, ed. *The Works of Sir William Temple*. London: T. Woodward et al., 1750. BL, 91.g.1.

Gisborne, Thomas. *An Enquiry into the Duties of the Female Sex*, London: T. Cadell and W. Davies, 1797. BAN, HQ 1201.G5.

Gobinet, Charles. *The Instruction of Youth in Christian Piety*. London: F. Needham, 1741. ECCO.

Gough, James. *Memoirs of the Life, Religious Experiences, and Labours in the Gospel, of James Gough*. Dublin: Robert Jackson, 1781. BL, 1373.b.20.

Gregory, John. *A Father's Legacy to his Daughters*, 1774. In *Female Education in the Age of Enlightenment*, vol. 1. London: William Pickering, 1996.

Henry, Matthew. *Memoirs of the Life and Character of Mrs. Hulton*. London: Ogle, Duncan, and Company, 1821. BL, 4920.e.36.

Hervey, James. *A Present to a Youth about Entering upon a Trade, and to an Apprentice*. London: J. Cole, 1819. BL, 4377.aaa.55 (2).

Heywood, Eliza. *The Female Spectator, Being Selections from Mrs. Eliza Heywood's Periodical (1744–1746) Chosen and Edited by Mary Priestley*. Introduction by J.B. Priestly. London: John Lane, The Bodley Head, 1929.

———. *The Fortunate Foundlings*. London: T. Gardner, 1744. BL, 12614.eee.16.

Hurdis, Rev. James. *Tears of Affection, a Poem, Occasioned by the Death of a Sister Tenderly Beloved*. London: J. Johnson, 1794. BL, 239.k.3.

Hussey, William. *Letters from an Elder to a Younger Brother on the Conduct to be Pursued in Life*. London: Taylor and Hessey, 1809. BL, 10920.ccc.6.

Johnson, Samuel. *The Prince of Abissinia*, vol. 2. London: R. and J. Dodsley; and W. Johnston, 1759. ECCO.

Kames, Henry. *Loose Hints upon Education, Chiefly Concerning the Culture of the Heart*. Edinburgh: John Bell, and London: John Murray, 1781. ECCO.

Le Grice, Rev. C.V. *Sonnet on Charles Lamb, Leading his Sister to the Asylum*. Trereife, Cornwall, [1830]. BL, 11647 e.1.(169).

M—n, B. *A Master-Key to the Rich Ladies Treasury*. London: J. Roberts, 1742. BL, 10804.e.3.

Marchant, John. *Puerilia: or, Amusements for the Young*. London, the author 1751. ECCO.

Mestayer, Henry. *The Perfidious Brother*. 2nd edn. London: T. Warner, 1720. BL, 162.e.10.

More, Hannah. *Strictures on the Modern System of Female Education*, 2nd edn, vol. 2. London: T. Cadell Jr. and W. Davies, 1799. GA, R.O.L. N3/Mor.

Nelson, James. *An Essay on the Government of Children under Three General Heads, viz. Health, Manners, and Education*. London: R. and J. Dodsley, 1763. ECCO.

O'Brien, Lord Edward. *Interesting Sentiments Uttered by the Late Lord Edward O'Brien*. Edinburgh: Waugh and Innes, 1824. BL, 1506/601 (1,2).

Palinurus, *Familiar Letters, from an Elder to a Younger Brother, Serving for his Freedom in the Trinity-House, Newcastle-upon-Tyne*. Newcastle: L. Dinsdale, 1785. BL, 1455.f.15.

Pennington, Lady. *An Unfortunate Mother's Advice to her Absent Daughters*, 1817. In *Marriage, Sex, and the Family in England 1600–1800*, ed. Randolph Trumbach. New York and London: Garland Publishing, 1986.

Secker, Thomas. *On the Relative Duties between Parents and Children*. Dublin: John Exshaw, 1790. ECCO.

Smith, Jeremiah Finch, ed. *The Admission Register of the Manchester School with Some Notices of the More Distinguished Scholars*, vol. 2: *1776–1807*. Manchester: Chetham Society, 1868.

Smith, Richard. *The Fratricide or the Murderer's Gibbet*. Bristol: Mirror Office, 1839. BRO, 14754/5/c.

Sondes, Sir George. *Authentic Memorials of Remarkable Occurrences and Affecting Calamities in the Family of Sir George Sondes, Bart*. Evesham, Gloucestershire: J. Agg, and London: T.N. Longman, [c.1790]. BL, 1373.b.17.

Tomlins, Elizabeth Sophia, and E. Tomlins. *Tributes of Affection*. London: T.N. Longman, 1797. BL, 11644.cc.21.

Travell, Ferdinando Tracy. *An Attempt to Render the Daily Reading of the Psalms More Intelligible to the Unlearned, with a Paraphrase Selected from the Best Commentators, and Illustrated with Occasional Notes*. Gloucester: R. Raikes, 1794. BL, 1004.i.2.

———. *The Duties of the Poor, Particularly in the Education of their Children*. 5th edn. London: F. and C. Rivington, 1799. BL, 224.c.31.

Volney, C.F. *The Law of Nature, or Principles of Morality, Deduced from the Physical Constitution of Mankind and the Universe*. London: D. Steel, 1796. ECCO.

Watts, Isaac. *Divine Songs Attempted in Easy Language, for the Use of Children*. London: Richard Ford, 1727. ECCO.

———. *Prayers Composed for the Use and Imitation of Children, Suited to their Different Ages and their Various Occasions*. London: John Clark et al., 1728. ECCO.

West, Jane. *Letters Addressed to a Young Man on his First Entrance into Life, and Adopted to the Peculiar Circumstances of the Present Times*. Charlestown, MA: Samuel H. Parker, Boston, 1803.

———. *Letters to a Young Lady*, London: Longman, Hurst, Rees, and Orme, 1806.

Willets, William. *Christian Education of Children*. London: the Author, 1750. ECCO.

Wollstonecraft, Mary. *Thoughts on the Education of Daughters, with Reflections on Female Conduct, in the More Important Duties of Life*, 1787. Introduction by Gina Luria. New York and London: Garland Publishing, 1974.

Wright, Louis B. *Advice to a Son: Precepts of Lord Burghley, Sir Walter Raleigh, and Francis Osborne*. Ithaca: Cornell University Press, 1962.

Published diaries and correspondence

Allen, John. *Copy of Two Letters from a Missionary in America, to his Brother and Sister in England*. Bristol: Bonners & Page, 1804. BL, RB.23.a.20985.

Anonymous. *My Travels*. London: F. Westley and A.H. Davis, 1837. BL, RB.23.a.20086.

Anonymous. *The Shipwreck of the Dryade in Letter to a Sister*. London: Jonathan Hatchard and Sons, 1842. BL, F.3.23.1.17663.

Aylmer, G.E., ed. *The Diary of William Lawrence Covering Periods between 1662 and 1681*. Beaminster, Dorset: J. Stevens Cox at the Toucan Press, 1961.

Black, Clementina, ed. *The Cumberland Letters: Being the Correspondence of Richard Dennison Cumberland and George Cumberland between the Years 1771 and 1784*. London: Martin Secker, 1912.

Boswell, James. *The Life of Samuel Johnson*. London: Charles Dilly, 1799. ECCO.

Dresser, Madge, ed. *The Diary of Sarah Fox*. Bristol: Bristol Record Society, 2003.

Freemantle, Anne, ed. *The Wynne Diaries, 1789–1820*. London, New York, and Toronto: Oxford University Press, 1952.

Fry, Elizabeth Gurney. *Memoir of the Life of Elizabeth Fry with Extracts from her Journals and Letters*, ed. Katherine Fry and Rachel Cresswell (London: J. Gilpin, J. Hatchard & Co., 1847). British and Irish Women's Letters and Diaries, Alexander Street Press, http://alexanderstreet.com/products/british-and-irish-womens-letters-and-diaries (accessed March 2011).

Galbraith, Georgina, ed. *The Journal of the Rev. William Bagshaw Stevens*. Oxford: Clarendon Press, 1965.

Greet, Carolyn S., ed. *Six Years 1865–1861: The Diaries of Edward Welch of Arle*. Cheltenham: Carmichael Books, 1997.

Hawkes, William, ed. *The Diaries of Sanderson Miller of Radway Together with his Memoir of James Menteath*. [Stratford-upon-Avon]: Dugdale Society in association with the Shakespeare Birthplace Trust, 2005.

Johnson, R. Brimley, ed. *The Letters of Hannah More*. Introduction by R. Brimley Johnson. London: John Lane. The Bodley Head, 1925.

LeFanu, William R., ed. *Betsy Sheridan's Journal: Letters from Sheridan's Sister, 1784–1786 and 1788–1790*. Oxford: Oxford University Press, 1960.

Macfarlane, Alan, ed. *The Diary of Ralph Josselin*. Oxford: Oxford University Press, 1976.

Plumer, Frank. 'Copy of Part of a Letter I Wrote to my Brother at Lilling-Hall, September 17, 1776'. BL, 12355.f.14.(6).

Rumney, A.W., ed. *Tom Rumney of Mellfell, 1764–1835*. Kendal: Titus Wilson and Son, 1936.

Shaen, Margaret J., ed. *Memorials of Two Sisters: Susanna and Catherine Winkworth*. London: Longmans, 1908.

Stocking, Marion Kingston, ed. *The Clairmont Correspondence: Letters of Claire Clairmont, Charles Clairmont, and Fanny Imlay Godwin*. Baltimore: Johns Hopkins University Press, 1995.

Vaisey, David, ed. *The Diary of Thomas Turner, 1754–1765*. Oxford and New York: Oxford University Press, 1984.

Verey, David, ed. *The Diary of a Cotswold Parson: Reverend F.E. Witts, 1783–1854*. 2nd edn. Stroud, Gloucestershire: Sutton Publishing, 2003.

Unpublished family papers, correspondence, and local history

Atkyns Family Papers. Letters, property disputes, and estate papers. GA, D4582/2/1–7.

Coxwell and Coxwell-Rogers Family Papers 1649–1833, Family Correspondence 1736–1857. Coxwell and Coxwell-Rogers Families of Dowdeswell and Bibury Collection, GA, D269a.

Dodwell Family Papers. Deeds, wills, money releases, and pedigree, c.1702–1814, Lawrence Family Collection. GA, D444/T65, D444/E6, D444/F4 and D444/F24.

Edwards-Freeman Family Papers. Letters, wills, receipts. GA, D153 and D2002.

Engravings and prints of Cheltenham and Gloucester. Late eighteenth and early nineteenth centuries. GA, A78/66/1,2; A 78/1; A154.

Graves Family Papers. Genealogy, correspondence. GA, D5626/13/1.

Greet, Carolyn. *Cheltenham's High Street, 1800–1820*. Cheltenham: Privately printed, 2001. GA, GAL/C5/41070GS.

Guydickens Family Papers. Diplomatic letters, family correspondence. GA, D4582/3/18, D4582/3/19, D4582/3/26, D4528/3/29, D4582/3/32.

Hicks Family Correspondence. GA, D1866/F11.

Hughes Family Papers. Genealogy, biography, photos, sketchbooks, correspondence. GA, D245/IV/25, 26, 27, 28; D245/V/7.

Hyett Family Correspondence. 1735–75. GA, D6.

Jackson and Martin Family Papers. 1720–77. Jackson Family of Sneyd Park, Westbury-on-Trym, Gloucestershire, Collection, GA, D153.

Lawrence and Pearkes Family Papers. GA, D444/F3, D444/F13.

Leigh Family Papers. SBTRO, DR671, DR18.

Sharp Family Papers. Lloyd-Baker Family of Hardwicke Court Collection. GA, D3549.

Sharp Family Probates. Proved c.1758–83. GA, D3549//1/3, D3549/13/2/14.

Sheridan and LeFanu Family Correspondence, c.1747–1842. KCC, LeFanu Collection.

Smith, Richard. Notes on the murder of Sir John Dinely Goodere, including broadsheet from c.1740s. c.1839. BRO, 14754/5/c, 13847/3, 13847/4, 11373/2. 35893/36t.

Tracy Family Papers. GA, D444/E6; GA, D2153/Av/1–17, 19; GA, 4582; ORO Flick I/i.

Travell Family Papers. Genealogy, receipts, scrapbook, keepsakes, songs, and miscellaneous correspondence, c.1708–1826. Bowly Family of Cirencester Collection. GA, D4582; GA, D495; ORO, Flick I/xvi; WFP, 256.

Travell Family Probates. ORO, Flick I/i/3, I/i/4, I/i/5, I/xvi/1.

Travell, Anne Tracy. Letters, 1730s. Transcribed by Celandine Tracy, 1911. In private possession of Earl of Wemyss, Stanway, Gloucestershire.

Witts Family Papers, c.1750–1830s. In Bowly Collection, GA, D4582; in private possession of F.E.B. Witts. WFP 255, F256, F262, F263, F271, F287, F288, F406–13.

Unpublished diaries and journals

Agg, Jasper. Diary 1796–99. Included in Agg-Gardner Family Papers. GA, D855 E8 1796–1826, 1894.
Clutterbuck, Edmund. Diary, 1775 (typescript). GA, GE 179.
Ellis, Daniel. Diary (Gloucestershire and Edinburgh), 1800–41. GA, D2227/6
Gegg, Robert. Diary 1763–64 (typescript). Included in Hicks-Austin Family Papers. GA, D1770 (uncatalogued).
Holder, John. Diary, c.1691–1730 (photostat). GA, D1371.
Hughes, Thomas. Diary, 1763, 1769. GA, D245 IV/20/1–2.
Hughes, Thomas Bridges. Diary, 1786. GA, D245 IV/21.
Huntingford, Thomas. Autobiography, c.1830s (typescript). GA, PE98.
Leigh, Elizabeth. Diary excerpts, 1790. SBTRO, D671/79.
Prowse, Elizabeth Sharp. Diary and memorandum book. GA, D3549/14/1/1–2.
Sharp, Frances. Diary of a journey to Scotland, 1785. GA, D3549/15/1/1.
Sheridan, Charles Frances. Diary, 1802–04. KCC, LeFanu Papers, MS 6.
Snooke, William. Diaries, 1768–75 (typescript). GA, R.O.L. G3.
Travell, Anne Tracy. Diary, 1723–25. Transcribed by Celandine Tracy, 1911. In private possession of Earl of Wemyss Stanway, Gloucestershire.
———. Daybook, 1764–1804. GA, D4582/4/17/1–18.
———. Commonplace book and recipe book, c.1780s. GA, D4582/7/18.
Treby, Caroline. Diary, 1808–31 Treby Family of Goodamoor Collection, PWDRO, 1148.
Wintle (first name unknown). Copy diary, 1783. Transcribed by Miss Palser. Palser Family of Wotton-under-Edge Collection, GA, D1559/Z1.
Witts, Agnes Travell. Diaries, 1777, 1788–1824. WFP, F172–235.

Church of England records (parish, Poor Law, and testamentary)

Brooke, J.M.S., and A.W.C. Hallen, *The Transcript of the Registers of the United Parishes of St. Mary Woolnoth and St. Mary Woolchurch Haw, in the City of London, from their Commencement 1538 to 1760* (London: Bowles, 1886). FHL, British book 942.1/L 1 K29.
Church of England, Adlestrop, Gloucestershire, Bishop's Transcripts, 1580–1812. FHL, British film 417099.
Church of England, Haselbury-Plucknett, Somerset, Parish Registers and Poor Law Records, 1727–57. FHL, British films 1596988-9.
Church of England, Lower Swell, Gloucestershire, Parish Registers. GA, P322 IN 1/1–5 and microfilm PMF 322.

Church of England, St Michael, Gloucester, Gloucestershire, Parish Registers. GA, P154/14 IN 1/2.
Church of England, St Michael, Gloucester, Gloucestershire, Bishop's Transcripts. FHL, British film 425423.
Church of England, Stanway, Gloucestershire, Bishop's Transcripts, 1580–1812, FHL, British film 427778, item 2.
Church of England, Swerford, Oxfordshire, Parish Register Transcript, 1577–1943, FHL, British fiche 6142087 and ORO.
Church of England, Upper Swell, Gloucestershire, Parish Registers. GA, P323 IN 1/1–6 and microfilm PMF 323.
Consistory Court of Chester. Testamentary Causes, 1700–57. CALS, EDC 5.
Consistory Court of Gloucester. Testamentary Causes, 1700–1830. GA, GDR B4/2.
Consistory Court of Gloucester. Court Minutes, 1700–05, 1765–73. GA, GDR B3.
Court of the Exchequer. Estate and property disputes, TNA, E134.
Diocese of Gloucester Marriage Allegations. FHL, British film 431174.
Arthur J. Jewers, ed., *The Registers of the Abbey Church of SS. Peter and Paul, Bath*, vol. 2 (London: Mitchell and Hughes, 1901).
Overseers of the Poor, Gloucestershire parishes, c.1690–1840. GA, P29-P376.
York Court of Chancery. Testamentary Causes. FHL, British films 1752043-4, 1785841-85.

Internet sources

Cornish Probate Abstracts, http://webs.lanset.com/azazella/cornish_database.html (accessed 2009).
Old Bailey Online, www.oldbaileyonline.org, version 5.1 (accessed 2009–11).
London Lives, www.londonlives.org (accessed 2010–11).

Index

Note: married women are indexed under their married name

adolescence and childhood 3–4 6–7, 9, 18, 26–31, 34–8, 40, 42–6, 50n47, 51n64, 69, 85, 87, 100–1, 122–3, 150
affection *see* friendship
aunts *see* nieces and nephews

birth order 20, 31, 33–7, 45, 83, 85, 126–7, 143–5, 147, 150–4, 157–60, 166–70

care of the ill or dying 36–7, 62, 121–2, 124–7, 133, 158–9, 166–70
child care 38, 68, 121–5, 127, 159, 168
childhood *see* adolescence and childhood
class comparisons 7, 9, 16–18, 29–30, 44–6, 61, 71, 97, 115, 117–18, 123–7, 158, 170
courtship *see* marriage
cousins 9, 20, 40, 59, 67, 72–3, 100–1, 118–19, 158
Cumberland family 44, 57, 59, 67, 80, 118, 121, 131

death and burial 34–8, 50n47, 61, 124–6, 151–3, 158–9, 166–9

discord and disappointment 18–19, 41, 46, 69, 70, 73, 80–3, 86–8, 90–5, 102–4, 123, 133, 148–60

education and training 27, 30–1 33, 40–1, 43–5, 72, 83, 88–9, 94–5, 122–3, 127–9, 139n84
equality 2–3, 11–14, 31–3, 38, 71, 83, 85, 95–6, 103–4, 145, 148, 153–4, 160, 166, 169–70, 172–3

fictive kinship 11–14, 29, 71–3 103–4, 114, 116, 122, 159, 169, 172–3
financial exchanges and support 1–2, 35, 46, 68–71, 73, 80–3, 88, 90–3, 112, 116, 122–3, 125–8, 131–3, 136n32, 139n84, 145, 157–9, 181 125–8, 132–3
friendship 7, 18, 28–9, 41, 56–7, 59, 61, 63–71, 73, 84–5, 87, 103, 159, 166, 169–70

gender 6–7, 19–20, 29–33, 39–40, 57 83–4, 103–4, 122, 127–8, 143–50, 153, 157–9, 166, 169–70

half- and step-siblings 14–15, 61, 65, 96–8, 100, 106n40, 109n81, 128

hierarchy 2–3, 11–14, 27, 29–33, 38–40, 71, 83–4, 94–6, 103–4, 134, 144, 148, 153–4, 166, 169–70
households
 establishment of 55–6, 112–17, 158
 management of 30, 68, 117–21, 124–6, 132–3, 158, 166–9
 power within 19–20, 27, 38–40, 120, 158

in-laws 14–15, 58–9, 66, 89, 98, 107n43, 107n45, 130, 133, 149–50, 156–60, 167
incest 83–4, 90, 98–104, 109n88, 110n96, 110n104, 170–2
inheritance and probate 16–17, 33, 85–91, 94–7, 116, 118, 125–7, 131, 146, 148–57, 160, 166

Jackson family 16, 40, 44–5, 61, 65, 67–8, 72–3, 118, 129

LeFanu, Alicia Sheridan 41, 46, 59, 86–7, 92–4, 103–4
LeFanu Betsy Sheridan 41, 59, 86–7, 92–4, 104
letter-writing 44–5, 61, 64–7, 70–3, 80–2, 97, 116, 121, 159, 169
love see friendship
Lyttelton, Apphia Witts 2, 59, 61, 65–7, 112, 130

marital status 8, 14–15, 16–17, 68, 90, 97, 117, 120, 123, 126–7, 134, 135n17, 140n91, 143–7, 151, 154–60, 162n21, 163n40, 167, 170
marriage and courtship 2, 59, 61, 67, 70, 94, 97, 129–32, 154–60, 171–2

nicknames and naming patterns 14, 37, 51n64, 60, 64, 66, 97–8, 124

nieces and nephews 20, 60, 63, 67, 91, 113, 115, 121–4, 126–7, 133, 138n65, 139n84, 139n85, 144, 152, 157–9, 166–8

occupational support 43, 69, 119, 122–3, 127–9, 167
occupational training see education

parenthood and parenting 27–31, 38, 42, 45, 58, 84–8, 95–6, 123, 131–2
Poor Law and poverty 17, 38, 91, 123–4, 140n91
prescriptive literature 28–9, 31, 38, 56–8, 63, 68–9, 70, 83–6, 95–6, 100–3, 122, 127, 129–30, 145, 151, 153, 158, 170–1
primogeniture 9, 19, 35, 86, 94–5, 144, 146–7, 150, 160, 163n36, 172
probate see inheritance
Prowse, Elizabeth Sharp 43, 59–60, 64–5, 123, 129, 131

Sharp, Ann Jemima 60, 67–9, 123
Sharp, Frances 64–5, 123
Sharp, Granville 43, 58, 60, 64–5, 68–9, 122, 126, 129
Sharp, James 43, 60–1, 64–5, 67, 126, 129
Sharp, John 60–1, 64–5, 67–9, 126, 131
Sharp, Judith 59–61, 64–5, 69, 123
Sharp, William 43, 60–1, 64–5, 69, 126, 129, 131
Sherdian, Charles 86–7, 92–4, 104
Sheridan, Richard Brinsley 57, 86–7, 92–4, 104
sibling rivalry 4, 19, 73, 83–94, 102–4, 145–6, 162n32, 169–70
step-siblings see half-siblings

Tracy family 26, 34, 39–40, 46, 68, 103, 133, 143–4

Index

Travell, Anne 1, 17, 33–6, 55–6, 58, 62, 65–6, 80–3, 112–17, 121, 123, 125–6, 130, 133–4, 144, 157–8, 166–9

Travell, Anne Tracy 26, 33, 35–6, 39–41, 46, 55, 103, 151

Travell, Catherine 1, 33–6, 55–6, 62, 12–16, 121, 125, 133, 144, 158, 166–9

Travell, Ferdinando 1, 33–6, 55–6, 58, 80–3, 92, 112–14, 121, 125, 133, 144, 152, 157–8, 166–9

Travell, Frances Mary 33–6, 55–6, 112, 114, 116, 125–6

Travell, Francis 1, 33–7, 55–6, 58, 113–14, 133, 144, 152, 157–8, 166–9

Travell, Jane 34, 113, 116, 144

Travell, John (father) 33, 35–6, 55, 144, 151

Travell, John (son) 33, 116–17, 152, 167

Travell, Martha Rollinson 55–6, 80, 113, 125, 158–9

Travell, William 34, 112, 144

uncles *see* nieces and nephews

violence 69, 83–4, 91–2, 94, 97–8, 103, 120

Witts, Agnes Travell 1, 33–6, 55–6, 59, 65–6, 80–3, 112–14, 116, 120, 130, 133, 144, 152, 157–8, 167–9

Witts, Edward 46, 58–9, 61, 66–7, 81, 120, 130, 133, 152, 157, 167

EU authorised representative for GPSR:
Easy Access System Europe, Mustamäe tee 50,
10621 Tallinn, Estonia
gpsr.requests@easproject.com